CW01661765

FACE TO FACE
WITH JESUS CHRIST

This is a true story of three face-to-face meetings with the Lord Jesus Christ, the first in October 1994, the second on Easter morning 1997, and the third on February 16, 1999; a meeting with the Virgin Mary on January 10, 1999; two visits through Seven Ascending Heavens of Clear Light, December 22 and 23, 1986, and the Lord's message to humankind as it moves into the new millennium.

The Lord's face shined brighter than a thousand suns and the Glory of Innocence, Love, Ecstasy, Peace, Power and Graces was inescapable and even brighter than the light the Lord beholds. It was nearly impossible to gaze upon Jesus' face for more than a second each glance. As I was unable to stand, fallen at the Lord's feet, the Lord delivered this message to me and to all of humankind.

FACE TO FACE
WITH
JESUS CHRIST

David Sereda

BLUE DOLPHIN PUBLISHING

Published by Blue Dolphin Publishing, Inc.
P.O. Box 8, Nevada City, CA 95959
Orders: 1-800-643-0765
http://www.bluedolphinpublishing.com

ISBN: 1-57733-032-3

Library of Congress Cataloging-in-Publication Data

Sereda, David, 1961–
Face to face with Jesus Christ / by David Sereda.
p. cm.
ISBN 1-57733-032-3
1. Jesus Christ—Apparitions and miracles. 2. Private revelations. I. Title.
BF580.A1S47 1999
232.9'7—dc21 98-55525
CIP

First printing, January, 2000
Second printing, October, 2000

Printed in the United States of America

10 9 8 7 6 5 4 3 2

Contents

Introduction

What power and glory could be so great that it could cast the shadow of the sun? This is a true account of three face-to-face meetings with the Lord Jesus Christ, first in October of 1994, second on Easter of 1997, and third on February 16, 1999, and a direct account of the Lord's message to humanity as it moves into the millennium. The heart of this message will not alienate all other religions and call them evil, as many Christians would believe. Rather, the messages show the cause of human war and suffering, and integrate what we already know about human spirituality, suffering, and different religions into a more synthesized picture.

The Lord's face shines brighter than one thousand suns. It is physically impossible to stand up in the Lord's presence or even gaze directly upon the face of the Lord unless it is the will of the Lord to allow it. No humility is greater, no innocence brighter, no ecstasy sweeter, no peace more serene, no power comparable to, and no beauty more splendid than what I experienced in the Lord. Even so, the Lord said, "No one has seen me in my entirety," meaning spiritual capacity. As I was collapsed at the feet of the Lord, I had no doubt that I was in a presence so great that whole galaxies would bow in grace if they could perceive what I saw, felt and experienced in those timeless moments.

I had been searching for God and the meaning of existence for over 15 years with a daily meditation practice, learning from many masters of the far east and west, my own father, and serving intensely as an environmentalist. I had by then planted over 700,000 evergreen trees in the forests of British Columbia (the foremen and women deserve much credit), helped clean up oil spills, protested, directed an environmental foundation called "The Tesla Foundation" promoting great new technologies in "Science For a Better Environment," spoke in the United States Congress on nuclear fusion in 1992, and still continue to work today, despite all odds against me to serve.

If you would not believe that any human being could ever see God, then you might be preventing even your own self from ever seeing God, until you removed such a doubt. Remember, it is written that Jesus said in the Bible, Book of Matthew, Chapter 5, Verse 8: "Blessed are the pure in heart: for they shall see God." Here you will see my evidence of that, from a witness to the Lord, and the Lord's Heavenly Kingdoms. Even more than sight, you will receive the Lord's message to humanity as we move into the new millennium.

Love without wisdom is as a child's innocence. It is surely to be lost. To understand the spiritual physics of the soul's conflict could make us wise to learn how to undo the knot. To understand the spiritual physics of how to untie the knot may allow us to experience what it means for the soul to become free from the suffering that it creates all on its own. Now that the soul could become free, we may enter and begin to understand the spiritual physics and wisdom of the soul in God's Heavenly Kingdoms.

CHAPTER ONE

First Meeting with the Lord, Jesus Christ

October 1994

I

Approaching the first meeting with Jesus. Face-to-face meeting with Jesus Christ for approximately 1/2 hour in mid- to late October 1994.

I, David, swear that the following story is true, and if it is a lie, that I be cast into hell for telling such a lie. I will not be cast into hell, because I am one hundred percent sure that the following is a true story and did happen to me. Now, unto you, this message may be delivered.

The following true story may sound difficult to believe, so I ask you to note: *King James Bible:* Acts 2:17, "And it shall come to pass in the last days, saith God, I will pour out of my spirit upon all flesh: and your sons and your daughters shall prophesy, and your *young men shall see visions,* and your old men shall dream dreams:"

How do visions of the Lord, Saints, Spirits and Angels appear to us? How can they appear in your own spirituality? In Matthew, Chapter 1, Verse 20, we find one way that Angels appear: "But while he thought on these things, behold, the angel of the Lord appeared unto him in a dream, saying, Joseph, thou son of David, fear not to take unto thee Mary thy wife: for that which is conceived in her is of the Holy Ghost." There are multiple ways that the Lord, Saints, Spirits and Angels make appearances. This example is to show that an Angel may come to you in a dream.

The next example is to show that an Angel or Saint of the Lord (or Mother of God) can appear directly to the masses: In 1968-1970, the Virgin Mary made over 700 apparitions (holy appearances) in Zeitoun, Egypt. She appeared hovering above a large Coptic Church in a body made of very bright light. She was plainly visible to perhaps thousands of people at any given time and even photographed. The area was checked by local police for a possible hoax and they found nothing technological that could have been a false cause to manifest these apparitions. To confirm her apparition, hundreds of documented healings took place during the apparitions.

The greatest message of peace came to the war-stricken Middle East when Jews, Muslims and Christians all prayed together in her midst saying, "Mary is the most beautiful woman in the world" and obviously is the Mother of God. This was a powerful message of peace set in the heart of one of the most violent religious war zones on earth—an act of God and perhaps the greatest public apparition in recorded world history. Over a 3-4 year period, over one million eyewitnesses saw Mary in her shining body of Light.

Luke, Chapter 1, Verse 11 shows us that an Angel can appear in private to someone: "And there appeared unto him an angel of the Lord standing by the right side of the altar of incense." This was the Angel Gabriel appearing to Zacharias, the father of John the Baptist, telling him that his wife Elisabeth will give birth to John in Verse 13: "But the angel said unto him, Fear not, Zacharias: for thy prayer is heard; and thy wife Elisabeth shall bear thee a son, and thou shalt call his name John."

The Angel Gabriel also appears soon after to the Virgin Mary to tell her about her mission in Luke, Chapter 1, Verses 30-31: "And the angel said unto her, Fear not, Mary: for thou hast found favour with God. And, behold, thou shalt conceive in thy womb, and bring forth a son, and shall call his name JESUS."

In the Book of Revelation, we can see that the Lord can appear to someone, in this case St. John the Divine, years after the resurrection while the receiver is in the Spirit (what we now call out-of-body). This is revealed in Revelation, Chapter 1, Verse 10: "I was in the Spirit on the Lord's day, and heard behind me a great voice, as of a trumpet, . . ." Obviously John was in the Spirit (either in a dream or actually out of his body) because the Revelations John was about to see were so elaborate, with visual portrayals of things to come, that I believe John was seeing these Revelations out-of-body.

Further evidence of out-of-body experiences of Biblical Saints are the Visions of Enoch, who was the first "saint" in the Bible. From the Book of Enoch (translated by Richard Laurence, Archbishop of Cashel in 1821), Chapter XIV, Verse 1, reads: "This is the book of the words of righteousness, and the reproof to the Watchers, who belong to the world, according to that which He, who is holy and great, commanded in the vision. I perceived in my dream. . . ." In Verses 9-10 Enoch reveals that he was flying as if by Spirit in this great dream, for he was about to meet the Lord in person: "Behold, in that vision clouds and a mist invited me; the running of stars and flashes of lightning impelled and pressed me forwards, while winds in the vision assisted my flight, accelerating my progress. They elevated me aloft to heaven."

Many Christian fundamentalists do not believe that the soul can separate from the body. By their philosophy, they discredit all apparitions and near-death experiences that claim to involve separation from the body and going into the light.

Evidence suggests that the soul perhaps can separate from the body, however contradictory it may seem to fundamentalist Christian belief that the body and soul are linked together and inseparable. In II Corinthians, Chapter 12, Verses 1-4: "IT IS not expedient for me doubtless to glory. I will come to visions and revelations of the Lord. I knew a man in Christ above fourteen years ago, (whether in the body, I cannot tell; or whether out of the body, I cannot tell: God knoweth;) such an one caught up to the third heaven. And I knew such a man, (whether in the body, or out of the body, I cannot tell: God knoweth;) How that he was caught up into paradise and heard unspeakable words, which it is not lawful for a man to utter."

These examples have set the stage to prove and reveal some of the many ways that God, Saints, Spirits and Angels can appear and have appeared to persons throughout history. They also set the stage to my own experience and reveal how the Lord made his appearances and graced me with visits through the Heavens.

In mid-late October 1994, out-of-body, I met Jesus Christ in person, face-to-face for nearly half an hour (time was difficult to read). His face shined with a light brighter than one thousand suns, his robe like that of our sun, and with spirit immeasurable, so no physical eyes could bare such a glorious light. His Glory and power literally roared many million times greater than the roar and power of all the lions on earth, and yet was utterly silent.

The entire force of power on earth—spiritual, political, military or otherwise—cannot even equal one billionth of Jesus' power and spiritual Glory. Humanity in its entirety is incomparable to any fraction of the Lord, and so is an entire galaxy. The truth is, the Lord is so much greater than the Bible makes the Lord out to be, and the written word has little impact upon those who have seen the face of the Lord. As the shining Lord spoke to me for nearly half an hour or more, I was fallen at the Lord's feet and could barely gaze upon Jesus' face (but I did) because of the ultra-blazing light, spiritual power and Glory that the Lord eternally beholds. Jesus' face is the most beautiful I have ever seen. It is impossible to imagine any such beauty, and even more impossible to gaze upon, but by some unknown miracle and will in the Lord it was allowed.

Over the past fifteen years, I have traveled to India to meet many spiritual teachers, saints, and spiritual leaders, and have also met with many of them in the West. I believed that the spiritual enlightenment taught by great masters was an "It's all one," that only one final enlightenment was attained by these teachers and that Jesus was also one of them, one who attained enlightenment. These teachers taught that there is only one enlightenment, and that's all there is and that it's possible to make the leap from the human state of consciousness to full realization in one giant swoop. After meeting the Lord Jesus, I know that is simply not true. There is so much more, it is inconceivable.

I have met and studied meditation and prayer with teachers such as Baba Hari Das (Hindu Saint), Bhagwan Rajneesh (controversial Meditation Master), Krishnamurti (a Hindu genius Meditation Master), Guru Mai (Hindu full of Grace), Ma Amrit Anandamai (Hindu), Bhante Shibuya Subhuti (enlightened Theravada Buddhist Monk), The Dalai Lama (Tibetan Political Leader and Spiritual Master), Kalu Rinpoche (Tibetan Master), Takar Sing (Hindu Master), Poonjaji (Hindu Teacher who met Krishna in person), Wallace Black Elk (Native American Spirit Being), etc., and many others who are not as well known.

My first conscious memory of an out-of-body meeting with spiritual beings happened when I was a young teenager. My father had forced me against my will to go to a yoga retreat led by a meditation master from India named Baba Hari Das. I had never before heard of meditation, and I had recently begun living with my real father, a psychologist at the University of California at Berkeley who traveled to India and practiced yoga, vegetarian diet and meditation. I thought it was all ridiculous, but I kept a quasi-open mind.

At the retreat, by my father's hand, I met the master and didn't think a whole lot of him. Baba Hari Das did not speak, but wrote his answers on a chalk board. He seemed quiet inside but I didn't see white light shining from his head, nor did I feel elevated or enlightened.

One night, while sleeping near the master's house, something peculiar began to happen. A strange energy like a paralysis began moving up my spine causing me to become unable to move my body. I was very conscious of this happening. I watched the paralysis move past my neck and then it was like I died. I just saw blackness like the night sky with no stars. Suddenly, I was standing in front of these three beautiful beings who were shining with the most powerful light-blue light that I had ever seen. It was so powerful, I began to shake and tremble and fell to the ground, unable to stand up. I gazed very easily and clearly upon their faces. There was one being in the middle who I could not take my eyes off of because he had the face of a monkey and a man blended together. I was so fascinated by these beings, but especially the monkey man. To the right was a woman who was so beautiful and powerful, I cannot describe her. To the left was another man, who was exquisite. They all blazed with blue light and I was unable to stand up in their presence. I could not believe how powerful and radiant they were.

The next morning I told Baba Hari Das about my experience, and he laughed. He wrote on his chalk board that I had seen

Hanuman, a great Hindu God. He said that the reason I was fallen at their feet was because my Ego was being humbled in their presence. "Oh," I thought, how fun. I met a Hindu God. Later, someone showed me pictures of Hanuman and I was really amazed. The pictures looked so much like Hanuman, but who were the other two beings with him? No one ever told me.

Many years later, I read the whole Hindu *Bhagavad Gita.* I learned there that Hanuman is always seen with Rama who is one of a number of forms of Krishna, the Hindu Supreme God. In the *Gita,* Krishna is seen as the incarnation of God, the Supreme Being's absolute self, who is higher than all saints of all religions. Krishna lives on the most supreme paradise planet in the universe known as Krishnaloka. The woman I saw with Rama is known as Sita. The two, the *Gita* says, are always seen with Hanuman.

Even though I still love and appreciate the guidance and meditation teachings of all my past teachers, after meeting all of these beings, no one person (and I have met many great world spiritual leaders in person) even has a grain of sand of Power and Glory compared to Jesus Christ. For me, this was terribly devastating in the most positive way. I had been a Buddhist Vipassana meditation practitioner for fifteen years, and had loved Jesus, but did not think a whole lot about him. Now I was seeing Jesus face-to-face.

Previously, I had no idea who Jesus really was and is in truth. In a positive state of terror and awe, I experienced the Glory as Jesus spoke to me. The Lord's message is urgent. Herein, Glory always means the Innocence, Love, Peace, Ecstasy, Power, Beauty, and Grace that is billions of times greater than the human capacity to withstand, a Glory beyond time and space. I would like to explain some of the background and most of my encounter to you all.

I was experiencing the most difficult time in my life. The environmental company owned by myself and Ghassan (The

Green & Blue Corp.) and all our efforts had just gone bankrupt. Our company raised funds for genius scientists to develop technology that would solve the serious environmental crisis that the world faces today. There were many others in the world who were fighting for the same technology and changes to happen.

We represented and tried to raise funds for one technology that was supported by Nobel Prize winners. It was Dr. Bogdan Maglich's non-radioactive fusion. We, amongst many others, were trying to raise large funds for Harry Braun's "Phoenix Project": Sterling Solar Power-Hydrogen Fuel. Harry Braun's dream was proven technology. The idea was to fill an area of the desert in Arizona with these giant solar collectors and produce hydrogen fuel for heating homes, driving cars and flying aircraft, meeting the most ecological goals for clean energy. The project even had matching funds from the U.S. Department of Energy. It all seemed like it was going to be so easy. Of course, we thought, the wealthy persons in the world would certainly want to invest in non-radioactive fusion, the Phoenix Project, and five other technologies we were working with.

With Ghassan's contacts to many of the world's millionaires and billionaires and my other associates like Nancy Pfister (a great humanitarian) and her friends in Aspen Colorado, we had personal contacts with many of the most wealthy persons on earth. All we had to do was get the money people to sign checks to the genius scientists. It sounded so easy at first, but it all failed. None of the people we contacted were interested. If the money people and the genius idea people couldn't change the world, in the here and now, who could? What was all this so-called environmentalism, even amongst the world's elite, if, when it came down to spending funds on changing the world, they would do nothing. How else could the world change? I became furious with humankind to the point of emotional and mental collapse. I doubted God and the future of humanity when our plan failed because it didn't seem to me that there was a serious effort in Heaven or on earth to evolve past the problem of ecological disaster. I used to yell at the Angels and call them lazy.

Our Green & Blue corporation went bankrupt and I had to move to my father's house in Topanga Canyon, California, due to lack of funds. Even worse, I had just gone tree planting for two-to-three months and the tax people repossessed most of my earnings from that intensive labor. I was exhausted from tree planting, had no money, and had no girlfriend standing by me, nor rarely ever had.

There was only one catch to living at my father's house: he was just developing his land and had no spare rooms in the house so I lived in my tree planting tent (a very small tent) in the front yard. The yard consisted mostly of dirt and a few weeds.

One night in October of 1994 it was raining hard in the early morning, and I was fast asleep and dreaming. My tent was pitched in a gully, so the floor was filling up with very cold water. I was freezing to death and I knew it. However, I had no will to live in a world filled with unloving and uncaring human beings any more. Freezing to death, I awoke, removed the covers, and decided just to lie in the water until I froze to death.

II

Suddenly I am in a powerful out-of-body vision standing in front of a huge fifteen-foot stone crucifix with a pool of water shaped like a cross on the ground below.

When a person moves out of their body, many phenomena that are not visible to the naked human eyes can be seen. The first stage above normal human consciousness, out of body, can be more illusionary than the physical or natural world. In the natural world, landscapes appear solid and unchanging, even though they are not. In the out-of-body state, depending on your spiritual ability and the grace of God, you can view the natural world and it will show many additional features such as auras around trees, plants, animals and humans—all of which I have seen. It is fascinating to experience these additional features, but is still very limited. In a higher vibration, the natural world dissolves from view, and you may enter a new and more spiritual dimension in the out-of-body state of awareness. A true out-of-body state is not a projection of the mind. It is not a remote viewing state. It is not a channeling or trance-like state. It is as actual as reality in the human waking state; however, with the awakening of spiritual senses that are so evolved, it makes the human waking state of awareness seem like sleep.

Even though Jesus can appear in any dimension He wishes to, including the earthly dimension, I feel it is much better to see the Lord in a higher dimension because the communication of more wisdom and spiritual experience is possible. But, perhaps others have experienced great wisdom upon meeting spiritual masters from beyond while still in their bodies. By the power of Grace, nothing is impossible with the Lord.

For the Lord, Mary, or any angel to appear before all eyes on earth, a lowering of the vibration rate of their Glorious spiritual body to that of the rate of our sun's light (or lower) is accomplished. This is how visionaries see apparitions while they are still inside the body, or through human eyes. Even in some of those cases, depending on the spiritual ability of the recipient, a light even brighter than our sun could be seen. This has happened, as in the case of Mary appearing at Zeitoun, Egypt from 1968 through 1970.

Although much can be spiritually felt and seen by all humans in an apparition like this, it is possible to experience and see more when taken in spirit, out of body. The difficult part of seeing and receiving a message out of body is to "down load" the experience into the brain when it is all finished. Only then can the knowledge received be of any use to others.

Very soon after removing the covers from my body, freezing to death, I moved out of my body into the first state. Having moved out, I could see the sky was dark and cloudy just like it was in Topanga that morning. As if sent from above, a large stone crucifix with a pool of water shaped like a crucifix below appeared in front of me. The meaning of this was very significant for what was about to happen. It was a sign of who was about to appear, as a form of reassurance, in case I doubted who it was to be. It was also a purification to prepare me to be in the presence of the Lord.

I could feel and actually hear the most holy of holy vibrations emanating from the cross-shaped pool of water. I knew instinctively that I was to surrender and fall into the water. When I did, a most holy force (The Holy Ghost) of spiritual energy cleansed my spirit. I then floated upwards, moving higher into the sky. Instantly, the clouds opened and the sky cleared. I stood in a clear blue sky above the clouds with the rain below. The edge of the higher spiritual world was opening in front of me.

Suddenly, billions of atoms came rushing together from the far reaches of the universe (literally from every direction at once) to form the body of Jesus Christ in front of me in a matter of seconds. The sound of the atoms rushing together was an enormous oceanic, cosmic sound, louder than thunder.

Instantly, there the Lord was in front of me shining in holy Glory. Jesus' face shined brighter than a thousand suns and that is no exaggeration. The eyes of the human body could never gaze upon a light so bright as this. The million-fold power and Glory of Innocence, Love, Ecstasy, Peace, Power, Grace, and Beauty was instantly staggering. I experienced Jesus as God, and that the power and Glory of the "whole universe" and the "Heavens beyond" was coming from Jesus, flowing through and making itself apparent to me.

When Jesus stood in front of me, the power and energy emanations were so great and constant that "i" could not bare to look at the Lord's face for more than a second at each glance. Like an earthquake in my veins and soul, trembling like a leaf, my spirit body collapsed and I fell to the Lord's feet; the power so great it was impossible to stand up. I held Jesus' feet, below his long brilliant shining white robe, his face blazing eternally innocent and beautiful. The humility was instant. The sense of self (as I knew it) was destroyed in the Lord's presence. I knew it was Jesus because of the sign of the cross, and the glimpses of his face, and the Glory and power that he beholds for eternity.

Jesus' hair is long and blazes with an ultra-shining copper light. His face is immeasurably more beautiful and innocent than all the children on earth, shining with Glory and light. Jesus stands tall. His robe shines blazing white (perhaps as bright as the sun itself) and hangs just below his knees; his feet are exposed bare in sandals.

When Jesus speaks, his voice is as silent as a calm lake but is heard very clearly to the ears of the spirit. He speaks perfect English. If educated humans can speak multiple languages, I am sure Jesus speaks all languages perfectly. It should be no surprise. Jesus spoke to me in English because I am from the English speaking world. If I were French, I am sure he would speak to me in French.

There is a great added feature beyond human language that Jesus showed me as the Lord spoke. It is called the "word" and all that is "implied by the word"—both experienced directly and clearly. This means that both the word and the extended implications of the word are delivered simultaneously. The word is heard by the spirit ears and the implied is seen clearly like our eyes can see the expanding "ripple effect" when a stone is dropped into a clear lake. Because the implications are so clearly revealed, throughout this message you will see Jesus' spoken words, which appear simple, and the subsequent text will reveal a portion of the implied. I could not write the whole implied because each word the Lord speaks reveals countless implications which each branches off into more implications. Therefore, I have selected what I feel is sufficient to explain the implied.

The first thing Jesus said to me was: **"I have appeared to a number of people throughout history, but at different levels of their spiritual ability. No one has seen me in my entirety. Even now, you are not seeing me in my entirety. It is not possible at this time."**

Jesus is implying that he is not a one-dimensional being like humans appear to be. The Lord appears to you within your scope of spiritual ability, and we certainly are unable to see the Lord in the Lord's spiritual entirety. The term "entirety" here is so spiritually mysterious as to contain the universal micro and macrocosm, the Alpha and the Omega, all in one. It will be more possible to glimpse this implication at the end of this message rather than now. Even to show a human who is not ready a small part of Jesus' Glory is like sending a billion watts of electricity into a one-watt circuit. It would short out a person's nervous system and soul. We have to evolve toward God in stages before we can survive even one direct gaze by the Lord.

Jesus is so much more than I could see at that time, and I could barely withstand as much as I was experiencing. It is so powerful just to gaze upon the Lord. I could gaze upon the face of any other spiritual teacher with relative ease, but this was impossible with Jesus. Even with Ray Ban sunglasses on, there would be no difference. The light of the Lord was full of extreme levels of inescapable Glory.

I knew what the Lord meant when I first saw and experienced the Lord's body manifest from all the atoms of the universe. He showed me he actually was everywhere and in everything and had the power to command any of the spiritual or physical universes at will. Jesus is "one" with and is all of that, including the expansive spiritual universes which I could not see at that time. This is how he performed all those miracles when he was on earth. Having seen how much power and Glory Jesus has, I have no doubt that those Biblical miracles—raising the dead, turning the sea into wine, manifesting the loaves of bread for the multitudes, curing the sick and the blind—were real. In fact, they were tiny compared to what Jesus could really do.

The full meaning of the Lord's words, "No one has seen me in my entirety," is so vast, it means that the Lord Jesus Christ, in the Lord's entirety, would have to be so great in Glory that no other being, no matter how enlightened or angelic, can see that entirety.

There is startling evidence for this in the Nag Hammadi Library. These ancient texts were discovered in Egypt in 1945. They used to be the Gospels of early Christianity before Rome had them destroyed, for reasons that become apparent after studying them. Someone buried the books in ancient Egypt. I believe their discovery is of such paramount importance to Christianity, that to live without them for millennia, as we did, was a tragic loss. Today, the Nag Hammadi was translated into English by members of the Coptic Gnostic Library Project, of the Institute for Antiquity and Christianity, Claremont, California. It was introduced to me by Professor of Religion at Princeton, Elaine H. Pagels. I will use it as a reference throughout this manuscript to give evidence to many of the wisdoms I received directly from the Lord. Because of the similarity of messages I was about to receive with these Gnostic Gospels, I had to deduct that they are not heresy, as the early Church declared, but true teachings of Jesus Christ.

In the Nag Hammadi Library, Gospel of Philip, pages 144-145, we see clear evidence to what Jesus' first words in this modern message mean: "Jesus took them all by stealth, for he did not appear as he was, but in the manner in which they would be able to see him. He appeared to them all. He appeared to the great as great. He appeared to the small as small. He appeared to the angels as an angel, and to men as a man. Because of this his word hid itself from everyone. Some indeed saw him, thinking that they were seeing themselves, but when he appeared to his disciples in glory on the mount he was not small. He became great, but he made the disciples great, that they may be able to see him in his greatness."

This first piece of evidence shows that Jesus "took them all by stealth," meaning Jesus hides his true power and glory because if the Lord revealed all the Lord's Glory, it would be much too powerful for anyone to bear. Imagine being flooded in your heart with more Innocence, Love, Ecstasy, Peace and Power than it took to create the universe. No one could bear it. But if no one could bear all the Lord's Glory, just who then is Jesus Christ in the Lord's entirety? While I will provide more evidence from the Nag Hammadi Library, the impact of this evidence will be recapitulated at the end of this message where it will have a more profound meaning for the recipients of this message.

Nag Hammadi Library, Trimorphic Protennoia, page 521: "So, now, I was dwelling in them in the form of each one. The Archons thought that I was their Christ. Indeed I dwell in everyone. Indeed within those in whom I revealed myself as light I eluded the Archons. I am their beloved, for in that place I clothed myself as the Son of the Archigenetor, and I was like him until the end of his decree, which is the ignorance of Chaos. And among the Angels I revealed myself in their likeness, and among the Powers as if I were one of them, but among the Sons of Man as if I were a Son of Man, even though I am Father of everyone."

I will keep this statement unfulfilled for now and return to it near the end of this message. There is too much information needed to deliver in this message to explain the fuller meaning of what the Lord is saying here. The key point in showing this segment now is that the Lord says that the Lord appears and manifests (perhaps incarnates) at different spiritual levels of our universe, as the Lord reveals here "even though I am the Father of everyone."

Kneeling before the blaze of light and Glory of the Lord's most innocent face, the Lord spoke to me these words: **"Things are very bad down here on earth and there is little hope for much of humankind making the leap into God's Kingdom of Heavens. I have had to break the natural law of "human free will" to give people, who had previously made commitments with me to do the healing work and spiritual work, a wake-up call because even they are becoming distracted by the meaningless phenomena of the world. They are not doing what I sent them to earth to do. This was why your environmental company was failing. Many of the team players were being distracted by the meaningless phenomena of the world and only a few of you were doing the work."** The team players included wealthy persons who were to finance the technologies and developments. They are the most problematic ego complexes, and the most distracted.

It is important to understand that, from a divine perspective, Jesus, Mary or the enlightened Angels can assist us in our lives with meeting all the right people to make a project of divine plan be successful, *but the Angels cannot force any being to make the choices.* They cannot even intervene unless we ask them to. This means that if you need guidance in your life, you actually have to ask for intervention. Angels also don't intervene when we ask for help, to remove us from an experience, however painful it may be, that is an integral part of our spiritual development. Wisdom and free will prohibit this kind of force. This will be easier to understand as we get further into the most significant part of Jesus' message.

Again, I attempt to gaze, only for a few seconds, upon Jesus' face, brighter than a thousand suns, "crushing" me with Glory.

Then, I look down at my hands on his feet and sandals as he continues: **"It is wrong for Christians and others to believe in the abuse to the environment thinking that I will come along and clean up their mess in the Revelations. It is even worse to try and bring on the Revelations as an act to try and provoke the Second Coming. I have the power to make a whole new earth in a blink of an eye, yes! But, that is not the purpose of human evolution and the end of sin. Human beings do not evolve if they refuse to make loving choices for each other, the planet they live on, and all the beings that live on earth. They do not evolve if they do not grow up and learn to make loving choices on their own. Love is the catalyst that transforms the human soul into God's Kingdom. Without love in a person's soul, there is little that can be done to save them."**

I know Jesus sounds angry, and the Lord is angry out of compassion for us, but as he spoke those words I was being crushed with a million times more Love and Glory than all humans on earth could possibly give. Imagine anger filled with Innocence, Love, Ecstasy, Peace, Power, Beauty and Wisdom. That is the Lord. Try and understand this as you integrate what the Lord is saying to us throughout this message.

Think about what the Lord is saying here logically for a moment. If God is Love and even more so Glory, and a person refuses to grow in love, and perhaps Glory, how well are they going to receive the transformation of God's Love and Glory, which is millions of times greater than human love, at the hour of their death and make it into God's Love and Glory? For those who cannot stand to be loved and give love, what will happen to them when they even more so cannot stand the Lord's omnipresent and all powerful love and Glory? They will flee in terror.

Human love is the easiest preparation, but still it is a quantum leap to make it into the Lord's love, let alone Glory. What will happen to those who have labeled themselves Christians, Jews, Muslims, Buddhists, Hindus and atheists, yet are egotistically righteous and unloving towards anyone other than those who are of the same faith or agree with them? What about those who were afraid of falling in love? This message reveals that the consequences could be devastating for those souls.

This message is showing that it will at least be very difficult to be able to stand the idea of building a loving relationship with each other on an international and inter-religious level. But, even within our own societies and structure of living, real love, Glory and enlightenment is the transformation that merely prepares us for the quantum leap into God's Kingdoms of Heavens. It is not the final product. It is not that we remain the same as we become when we die. There is a quantum transformation, even of our most evolved state, at the hour of death. It is not that if we pass the test of who has the right god, gets to go into heaven.

The Lord is revealing a great sense of urgency and compassion for us, for the Lord understands the outcome of our souls after death. Therefore it is wise to listen to what Jesus is saying here.

In the Nag Hammadi Library, Jesus warns us that we should not rely on the afterlife to attain to spiritual enlightenment or the resurrection, but should transform ourselves "before death." This is contrary to the classic Christian belief that just by being baptized, one is "saved." While this point is an iconoclasm to the Christian world at large, upon seeing the Lord, I can attest that it is much closer to the truth than the position Christianity holds to be true today. This message is revealing that only if a person lives a life of truth and real love, or at least evolves into true love after all of life's vicissitudes and inner tribulations, can they hope to be capable of withstanding the cleansing of the Holy Ghost and enter the Clear Light Heavens.

In the Nag Hammadi Library, Gospel of Philip, page 153, we find the evidence: "Those who say they will die first and rise are in error. If they do not receive the resurrection while they live, when they die they will receive nothing. So also when speaking about baptism they say, Baptism is a great thing, because if people receive it they will live." The last point here shows that even to think you can be saved by baptism alone is also an error.

In the Bible, Jesus did receive baptism by John the Baptist, but Jesus Christ did not baptize any of his disciples with water—he taught them the path of wisdom, prayer and right living, leading to the actual experience of the holy spirit which is real inner enlightenment. This is confirmed in Matthew, Chapter 3, Verse 11: "I indeed baptize you with water unto repentance: but he that cometh after me is mightier than I, whose shoes I am not worthy to bear: he shall baptize you with the Holy Ghost, and with fire." John never claims here that baptism with water actually "saves a soul" but by it asks you to live a life of "repentance." Repentance alone is not salvation.

Further evidence of this is found in the Nag Hammadi Library, Testimony of Truth, page 457: "For the Son of Man did not baptize any of his disciples. . . . But the Baptism of truth is something else; it is by renunciation of the world that it is found. But those who say only with the tongue that they are renouncing are lying, and they are coming to the place of fear."

Further, and the most staggering evidence to suggest that baptism alone does not give anyone salvation and heaven, is in the Nag Hammadi Library, The Paraphrase of Shem, Page 357: "Oh Shem, they are deceived by manifold demons, thinking that through the Baptism with the uncleanness of water, that which is dark, feeble, idle, and disturbing, he will take away sins. . . . For I foretell it to those who have a heart. They will refrain from the impure Baptism."

I don't feel that this is saying that you should not get baptized, rather, if you do, use it only as a reminder that you are walking on this path with Jesus Christ. By it alone, however, you are still not "saved." You still have to transform your life and work to attain real inner enlightenment by wisdom, prayer and a truthful life to gain the purification needed to withstand the cleansing of the Holy Ghost and be able to withstand the Glory of living in the resurrected body.

This message and experience I am receiving from Jesus Christ today, in 1994, concurs greatly with the evidence I have just presented from both the Bible and the Nag Hammadi Library. But, there are many more possibilities that you can discover as this message evolves. The real truth is not so "cut and dry," as you will see.

III

As humankind approaches the Millennium,
the notion of playing God spreads like a virus.

In 1493, Columbus said he discovered America. The Native Americans have said that they had already discovered America a long time ago, Columbus was lost, and that they discovered Columbus. Not only did the White Man raid America from the Indians for land claims and to conquer, the Catholic Church forced Native Americans to convert to Christianity by means so brutal and cruel, they make the crucifixion of Jesus Christ seem like passive violence. Millions of Native Americans were tortured and killed in the name of Jesus Christ.

When special Native Americans told stories to the White Man of how Jesus had appeared to them in powerful visions, shining with light, and how Jesus loved the Native Americans, and even told them they would inherit the new earth, the White Man and the Church did not acknowledge these visions. The violence and oppression continues to this day.

Bhante Piyananda, a very educated Buddhist monk from Sri Lanka, living in Los Angeles, told me a story of how the

Catholic Church, in the fourteenth century AD, sent its missionaries to Sri Lanka and forced Buddhists to convert to Christianity by the sword. It was a bloody massacre. Buddhist babies were thrown up in the air and down they came upon the swords of the Christian missionaries until the Buddhist women and men cried and were forced to convert. Still, only some of them converted.

While these are only some of the examples of humans thinking that they are "playing God," they are examples that Jesus laments. Jesus is very sad for humankind because it has not understood the Lord's message of conversion to love. Conversion to love is Jesus' message. Conversion to a form of religion by force is not.

When Jesus said that "It is wrong for Christians and others to believe in the abuse to the environment thinking that I will come along and clean up their mess in the Revelations," the Lord is perceiving a great need for us to change our ways and learn to live in harmony with our earth. The seriousness of this issue is astounding and will be revealed more clearly as this message evolves. It is even worse to try and bring on the Revelations by destroying our earth, each other and our creatures, as an act to try and provoke the Second Coming. Jesus and Mary have been giving us too many fair warnings. If we do not take heed, a terror by our own making will strike. Just watch the earth and the number of disasters increase. It is not the Lord who causes force majeure. It is the reaction of the natural world's forces that does back to us what we do to the natural world. We humans are so fragile, it is no problem to remove us if we continue to act as a cancer.

Since the Book of Revelation has been scrutinized by scholars, the Christian world has been obsessed with uncovering its meaning. When will the promised Second Coming of the Lord Jesus Christ happen? What does the Second Coming really mean?

There are numerous Christian, Muslim, Jewish and other groups who are trying to bring on the Revelations and Armageddon thinking that this is the "will of God" and Jesus or their own messiah will be coming soon if they perform this will.

The Lord is telling us that he is not willing an Armageddon, but predicted it in the vision to St. John the Divine (Revelations) based on our state of ignorance. "Ignorance" is the key operating word here. It is not the will of the Lord to have a war. It is the Lord's observation and prediction based on our state of inner and outer conflict that we will create many wars, thinking we are "playing God's will." Jesus is telling me that anything that is not done in love, and by his true message, is not the will of the Lord. He is deeply saddened by these acts.

Because of our internal psychological state of conflict, it is very easy to calculate the outcome. It is not necessary to fulfill Armageddon for the Lord. In fact, if we evolved in love and wisdom, there would be no need for such a great war and no need for the crimes we commit on each other at all.

There are many secretive groups the Lord is warning us about here. There are many unseen players who create world events. Perhaps this warning is to go out to all those who are trying to create the circumstances right now for World War III just because they feel it may be the will of god to provoke the Second Coming. Perhaps these fanatics see themselves as God's servants.

Today, with television operating as a demigod to the masses who believe what the media shows them, it is possible to manipulate the world and coerce them into planned action and even war. Television has become the demigod of the modern world. Whoever controls the media becomes the unseen demigod of our world. What I mean is, the media can help create World War III. Are secret players in our world governments trying to "play God" and bring us into the war of the worlds just to see if the Lord arrives on time?

While his intentions are driven by his own faith and religious understandings, even the Christian leader Pat Robertson has blamed environmentalists for inhibiting the Revelations and most importantly the notion of Armageddon by trying to save the planet. My personal observation of Pat Robertson is to say that he thinks he is playing God's assistant, and trying to help us all get to the battlefield in Armageddon, so that we can all hurry up and meet the Lord and get on to Heaven. Pat Robertson is not the only one. There are too many names to mention who feel the same way he does.

The Muslim world sees the Western world as evil and to make war against America is assisting the will of God. The attack on the New York World Trade Center is another example of the same phenomenon, while the CIA's attacks on the Muslim world are also examples of people, religions and nations "playing God" against each other. The Jewish world sees the Muslim and Christian worlds as its enemy. Almost every religion has created an enemy, but in their minds only. Because we believe in what goes on in our minds, we manifest it in our world.

Jumping ahead of this meeting with Jesus to 1995, in an article by Joseph Douglas Jr. titled "Chemical and Biological Warfare Unmasked," the author states, "The most recent event to raise consciousness is one Senator Nunn highlighted: the release of a sarin nerve agent in the Tokyo commuter train by the Aum cult earlier this year. Reports in the open press have credited this cult with more than 10,000 members in Japan, 30,000 members in Russia and ties to North Korea; sufficient chemicals to manufacture six tons of nerve agents; the ingredients to produce botulinum toxin; attempts to obtain the Ebola virus: testing sarin on sheep in Australia; planning a coup in Japan; a war chest between $300 million and $1 billion; a Russian helicopter and two unmanned drones, ideal Chemical Biological Warhead (CBW) delivery systems; setting up companies in America to obtain CBW supplies; *preaching global*

Armageddon [italics added]; and planning a Chemical Biological Warfare party for the upcoming Asian Pacific Cooperation forum in honor of visiting officials including President Clinton."

If that isn't frightening enough about President Bill Clinton being invited, read US Code Title 50/Section 1520 (01/16/96), *"Use of human subjects for testing of chemical or biological agents by Department of Defense, accounting to Congressional committees with respect to experiments and studies; notification of local civilian officials."* In the law it states: "The Secretary of Defense may not conduct any test or experiment involving the use of any chemical or biological agent on civilian populations unless local civilian officials in the area in which the test or experiment is to be conducted are notified in advance of such test or experiment, and such test or experiment may then be conducted only after the expiration of the thirty-day period beginning on the date of such notification." There is also an agreement (Title 50/Section 1524) for the same program to provide support to vaccination programs by the Department of Health and Human Services.

Could these cooperating forces be planning an Armageddon with biological weapons and already choosing the only survivors—those persons who qualify to take the vaccination? If this were true, this could mean that they are not even planning on the power of the Lord and the Second Coming, and that they will judge and decide who gets to live in the New World after the Armageddon they create.

The other notion is that because we have all been responsible for overpopulating our world, governments are forced to take the role of "playing God" for the sake of our very survival. Perhaps they see a drastic population decrease as such a measure. Perhaps it is a back-up plan in case the Messiah doesn't show up by the year 2010, and solve all of our problems for us. Perhaps it is an experiment to see if vaccines can prevent death from a chemical or biological warfare attack. We don't know for sure, but we do know that chemical and biological weapons, once released, cannot be contained very easily. The government can test a chemical weapon like Anthrax on civilians, if it gave them a vaccine, and it may be able to contain part of the effects. However, the effects of a biological weapon test is far more difficult to contain in a civilian population. That is because a virus can spread throughout a whole country. Unless a person was vaccinated, they would die.

If our governments decide that we have overpopulated our world, and this cannot be blamed on the governments, and our governments feel the only way to survive into the next century is to create a drastic population decrease, they could easily do it by this measure: give a vaccine to "chosen ones" and drop a deadly virus, making it look like an act of God, and all those without the vaccine will die. The world will be saved from overpopulation.

I have seen large US government files showing great concern over the issue of overpopulation and the effects it has on sustaining life on earth. If the government has to "play God" to solve a problem, it can now do it without anyone knowing it wasn't an act of nature. Because we believe what we see on television, it is easy to manipulate the masses into believing almost anything. Television and its demigods can create almost any situation in global politics they want.

How will we solve our problems on our own if the Messiah doesn't show up when we expect the Messiah to arrive? How many national leaders and conspirators will presume to take on the role of "playing God" just in case God doesn't show up and solve all of humankind's problems? What are we all going to do if we move into and past the year 2000 and God doesn't show up and we have to solve very serious problems such as overpopulation, environmental crisis, and religious and social conflicts on our own?

The Lord has expressed great concern in this message to all human beings. Jesus knows we have problems of these many kinds. The Lord knows they need to be solved but Jesus is saying we need to clean up the mess ourselves and not rely on the Lord to clean up our mess after the Revelations are fulfilled.

If we are living in an overpopulated world, what are you personally prepared to do about that? Are you willing to have smaller families? Are you willing to use birth control? If not birth control, are you willing to be conscious over the power of your own sexuality and learn to use it in ways that do not abuse your right to create life?

If we are living in a world that needs clean energy technologies to be implemented, what are you personally willing to do about it? Are you willing to invest or donate money to the solutions and the scientists who can make it happen? Are you willing to become educated into the ecological sciences and contribute to them? Are you willing to become involved in the political process that forces these new technologies to become implemented?

The late great Carl Sagan once said, "Science has already come up with the technologies that would allow us to live in harmony with our earth. They just have not been implemented." He was speaking about solar power and hydrogen fuel, amongst others.

If our world insists that we go to war with each other, and you learn that the only answer is "love," what are you willing to do about war? Are you willing to educate yourself about the "cause" of war and how to prevent war?

Will we rely on the Lord to solve our problems because we refuse to solve our own problems? If we refuse to evolve on our own, what will the Lord do to try and instigate our evolution?

When Jesus said to me that he had the power to create a whole new earth with such ease, I did not doubt him for a second because his presence and Glory contained more than enough power to create whole galaxies. I cannot explain to anyone how positively devastating this was to me to see one Lord with so much power and Glory at his command. It was positively devastating because I could see how little power humans really have. If any religious leader or any great spiritual human being I have met told me they could make a new earth, I would seriously doubt them. This would not mean that other spiritual teachers are evil at all. In fact, I still feel that many of them are benevolent towards our spiritual growth. I do not want to take the classic fundamentalist Christian ideal that all other religions are evil. After all, that is the philosophy that has gotten so many religions to divide and go into holy war status with each other. That is also the heart of why the fanatics who are "playing God" will be at war with each other, thinking it's all just one big football game. That is not the message I was receiving from the Lord.

Now that we have created this mess on earth, the thousands of years of violence, the destruction to the environment, the oppression of the poor by the super financially wealthy, the sexual and mental abuse—all of it—what are we prepared to do? Are we going to play stupid and wait for God to arrive and sweep up the floor?

If a child is left in his or her room to make a mess, and the parent never teaches the child how to clean up the mess, or the child never learns, then the room is always a mess unless the parent cleans up after the child. This is how Jesus sees us right now: as children who are looking for God to clean up the mess, when they know how to do it themselves, but refuse.

Fallen at the feet of the Lord, barely withstanding the emanations of the Lord's Glory, it was amazing to feel so much love, power and the rest of the Glory as his compassion towards humanity holds the tone of what we would call anger. Imagine being filled with ecstasy while the Lord is scolding you and calling you an unwise fool. It is indescribably brilliant to be filled with bliss while feeling scolded at the same time. The Lord was speaking like this.

Jesus: **"If humans act as unloving terrorists towards each other and the earth, they show no signs to me of proving themselves to be maturing into loving souls ready for the evolution that God has in store for them."**

This means that all those religious leaders and politicians who instigated great crimes of violence, all the unseen players of the cause of violence, regardless of religion, the Lord is deeply saddened for. For the Lord knows that it is only by love that a soul may enter Heaven.

This does not mean that if you get the right god and pass "Go" you collect an entry pass into Heaven, and if you don't pass your written exam by getting the wrong god, you go to Hell. The doors to Heaven are always open, but those who have no love in their hearts will find the Glory shining from the gates of Heaven unbearable and flee in terror, just as they have done the same with love and Glory in their lives. The term "Glory" in no way here means the glory that soldiers or football players feel when they beat the enemy or the other team.

God's Glory is not a puffing of the chest. It is not as though Saint Peter at the Gates of Heaven is one of those body-builder bouncer guys who stands at the door to a night club saying "yes" and "no," letting people in and turning people away. The proverbial "gates" have always been open, but who dares to enter? It is that much of a terrible irony, terrible in the sense that God's heart and Kingdom is constantly "wide open" so to speak, but we fear entering the Lord's emanation while we are in the spirit.

Remember, Jesus said in the Bible that even he does not know the hour or minute of his own Second Coming, and that only the Father knows. That is how mysterious the Father in Heaven is. Hence, this message says that we must create and coexist with nature in a harmony rather than terror because our future children and we have to live here. This means that we are to continue to evolve and create a better and more loving world for ourselves, our children, the animals, and all other living beings on our earth while the great moment is still a mystery. To try and bring on the signs of the Revelation by trying to start catastrophes and condemning environmentalists or humanitarian efforts and asking for Armageddon does not bring us closer to the Second Coming. It takes us further from God and a better world.

Jesus: **"It is true that I can make a new Heaven and a new earth with ease, but so many human beings are so deeply unloving in every way, towards each other and God's creation, there is little hope for them becoming evolved enough to live in Heaven or a new earth. Love is the necessary catalyst for humans to make the leap to God and towards the supreme happiness in God's Kingdom.** [Jesus is speaking with compassion and worry about too many unloving souls.] **Very few people have truly understood my message of love to all of God's creation. So many humans have become so terribly unloving, there are too few humans who will be able to even withstand the Holy Ghost, let alone the Glory of the Kingdom of God."**

This is a crisis situation in the eyes of the Lord. The Lord loves all beings so much but also understands the spiritual physics of the soul and how the soul needs to evolve into the Heavens. Can we really understand the meaning that "the doors to Heaven are always open," that there is so much love shining out of Heaven that who dares to enter? The Lord is understanding and compassionate to humankind in this message, yet knows that humankind must evolve in real love if they are to be able to withstand the love in Heaven. There is no other way. This is so challenging to our churches, temples and synagogues, many of whom have taught that just by announcing blindly that they are a Christian, a Jew, a Muslim, or a Buddhist that this suddenly makes them able to enter Heaven. Heaven is not a place that feels just like you did in your mother's womb, which was the most peace many of us have ever experienced. Heaven is a quantum leap in Joy compared to our mother's womb. Perhaps we may have to rebuild our intentions and actions into more actualized loving ones so that we may actualize and be able to feel love.

This is not a personal attack on the religions of the world, an iconoclasm, it is an integrational message. It is the wisdom of the Lord, because the Lord knows that it is only by real Love, Wisdom, Glory and Enlightenment that you can enter the Heavens. It is impossible to cheat yourself on the true experience of becoming the living truth. God cannot be fooled.

IV

Jesus: ***"Stop complaining. You worry too much. Please continue to carry the burden (your environmental work) that you agreed with me to carry before you came to earth."*** Pleading, Jesus: ***"Please continue to serve the scientists that you are working with. They are very important to me. Please do not give up. It is very important."***

This first point is alarming to many Christians: that I made an agreement, as many others have, to do this healing work for the environment, **"before you came to earth,"** as Jesus said. The Official Christian Church position on creation of the soul is that there is no pre-existence to our souls, that we were all made living Spirits at the time of our birth into the flesh. So, how could I and other healers, and other people, have pre-existed? And if so, where did we pre-exist? In this case, healers, Jesus is inferring, were sent by the Lord to humanity and the environment out of compassion and wisdom. But, where did we receive such divinely instructed compassion and wisdom, if we did not pre-exist?

The scriptures do reveal the clues. From the Nag Hammadi Library, in The Gospel of Thomas, Verse 49, Jesus spoke about the pre-existence of certain souls: "Jesus said, "Blessed are the solitary and elect, for you will find the kingdom. For you are from it, and to it you will return." About the classic Christian view that man and woman were born as living spirits when our flesh came into being, Verse 29 reveals: "Jesus said, "If flesh came into being because of spirit, it is a wonder. But if spirit came into being because of the body, it is a wonder of wonders. Indeed, I am amazed at how this great wealth has made its home in this poverty." These scriptures reveal that Jesus does not agree with the notion that we, as spirits, did come into being because of the birth of our bodies.

Jesus' pleading went on a bit. I have never experienced such sweetness and love in a pleading in all of time. How could I say "no" to Jesus? I couldn't. I knew the scientists and projects Jesus was talking about. It was people such as physicist Bogdan C. Maglich, inventor of a type of non-radioactive nuclear energy that could supply us all with clean, abundant energy, who were still struggling for funding. Dr. Maglich's aneutronic fusion reactor was developed with over $25 million and was just a shot away from a working power plant. He had many Nobel Prize winners in support of his work, but no money to finish the project. But there were others like Harry Braun, Roy McCalister and Leroy Essel with the Sterling Solar Power Hydrogen Phoenix Project. They were going to use the world's most advanced solar power systems to make the world's most ecological fuel (hydrogen) in mass supply. We could be driving our cars and heating our homes with no pollution to the environment whatsoever. The project had little or no funds. There was Scott Tucker with his co-genesis project: burning trash in a closed system (non polluting) to produce electricity and carbon by-products. This would not only help reduce the solid waste disposal problem, it would recycle the recyclables and produce electricity. The project didn't get funding. Also, my work with the forests (tree planting) was all part of his pleading for me not to give up. The Lord was also speaking to anyone who can hear this message not to give up on serving the healers of humankind and the ecology of the planet.

My observation has been that there is no shortage of brilliant minds and scientists who have already invented technology to allow humankind to live in harmony with nature, just as the late great Carl Sagan had said, but there is a shortage of servants to them and, most of all, financial supporters. This message is a call to support and serve those scientists in any way that you can. Of the brilliant, I, of course, do not know all your names but I can assure you that the Lord does. At the end of this book, you will find an index of some of those projects.

The very fact that Jesus knew I was thinking of giving up and just having a good time was shocking to me, really shocking. I really didn't think anybody up there could hear anyone, including me. I thought I was yelling at an empty sky. They really do listen and messages do get sent. Wow! There is no distance?

If the Heavenly planets are suspended in the light that gets brighter as one travels nearer to the center of the galaxy, and those planets of paradise are millions of light years in time from earth (whose solar system resides on the outer edge of the Milky Way galaxy), then there can be no time and space for angels to travel and hear the words of men, women, children, mammals, animals and all of God's creation, here on earth. My little screams went beyond time and space to Heaven. Perhaps yours can too.

The very fact that Jesus knew about my calling the angels lazy and unwilling to bless those who work so hard to save the earth, proved to me that angels and the Lord must all exist beyond apparent distances; thus beyond time and space.

In my moments of doubt about why I was working so hard on the ailing ecology, I remember this really attractive young woman once telling me, "Nice guys finish last, David." This was a joke on me. I felt like I was wasting my time trying to work so hard and suffering so much, as some of my friends were also, like Jeffrey Harrison, Leroy Essel, Tim Rhode, Nancy Pfister, Ghassan Ibrahim, Cassandra Delaney—and for what? To save a planet so that a bunch of greedy bankers, corporate heads, gangsters and prostitutes can party?

I was really mad because I was the one carrying eighty pounds of seedling trees around my waist, climbing mountains in the pouring rain, covered in dirt and mud, planting trees while I could not even afford to live in my own house, and Greenpeace would raise $300 million per year to tell the people the bad news! That is why I wanted to quit. I even tried to get a job with Greenpeace and the Environmental Defense Fund, with all of my experience, just to try the political protesting approach. I did not even receive an answer. Not even one of those wonderful rejection letters showed up in the mail.

Jesus told me to stop complaining because I had been so mad at God and had angry conversations with God (talking to the ceiling of my tent and the sky) because the healing work with the Green & Blue Company was failing and I thought God was not helping at all.

Jesus also told me why things were not working with human beings making the transition to loving choices and responsible choices for humanity, explaining the failure of new technologies to allow humanity and science to live in peaceful harmony with the earth. Also, this was in relation to other spiritual and healing work being done by myself and others.

I feel that many humans do not understand that although it is possible to make a whole new earth—and it will happen (the same earth reborn?)—we do not qualify to live on it if we do not show God and each other our love. We are, indirectly, God's creations and to not love God's creation is to disrespect God and each other. What St. Francis said concurs with this.

Just because God can make a new earth paradise, does not give us the right to live as abusive humans, destroying it and each other, and then have Jesus come and fix everything later. Earth is not a disposable diaper for babies. Try and understand the logic of this. This type of thinking means that humans live in suffering all those moments (and they are long) that the Saints and Jesus are not with us.

V

King James Bible, Book of Genesis, Chapter 2, Verses 16-17: "And the Lord God commanded the man, saying, Of every tree of the garden thou mayest freely eat: But the tree of the knowledge of good and evil, thou shalt not eat of it: for in the day that thou eatest thereof thou shalt surely die."

It is important to note that when Jesus speaks about advanced spiritual knowledge, such as we are about to enter, he speaks with large, sophisticated energy thought-parables that enter a recipient's soul, in this case me. Therefore, this is a translation into English. This particular knowledge was first imparted to me on my Near Death Experience in December 1986 (see chapter 3), then was recollected on this meeting with Jesus in a matter of seconds.

Gazing once again upon the Glorious and innocent face of the Lord, in a blaze of light! This following parable was delivered in the most sophisticated form of telepathy in a matter of seconds. A few seconds in the Lord amounts to many pages of human time and space, as you will see.

When Jesus said that he had to break the natural law of free will to give people wake-up calls, the Lord meant that we humans have free will and we can do whatever we want because *we wanted to decide good and evil for ourselves;* and this desire made our will and self separate from God's. This knowledge of good and evil will be the key focal point for sin, as you will later see. That is why we live in a body of sin. A body of sin is an ego-centered body and soul whose nervous system is separated from God.

This subject is incredibly simple, but very evolved is the outcome. I will try and explain the meaning of Jesus' biblical parable from Matthew, Chapter 6, verses 22-23, as he explained it to me in person: "The light of the body is the eye: if therefore thine eye be *single,* thy whole body shall be full of light. If thine eye be evil, thy whole body shall be filled with darkness."

Try to acknowledge that we are what we eat, in both food and in thought, and we become what we believe. Our actions stem from who we have become, by that which we think or believe in. We have become exactly what we are internally. We project our internal world into, and create by it, the outer world which we all live in. This means that all you see outside, and even many natural disasters, were created by what we started within our souls. Knowing this, open a King James Bible and start by reading the Book of Genesis with me again. Herein lies the greatest secret parable.

In Genesis, Chapter 2, Verses 16-17: "And the Lord God commanded the man, saying, Of every tree of the garden thou mayest freely eat: But the tree of the knowledge of *good and evil,* thou shalt not eat of it: for in the day that thou eatest thereof thou shalt surely die." It does not say that God will kill us or kick us out of paradise, it says we will "surely die."

Later, Eve is tempted by the serpent in Genesis, Chapter 3, Verses 1-7: "NOW THE serpent was more subtle than any beast of the field which the Lord God had made. And he said unto the woman, Yea, hath God said, Ye shall not eat of every tree in the garden? And the woman said unto the serpent, We may eat of the fruit of the trees of the garden: But the fruit of the tree which is in the midst of the garden, God hath said, Ye shall not eat of it, neither shall ye touch it, lest ye die. And the serpent said unto the woman, Ye shall not surely die: For God doth know that in the day ye eat thereof, then your eyes shall be opened, and ye shall be as gods, knowing good and evil. And when the woman saw that the tree was good for food, and that it was pleasant to the eyes, and a tree to be desired to make one wise, she took of the fruit thereof, and did eat, and gave also unto her husband with her: and he did eat. And the eyes of them were both opened, and they knew that they were naked; and they sewed fig leaves together, and made themselves aprons."

Remember that it is the serpent Satan (the fallen angel) who is tempting her, not God, so there has to be something terrible about this knowledge of good and evil. Eve did not know that Satan and the fallen angels did this very same thing, and they all became separate from God by doing so. She and Adam did not know what it meant to decide for themselves what is good and what is evil and what the outcome would be. Neither did the fallen angels, who previously partook of the fatal knowledge, know how deadly the outcome would be for them also. Please follow closely now because Jesus did explain this to me and I saw it in the LORD. It is the "root cause" of all sin and war. If you can undo it inside of yourself, you will slowly become free of self-created sin and be filled with light (Glory).

The analogy of thought/knowledge (fruit) as food for the soul is used here. The knowledge of good and evil in its *"entirety"* is a *conflict* and nothing but a conflict. Try and step back in your mind and soul and see good and evil as an entire thought form. If you are what you eat and you become what you think and believe, as soon as you eat from this poisonous knowledge of good and evil, what happens? *You become a conflict* because you are what you eat. Your spirit ingested a conflict. Now the neurosis is turning inside of your soul, having destroyed the innocent, pure, undivided mind and soul that lives in God's "undivided" love. Now you divide yourself into good and evil and become as if split in two.

Innocence is lost and now there is this problem called "conflict" to solve. Now you have to "solve" the conflict that you ate and make it solid, define it, before it destroys your nervous system. Eventually, having solidified and defined it, you can act upon your version of good and evil as the true definition of "right." By then other souls and humans will have taken in the same knowledge of good and evil and will have solidified it and defined it, but their definition of good and evil is slightly or strongly different from yours. Now you will see your version of the defined good versus the defined evil as "right" and others as wrong, thus creating conflict in the inner and outer world around you. This conflict, which resulted in a separation from God, is what also happened to Satan and all the other fallen angels.

Enoch was perhaps the first Biblical saint. In the Book of Enoch (Richard Laurence Translation), page 85 Chapter LXVIII, we read about the fallen angels: "6. The name of the third is Gadrel: he discovered every stroke of death to the children of men. 7. He seduced Eve." This book shows that there were many fallen angels. The message from Jesus is to reveal that even the fallen ones did not fully understand how this knowledge would not only separate them from God, but also from each other. They would always be at war, even amongst other fallen angels, and now humankind would be at war with each other and even with the fallen angels.

Now that these angels were fallen, this would be the only way that Satan and the fallen angels could gain total mastery over an entire race of human beings: by making them separate from God and then lure them into the laws of conflict and mere survivalism, thus becoming subservient to worship them as gods.

There are many Christians and Satan worshipers who think that God actually kicked Satan out of Heaven—as if it was a war between God and the devil. But the way this truth was revealed to me by the Lord is different.

Knowledge of good and evil is a "conflict" in its entirety. God and God's angels do not fight fallen angels. Understanding the spiritual physics of love and Glory in Heaven, you can see that "conflict" is a lower vibration than "love" and literally "conflict" cannot exist in love because the physics of "love" create a state of union in which there is no "conflict." The angels who took on the possibility of knowing good and evil for themselves did it because it existed in the total realm of possibilities, not because God created it. When the fallen angels took in "conflict" they did not even really know what they were about to get into, and neither did the human souls who partook in the same and came to live here on earth.

"Conflict" is a lower vibration than love. It cannot stand the vibration of love (Heavens) and the souls and human beings who partake of the fatal knowledge leave Heaven and fear love, thus falling from grace with no violent hand from God or any angel. They thereby create their own will, separate from God and each other, and create their own worlds, which are all based in internal and external conflict.

Let's go over this again. Really try and see this inside your own self as you read this. It is a great key. If you really get it, this can save you and help you return to heaven and paradise.

Now that you are made separate from God, all of your soul's cells are vibrating with conflict (good and evil) making your nervous system neurotic. Eventually you try to end the conflict by solidifying it. The problem is, so did everybody else in their own individual ways, all separate from God. If ten million persons have taken in the fatal knowledge (before coming here) and became the conflict, they all became ego-righteous in their own isolated views of good and evil, thus giving rise to inward and outward world tension. Mathematically, it would be impossible for everyone to totally agree on anything, thus making life full of conflict, egotism and even worse, there would be no love and togetherness. Worse still, God would no longer have direct communication with humankind, but Satan and the fallen angels would.

What is the first thing that happens to Adam and Eve's offspring in the Bible? Cain and Abel have an argument. Arguments happen because one or both people see their own view as better than the other (ego-righteous), because their individual defined versions of good and evil are different. Cain and Abel have a serious battle and one of them dies. There is always one who is more angry than the other, or more skilled in battle, and someone dies or is oppressed.

Now, those humans who could basically agree with each other, they formed congregations of thought or sects of religions, but they would always be opposed to other congregations of thought that were different, thus different sects of religions and/or different sects of Christianity are formed. Even a single religion becomes divided against itself. Buddhism, Hinduism and Muslim religions are also divided into many schools of thought. This is the mathematical outcome of individualized good and evil. Egotism results. Views clash.

I have studied with so many different religions and Christian religions and they all say that they are right and the other Church or religion is wrong, even to the degree that they thought the other Christian Church or group was going to hell because they got it all wrong. Do you SEE the illusion of this poisonous knowledge? It separates humankind from each other, they suffer from lack of love for one another, and worse, God will not enter the spirit of a human unless they dissolve the self-created illusion barrier.

What is this barrier? We know it exists because all of us know that we are not living in direct communion with God, and are not living in the Glory and power of God. The barrier is created magnetically when good and evil turns inside of the soul. This magnetic turning of positive and negative creates a circular/oval force-field around the soul, which shields out God's Glory and light. Without God's Glory and light, and with inner conflict, the soul suffers great losses.

Even though people could religiously agree on a number of facts, they would disagree on others, thus causing separatism and war even within their own religions. Even in the name of God they fight so-called holy wars. Millions of lives are lost in the battles of ignorance. This terrible suffering was not created by God, as you can see.

Wars result from the clashing ego-centered views of good and evil, and paradise is lost not because God kicked us out of Adam and Eve's proverbial paradise but because we create violence and war and no longer know how to create and live in paradise. This is because we create the world around us by what we internalize. Internal conflict manifests as external conflict. External conflict is hell.

Paradise is lost not because God got mad and actually kicked us out, but because ignorance was produced in the mind and soul by this poisonous knowledge. Each one of us holds our internal views of good and evil like a solid architecture. But that is only part of what we lost. We would also lose our direct evolving communion with God and life in God's paradises or Heavens. This is because our obsession with the inner fire of conflict, and the insatiable impossibility of trying to "get it right" disables us from living inside of God's love and emanation qualities. This is very difficult to describe, but I witnessed it directly in the Lord.

What we are about to discover is that this knowledge of conflict (good and evil) is the root cause of all the deadly sins and defilements. So, with this fatal knowledge, humans will be at war many times with each other, and even in the names of their gods. Although the one God and the Heavens are suspended in undivided love, humans become divided against each other, each thinking their group/religion (including Atheism) is right and the other wrong. This is the very basis for all conflicts, violent confrontation and clashing views. War does not exist without first establishing an inner conflict.

This is what Satan created for itself and others (although even Satan did not fully realize its own outcome upon first taking in this knowledge), and humankind became divided and caught in the illusion of thinking that one is right and the other wrong. This fatal knowledge gave birth to alienation, the end of love and unity, neurosis, psychosis, violence and war.

Believing in good and evil, the thought of the enemy and fear is born inside the soul/mind for the first time. What happens when we call another person or congregation the enemy? And what happens when the enemy or congregation we fear looks back at us and calls us the enemy? We alienate each other from living in harmony and we create all sorts of crimes and sins. Worst of all, we stifle love and union. We tell our children if they are Jews not to marry a Christian or a Muslim or a Buddhist. Even if a Buddhist girl falls in love with a Christian boy, we tell them this is against the will of God. By doing this, the walls go up, love becomes more and more of a rare phenomenon, depression follows, and even more problems arise.

Here, I will give another example from the Gospel of Thomas, Verse 61: "Jesus said, 'Two will rest on a bed: the one will die, and the other will live.' Salome [stepdaughter to King Herod who ordered the beheading of John the Baptist] said,

'Who are you, man, that you have come upon my couch and eaten from my table?' 'Therefore I say, if he is destroyed he will be filled with light, but if he is divided, he will be filled with darkness.'"

This verse alone is difficult to accept because Jesus is showing compassion even to a harlot and murderer of his own kind, Salome, the exotic dancer who danced the dance of the seven veils. By her request, she had John the Baptist murdered and Jesus is showing her even love, compassion and wisdom, by which even she may gain eternal life. In the divided mind, body and soul, there is no love for the enemy. In fact, the divided mind creates enemies and causes people to not love one another; this is the root cause of sin, as you will see. Jesus knows that this is the cause of Salome's sin, so he shows even her his love and wisdom. Hence, Jesus says, "If he is divided, he will be filled with darkness." Internal conflict caused by knowledge of good and evil causes one to be divided and to divide. To understand this wisdom is to become "undivided."

When the human soul is not nourished with affection and love, it eventually malfunctions in a number of possible ways. The underloved soul gains the feeling that it does not have enough and can become greedy, become an oppressor so that it can become adored in a position of power, gaining false love such as fame. The underloved soul may steal the affection of another by raping or manipulating another for sexual favors. And, if enough anger is developed, a person who is underloved may even only see love in their innocence and childhood, and start molesting children. The worst is oppression, rape and murder.

Now, Jesus is telling me there is so little love in the world (1994 AD) because we took in this fatal knowledge that builds the ego centered righteousness barrier that could never get along with another of the same. Even though we need to experience love and become loving towards each other and God's creation, so that the light of God can reach our love at the time of death, by taking in this fatal knowledge of inner conflict we have lost the capacity to fully love. To lose the capacity to love is the "root cause" of all sin.

I feel it is not sufficient for a soul's spiritual evolution to just recognize sin, but to understand "cause of sin." After all, if a person recognizes their sins and continues to live in sin, where is the repentance? Repentance comes much easier when a soul understands how sins are caused. Jesus is showing in this message how almost all sins are caused by a lack of real love. Lack of real love is caused by having partaken in this fatal knowledge of "good and evil."

From the Nag Hammadi Library, Gospel of Philip, page 149, Jesus reveals this mystery in a great parable once more: "In this world there is good and evil. Its good things are not good, and its evil things not evil. But there is evil after this world which is truly evil—what is called 'the middle.' It is death. While we are in this world it is fitting for us to acquire the resurrection, so that when we strip off the flesh we may be found in rest and not walk in the middle."

Because Jesus is saying that in our world, "good things are not good," scholars must have been baffled by this passage in Philip. To say that human good is not good is devastating to the ego. I feel it is so astounding to give more evidence to what the Lord has revealed in this section of the message but also to show us again not to egotistically hold our positions of good and evil against each other. Human good is not "good" because it is dwarfed by God's light, so much so that human "good" no longer appears as anything holy. Jesus shows here that none of the mind's possible interpretations of an ultimate human concept of "good" compares even as one grain of sand to the true light and Glory that is in God. In fact, by my own experience in the Lord, God's Glory dwarfs all human concepts about goodness or Heaven as a supernova would dwarf our total solar system. You will all be baffled when you truly enter Heaven and you will see that all of our religious debates are like meaningless quiverings of our minds. Our paintings of Heaven and angels in our churches are mere scribbles.

VI

At the time of death, the great light and Glory of the Lord appears to be reaching towards you. Now is the time for your own truth.

Judgment

This is the truth Jesus showed me about "judgment" and how it happens in the Lord. As you will see in the Lord's message, there is a judgment of each soul; however, it appears that each soul judges itself in retrospect to the "truth," the all shining light and Glory of the Lord and the Heavens. This truth about judgment was delivered to me directly by the Lord, mostly by parabolic telepathy.

There is a new religion on earth—one can do whatever one wants to do and it is a crime to judge them for what they wish to do, even if it is a crime itself. This notion of non-judgment was originally taken from the Bible book of St. Matthew, Chapter 7, Verse 1: "JUDGE NOT, that ye be not judged. For with what judgment ye judge, ye shall be judged: and with what measure ye mete, it shall be measured to you again." Verse 5 reveals the final truth to the matter: "Thou hypocrite, first cast out the beam out of thine own eye; and then shalt thou see clearly to cast out the mote out of thy brother's eye." John, Chapter 7, Verse 24: "Judge not according to the appearance, but judge righteous judgment." This truth reveals that only those who are clear or saint-like can see clearly to advise and help heal, but more importantly, that there is a judgment (further stated in the Bible in Revelations). If we were acceptable to God as we are in sin, why would there be a need for a spiritual cleansing? If all were acceptable to God, crime would exist in Heaven.

If a person were to say they were non-judgmental in life, and still that person did all sorts of unloving and ignorant things in their lifetime (sin), and they say that God does not judge and loves them no matter what, it would be a true statement. But such a person does not know that they "will" judge themselves when they approach the true light and Glory of God at the hour of death. If they did not truly evolve in love or Glory on earth, they simply will not be able to withstand the holy vibrations of the Holy Ghost, let alone the Glory of the Lord. They will throw themselves out of Heaven with no rejection on the part of Heaven or Jesus. And while they are living on earth again or in a hell realm, God still will not judge them, and will love them (even though such a person does not know love), but they will fear love itself and God even more, as they have feared and rejected true love in their life on earth in the past. People who reject true love on earth for materialistic or false loves will not grow in true love, and will fear the emanations of the Lord at the time of death.

This message will reveal that God does not have to Judge, but God is truth and clear bright shining Glory, and when we approach that truth, we have no other choice but to see if we are evolved enough to live in that truth which is Glory. This makes judgment inescapable. It also reveals that it is impossible to defile the natural laws of Heaven and the Lord by living a life of ignorance (sin) and by not choosing to evolve in real love in our lives. It is wrong to think that by living such an untruthful life, that we may be forgiven and enter Heaven—thinking this is so because theoretically "God loves all beings." God loves all beings but not all beings value and evolve in true love. If a soul can't evolve in true love, there is no hope for them in their development to enter the Heavens. It is only by Love or Glory that you can enter Heaven. Evolving in Glory is more difficult than Love. Glory is for those who know service, prayer and meditation.

The Heavens

I will show you what I have seen in God's light of the Heavens and try to explain what happens at the time of death as Jesus showed me. In the First Heaven (the Lord's emanation to the first or last degree), God's light is made up of several qualities but they are all greater in experience than most humans have ever known. The "Glory" is made of Innocence, Love, Ecstasy, Peace, Power, Beauty, Graces and more qualities all a million fold to what humans experience.

God's Glory shines on all beings pure or defiled alike. At the time of death, the soul departs into the light-Glory (which actually is the universal body of the LORD). This whole body is filled with billions of paradise planets. If the departing soul has even a bit of love in it, the light of God (as the Holy Ghost) unifies and merges with that love in the soul and the Holy Ghost can begin to wash the rest of your sins away and make you clean so you can enter the First Heaven. *The process of having your soul cleansed can be very traumatic,* but it passes. The time of trauma cleansing is longer for those with greater sin than those with lesser sin. Once you are made clean by the Holy Ghost, you are filled with all the qualities of the light of God, and thus enter the First Heaven. Get ready, the Glory is truly a million times greater than the greatest joy on earth, and it is unceasing.

This is what Jesus really meant when he said in the Bible, that you must die first and be reborn before you enter the Kingdom of God. The notion of "being born again" is merely symbolic, but rarely actual on earth. The only truly "born again" ones on earth are those who have found true enlightenment. And there are only a few of these saints who have ever been on the earth at any given time. The true notion of becoming "born again" requires a spiritual cleansing by God's emanation. In Christianity, that process is defined as the cleansing by the Holy Ghost. The cleansing process of the Holy Ghost is like dying unless you are already amazingly pure and experiencing the light of God while living on earth.

Once you are cleansed by the Ghost, you can then enter the First Heaven. The First Heaven is beyond time and space. You can experience it here and now because it can fold time and space to appear to you in the here and now, but you can also be taken beyond time and space to the actual place called the First Heaven. This is what happened to me when I met Jesus in this first message. I met him on the fold of time and space between the First Heaven and earth, just above the clouds in Topanga, California, in October of 1994.

The First Heaven is seemingly eternal in size and there are countless paradise planets there. What is meant by the First Heaven is a level of God's light and qualities, which unceasingly permeate all beings who live there, the very atmosphere of that Heaven and every planet suspended in it.

The First Heaven is so huge that I have only seen a fraction of it, but I do know that you will still have a human form body there just like the one you have now, but millions of times more beautiful and useful. The difference will be that you will be permeated unceasingly and unconditionally by those qualities, timelessly in the Glory.

Every atom in your new body contains all of the senses you now know and much more. You will hear music as though every atom in your new body were as sensitive as the human ear, and you will see and feel Glory by the same measure. Vision alone in the First Heaven is a million times more crystal clear than the human eye can see. That means you can see far away with great accuracy. Emotions on earth arise and pass away. The qualities in the Glory and light do not. They are constant.

Get ready to be permeated by those qualities of the light and Glory of God unceasingly all day long. Emotions can still extend from those qualities, but it is impossible to be bored or depressed or angry or violent there. Get ready, it is really a million times greater than the greatest ecstasy possible on earth and it is unceasing and eternal. This means that all those persons who have strayed from God because they thought Heaven would be a boring place are gravely mistaken. It is impossible to be bored in Heaven. It is not like a flower or desire that either affects you with pleasure or it doesn't, or one person likes it or another does not. The Glory in the light is not a response to whether you like the light or not, and then decide if you like it and then are happy like things in this world are. The qualities of the light actually permeate all beings in Heaven "unconditionally," therefore all beings in it evolve in God and become the likeness of God's light and unconditionally feel and radiate Glory.

You may have heard rare stories of persons so in love with each other that they are so happy together, even if they live in poverty, they are filled with beauty and riches, and never feel that they are missing something? This is rare because we put too many conditions on our love: house, car, high income, career, and so on. After we meet all these criteria, we think our heart springs open. It rarely finds true love even when conditional conditions are perfect. The soul does not work like television. It is not a condition.

If your soul is more pure, this cleansing process by the Holy Ghost is much easier and God may grant you access to the higher Heavens. In each ascending Heaven, the qualities of the light multiply another million times greater than each preceding Heaven. You will know for sure when you are entering another Higher Heaven. It is a major transformation, just as entering the First was.

At the extremity of the First Heaven (the border of the First and Second Heaven), the ecstasy is so great it becomes unbearable, like it is crushing you. Then you silently explode into the Glory and Light of the Second Heaven, where all qualities multiply another million times over the first. You have an even more transformed body there. The air is a million times more crystal clear, your body a million times more made of light, and is expansive, able to withstand the new Glory. There are also millions and millions of paradise planets there. The Second Heaven is so great; it is mathematically greater than one million times one million.

I am receiving this message, still fallen on my face, holding on to the Lord's feet, and intermittently gazing upon the Lord's shining face.

Try to imagine that even though you may have sinned in your life, if you have some love in your soul, this whole process can start. This is how Jesus can forgive us our sins. But first we have to learn how to love again, as Jesus told me this is lost in too many human beings. Even one who has lost this is too many, but there are many more than that. It is alarming.

The Lower Worlds and Hells

I don't mean to scare you, but as part of Jesus' message to us, there is a down side. He showed me how the hells are created. Those terrible suffering realms are created by the souls who live there and not by God. God has nothing to do with hells, other than God allows all souls the freedom to either live in love or not. This is the judgment, in that you get to experience, really experience, the truth of which you are in respect to approaching and living in the light of God. In the same way the knowledge of good and evil is a conflict and leads to wars—wars created by humans who believe in the conflict—so is hell created by those beings whom after death do not make it into the light of God. By rejecting love all by themselves, and thus repulsed by Heaven (a judgment each soul makes on their own in the face of God's true light) such souls exist separate from God after death. The ignorant souls try to create their own worlds. Lacking in wisdom, their egos create hells or terrible suffering the same way humans on earth do when they are not evolving in love and wisdom.

Because dark souls do not make it into the light of God (because they have too little or no love), they are left without love because they never chose to cultivate love, Glory or Enlightenment on earth, and they create hell on their own. They get to live only with unloving beings. That became their destiny when they chose not to cultivate love on earth. On earth, an unloving human being could rape, murder, or steal from a loving being. But in their own hell, they will not be able to do that because loving souls will be in the Heavens. So, the unloving souls fight with each other all the time and create their own hell. Anger and rage and thirst and suffering are all created by their own ignorance. Earth can become a living hell for the same reasons, and for many persons of the world it is a hell today, in each society respectively. Some live in material poverty and material suffering, some in material wealth and live with mental and emotional suffering.

What Jesus showed me about hell is so sad, I cannot bear to speak about it, but I must deliver this whole message faithfully as the Lord delivered it. Be prepared for what you are about to read here. If you have little or no love in your soul at the time of death, rich or poor does not matter, if this is so, and God's light cannot reach you because you reject love, you fall into suffering and hell worlds until you repent into true love. No God or angel has to fight with you and guard the gates of Heaven like a castle with knights and send you to hell. You simply cannot be carried up into Heaven if God's light cannot find any love in you. This is the judgment. Please do not think that you can fool your heart in life. Please face the challenges that stand between you and true love. Please do not be fooled by false loves. The reward is immeasurably great.

Jesus has told me that very few souls are making it into the Heavens from this planet. The Lord stood with me on the edge of the place where souls with no love in their hearts fall into the gravitational, as if a giant black hole (and I saw this); thus hell. This black hole is the entrance to Hell or war planets. The Lord showed me that hell is not eternal, but can last for eternity as long as those souls who have fallen so low refuse to love. Even a spark of real love is enough for one of those souls to be saved. The Lord was so deeply saddened. Jesus said that **"It appears to us that these souls are so deeply engrossed in self-created suffering (hell), that as we have watched them for measures of time beyond reasonableness, and they are suffering so much, it seems as though they will never get out. Because we cannot stand to watch such suffering, we are thinking of erasing their souls. The process of having a soul erased is extremely painful and lasts for a duration, but it ends with no memory or no more soul. Those souls, once erased, will no longer suffer."**

I cannot tell you how deeply saddened Jesus was to have to tell me this. The Lord loves us so much, and the Lord cannot stand to watch souls suffer (neither can the angels), that the only wise course they can see to end the suffering of those beings in hell is to erase their souls. The tragedy of this is so great in all the universe, and the Lord and the angels have so much compassion for these terribly unloving souls, that the Lord thinks it is "possible" that the Lord and the Angels may erase their souls. Can you imagine what that means?

There is another phenomenon: Even if your soul has love in it, but still a lot of sin, the purification process by the Holy Ghost is so traumatic that you may wish to reject the Ghost, and thus fall into the suffering worlds.

Please suffer the cleansing by the Holy Ghost. While you are suffering the cleansing, it will seem as if Heaven is going to be terrifying and that you will fear God all day. The fear passes with the cleansing and then true Peace and Glory follow. When you enter Heaven, you will wonder why you ever thought your corrupted lusts (sex without love), drugs, alcohol abuse, greed for money and power, misuse of power, selling yourself for fame, etc., could provide you with truly satisfying results. You will see how foolish you had been and start a new life in Glory.

Reincarnation was not exactly revealed to me at this time, one way or the other. I have since asked this question to Jesus. I am awaiting an answer. I do believe it is possible that if we do not graduate to Heaven and a soul is not too unloving, it gets another and another chance to evolve. This theory makes perfect sense to me, only because I know how evolved the Glory in the First Heaven is. It is not so easy to be able to bear it for many unloving beings. They would have no other choice but to throw themselves out of Heaven and go somewhere else to evolve. However, I was not told anything about this by Jesus at this time.

Because "Love" is so important to evolve in, let alone the even more spiritually advanced evolution in "Glory," I feel it is necessary to show the importance of wisdom. For without wisdom, love is sure to be lost, as most children lose their innocence.

The knowledge of good and evil, which ended love, causing souls to fall into inner and outer hell, was taken freely. Now because of the fear of the enemy, which is manufactured in the mind, the enemy has become as if real. Then we alienate all others who do not agree with our viewpoint and we become sectarians. When we alienate another human being, we separate them from our love, and they are prone to psychosis. That alienated, unloved human being may even kill someone for lack of receiving love. All human beings need love. We all know what love is, we just don't give it. Without giving and receiving love, the soul, body and brain eventually malfunction in all sorts of ways.

Greed and hoarding emerge in the soul because that soul feels that it does not have enough love, and never feels satisfied. These souls can become like greedy bankers or corporation heads who oppress the world for their own power. This kind of power gives the unloved soul a feeling of false love, such as fame and worldly power. These are the world's most dangerous people.

Corrupted sexual lust is caused by the feeling that one is not satisfied or totally loved, and always wanting more than one has.

Pure sexual lust can only be experienced when a person is in love with another and if there is real love. This is true marriage of love and both of those souls will evolve into love.

If the hearts are pure in love, sensual pleasures can help cultivate love and good feeling, but even those pleasures appear as nothing in the Light of God. But, if pleasures of love help a human to experience love, then humans can know the love that leads to God.

To condemn happiness and pleasures can damage a soul terribly. It gives the untruthful representation that God is against happiness. Although human pleasures are tiny compared to Heaven, we have to start learning the art of being loving and happy to prepare our souls to deal with the extreme levels of ecstasy in God's Heavens. This is a huge subject. The majority of Christian Churches have done such a poor job of portraying God, that many lost souls have strayed from God because they didn't want to enter the incorrect painting of Heaven made by most of the churches. There are many lost souls who do not know the truth of how cosmic, ecstatic, loving, expansive and beautiful God really is.

The question of sexuality and celibacy is of paramount perplexity in the spiritual philosophies of all religions. It has been observed that living in a state of consciousness that is ruled by the senses is a sin and that "lust" is the internal ingredient that constitutes the soul being trapped into living in the senses. It has been observed that one has to transcend the senses and the experience of being ruled by them. Most humans have a general attraction to pleasure and an aversion to pain. Knowing this, how then can we transcend the senses, both pleasure and pain?

Why has sex been so condemned by religious philosophy in general? Terrible reactions to the Biblical interpretations of corrupted lusts leading to hell fire resulted in monastic ritualistic orders requiring monks and nuns to live a life of self-denial and to live a life of physical suffering or tortures. Many churches taught that humility required suffering for God and that God somehow wanted us to suffer. This notion of suffering was somehow supposed to help one become pure of sin or lusts. There are countless stories of painful austerities and even cruel punishment for errors inside the monastic orders of the churches. Were they really transcending the senses by these methods?

Not everyone accepted asceticism as a superior virtue to reach the promised kingdom of God. Professor of religion at Princeton, Elaine Pagels, writes in her book, *Adam, Eve and the Serpent,*

> In Rome, when Melania and Pinian renounced the world (c. 390), the ascetic movement was explosively controversial, especially in rich and aristocratic circles. Even Christian parents like Melania's father protested when their children succumbed to the preaching of such enthusiasts of asceticism as Jerome, then secretary to Damascus, bishop of Rome. Later, he looked back on his experiences living in a cave and recalled,

> How often, when I was living in the desolate lonely desert, parched by the burning sun, how often I imagined myself among the pleasures of Rome. I used to sit alone, because my heart was filled with bitterness; my limbs stuck inside an ugly sackcloth, my skin as black as an Ethiopian's. . . . Day after day I cried and sighed, and when, against my will, I fell asleep, my bare bones clashed against the ground. I say nothing about my eating and drinking. Even when sick, solitaries drink only cold water, and a cooked meal is considered excessive. And yet he who, in fear of hell, had banished himself to this prison, found himself again and again surrounded by dancing girls! My face grew pale with hunger, yet in my cold body the passions of my inner being continued to glow. This human being was more dead that alive; only his burning lust continued to boil.

The story tells of the near impossibility of extinguishing the desire for human love and pleasures and tragically shows no illumination or bliss as a reward for living a life of such severe austerities. Where did humankind adhere to the idea that celibacy was required to enter the kingdom of God? How then could a person find the promised kingdom of God, if rarely, by such austere practices?

Many people tried to find their way on the path that leads to God, claiming to understand the requirements and many followed in their footsteps. It is written in Professor Pagels' book, *Adam, Eve and the Serpent,* that Saint Augustine, one of the early founders of the Christian church, argued with anger about the notion of celibacy:

> Who can control this when its appetite is aroused? No one! In the very movement of this appetite, then, it has no "mode" that responds to the decisions of the will. What married man chooses that the appetite ever be aroused? Yet what he wishes

> he cannot accomplish. . . . In the very movement of the appetite, it has no mode of corresponding to the decisions of the will.

Obviously even the Saints went mad trying to control their sexual urges. Even so, it was believed to be a requirement to enter the kingdom of God. Because of this belief, Augustine, although passionate, remained filled with guilt about his sexuality it seemed, and never married. But could there be a misunderstanding of the meaning to "the original sin?"

It is very clear in gazing upon the Lord Jesus Christ that there is no suffering in the Lord other than that which Jesus experiences as empathy for human suffering. The clear light of Jesus' Glory truly transcends far beyond the reaches of human pleasure, and also human pain. The Glory is pure and full of Innocence, Love, Ecstasy, Peace, Power and Graces in immeasurable quantities. It is clear to me that these old methods of torture and suffering are not needed to transcend both pleasure and pain, because to experience a life of mostly pain still traps the soul in the senses, which is sin. Pain is still a sin. Pain is not what Jesus has in store for us. To be aware of natural pain is part of the human experience of sin, as well as natural pleasures. But to force pain on one's self that is an addition to natural pain or to force it on others, that would be violence. Seeing the Lord, I do not believe that it is good for a human soul to experience any more physical pain than pleasure. Neither of these two experiences will have any effect on spiritual growth unless the miracle ingredient arises from within.

There is only one human experience that can help you transcend living in and being ruled by the senses, and that is real love and even compassion. Perhaps pain is part of the human experience because if we can know it in ourselves, we can see when others are suffering, when our friends the animals and mammals are suffering, and even when our very own living earth suffers—then we can experience compassion. Perhaps compassion is that one human experience that triggers real love for others. Perhaps compassion is what creates that inner spark of light that glows inside of your heart even brighter when you actually help to ease someone or something else's pain. That inner "glow" "is transcending the senses." That inner glow and life force is bigger than all of us combined. If you live a life that matures in love, you may begin to feel it for your lover, your husband or your wife, your children and your parents, your family, and even those beyond your family, and those beyond your nationality. This is love.

This love has to start somewhere in your life to save you from your own sufferings of pain and pleasures. If you have ever been deeply in love with another human being, you know that bright glow or deep river of love flows inside of you and abounds beyond your body and senses and sometimes into the whole universe when you are kind to this other human being. It does not happen, nor can it happen, when you are cruel. Love is not a cruelty. It only grows with more and more kindness. This love is transcending the senses.

You may make love and experience a deep sexual orgasm with this person that is actually helping you transcend the senses. The senses may first be used with love and kindness to create the foundation for your sexual orgasm, but the orgasm that is created by love will explode far past your body and senses. Anyone who has been deeply in love with another human being can tell us this. To be deeply in love with another human being is the true meaning of a marriage. Marriage is when two become as one. Two become as one by real love only. To legally marry another person has no spiritual value if the marriage is for financial profit, ego, physical attraction alone, legal or national status, or anything that is short of real love. By understanding the physics of God's Glory and Heaven, any marriage that is not based in true love is not a marriage in the eyes of the Lord at all! Therefore to have sex without this real marriage of true love is a sin. It is a sin because it keeps you bound in the senses and not transcending them. Sex without love is corrupted lusts. Far too many people on earth are not marrying out of true love. I pray deeply that all of you recognize this and transform this aspect of your lives. If you marry another person for any wrong reason, by the physics of God's Glory and Heaven, you will not evolve into real love with this person and you inhibit yourself from maturing into a true spiritual enlightenment of love. Without real love you will not make it into heaven.

A most shocking discovery to modern Christianity is in the Gospel of Philip, revealing evidence of the physical affection and love Jesus expressed for Mary Magdelene:

> As for wisdom who is called "barren," she is the mother of the angels. And the companion of the *(word missing)* Mary Magdelene, Jesus loves her more than all the disciples and used to kiss her often on her mouth. The rest of the disciples. . . . They said to him, "Why do you love her more than all of us?" The savior answered and said to them, "Why do I not love you like her?" In this long explanation Jesus says, "Fear not the flesh nor love it. If you fear it, it will gain mastery over you. If you love it, it will swallow and paralyze you."

What Jesus just said is identical to Buddhist insight into non-attachment (neither clinging nor aversion to pleasure or pain), or what Tantra Yoga teaches about lust, "neither give into it nor reject it" while you are experiencing it.

While most Christian and even Buddhist mystics acknowledged that living in the senses alone without inner spiritual presence is sin (ignorance), what wisdom is it to condemn pleasure and live a life of suffering as many monks and nuns were told to practice? Especially when you consider that the senses are both pleasure and pain. Why did the monks and nuns live a life of pain and reject pleasure when both pleasure and pain are "sin" or ignorance? How to transcend this duality? The notion that we had to suffer for God (as if God loved to watch us suffer) led most people away from a life of such austerity and apparent boredom. After all, something inside of our souls tells us that we would rather experience joy than suffering.

How do we find that inner joy or magical light that we call the Soul? How do we make it grow brighter and expand it deeper? One experience is common to all religions: that is, sitting in silence and allowing ourselves to go within and explore who we really are.

In Buddhist meditation, while practicing sitting or Tantra (sexual union meditation), meditators were taught to experience all sensations that arise in our consciousness, pleasurable or painful, as "impermanent," and by the wisdom of neither rejecting nor becoming attached to such sensations, the experiencer actually allows, without judgment, both pleasure and pain sensations to arise and pass away freely within the conscious experience; thus the meditator, after minutes, years, or lifetimes of practice, transcends the senses and experiences a bliss greater than the senses can provide.

In the *Nag Hammadi Library,* Gospel of Philip, Jesus expresses the same principle, after kissing Mary Magdelene: "Neither fear the flesh nor love it." But what else was Jesus saying if he was kissing Mary Magdelene? Could it be that you can experience the senses in a state of "Love" and that "Love" is the mystical dance that transcends the soul above pleasure and pain?

This single point Jesus makes is so contradictory to what ancient and modern Christian theology thought about sin and the flesh, it has baffled them to the point of having rejected the Gospel of Philip before Jesus' religion was 200 years old. Today, Christian theology teaches that one must "suffer for God" and have aversion for pleasure and reside in pain. Such monks and nuns living in monasteries struggled so deeply with their sexuality, many became angry and mentally diseased, while only a few transcended. It is no wonder there are so many stories about sexual misconduct inside church walls.

Even Saint Francis of Asissi was deeply in love with Claire, but could not express it because of theo-illogical beliefs. If Saint Francis knew what Jesus taught in the Gospel of Philip (hidden in the desert during St. Francis' time), would he have acted differently towards Claire? Would he have loved her and been a Saint all the same? We will never know.

But, looking back, why was Jesus kissing Mary Magdelene if Jesus meant for the disciples to "suffer for God" in order to transcend the senses? By this act, could Jesus have been showing the disciples that to love another human being so deeply, to feel love is "transcendence" above the senses; that love is the way to transcendence and no suffering for God is needed?

While there is much to discover in the *Nag Hammadi Library* about Jesus' lost teachings, many modern Christians would argue that none of these teachings lead to salvation and heaven. The only way to prove modern Christianity "wrong" and the ancient lost teachings of Jesus as true teachings would be to find evidence of such wisdom by a Christian saint.

Emanuel Swedenborg, the 18th-century Christian saint from Sweden, wrote in his journal of April 6, 1744, of his first meeting with Jesus. He experienced a shivering or shaking at around twelve midnight to two in the morning. He trembled violently from head to foot and he heard a great sound as if many storms were colliding. The power threw him down to the ground on his face. He is in the spirit (dreaming) when this happens. He begins speaking to Jesus, later noticing that Jesus is holding him in his arms. He sees the face of Jesus for the first time and is astounded at the beauty. Swedenborg's spiritual world of experiences open from this point on, and he later visits the Heavens and Hells, which he identifies as being made up of countless planets.

On some of Swedenborg's countless visits through these Heavens and Hells, he learns a terrible irony about celibacy and sexuality amongst the angels and angelic life in the Heavens. It is written in his book, *Conjugal Love.* Some newcomers to the Astral world below the first heaven are first shown by angels that the newcomers are still completely human in every anatomical way. They ask some angels, as Swedenborg is a witness: "Does a similar love exist between married partners in the Heavens as in the earth?" "Altogether similar," the angelic spirits said, even to "the ultimate delights." But it is "much more blessed because angelic perception and sensation is much more exquisite than human. . . ."

The first observation by Swedenborg is incredible because it reveals that angels, whom he identifies as completely human in every way, but countless times more beautiful, even more physically than humans, still have a form of sexual communion or lovemaking with one another. Because their senses are "much more exquisite than human," they experience much greater joy and ecstasy in their lovemaking than humans do. I can attest to the first part by my own experiences when Jesus took me through a number of Heavens (see chapter 3) that my own perception of seeing, feeling and hearing was about one million times brighter and clearer than the human body can experience. So, it is not just better than human, it is millions of times better than human. In Heaven, while I was there, the Lord's Glory is in part made of ultra bright Ecstasy which is truly orgasmic in quality. The human experience of loving orgasm is small in comparison to such Ecstasy that the Lord's Glory truly dwarfs human sexual orgasm. However this is so, the Lord's Glory is not offended by human love. It knows that human love will one day evolve into God-like love.

Swedenborg's experiences in Heaven included that false marriages cannot exist in Heaven; those souls that are united falsely on earth cannot be united in Heaven.

About celibacy, Swedenborg discovers the most controversial and terrible irony of them all, but as you will see, it is synchronized with what is revealed in this part of the message. In *Conjugal Love,* Swedenborg writes: "Those celibates who have altogether alienated their minds from marriage remain single if spiritual, but if natural they become 'whoremongers' in the lower world." The word "natural" in Swedenborg's work means those who have not yet transcended the senses, even pain, with real love. This would mean those monks and nuns who were renunciates, but still craved lusts and commited sexual crimes, and did not develop real love, may end up in the lower worlds or hells. Because only by real love can you transcend the senses, even if one was a monk or nun and they did not evolve in love, they cannot enter Heaven. This is a terrible irony.

Swedenborg's further discoveries of celibacy in Heaven are even more disturbing: "As to monks and nuns, they are given their choice. If they really prefer celibacy, they are conveyed to those who live in celibacy on the side of Heaven. This is because the sphere of perpetual celibacy disturbs that of conjugal love, which is the essential sphere of heaven. Blessed marriages are provided for those who in their single state have desired marriage, if spiritual, but not until they come to Heaven."

For Swedenborg to say celibates live "on the side of Heaven" means, by his language, that they live in the lower Heavens. The inner, or higher Heavens, is a place where love is conjugal. Conjugal love is not a love that one can hold for one's own experience. By nature, it is to be shared and experienced with all beings. Because the higher Heavens are relationship oriented, celibates are not ready to live there. How deeply disturbing this discovery is to our beliefs about God and the Heavens?

Lusts that are not pure with love are thus corrupted lusts. This craving for sensuality, void of any love or true feeling, is one of the many attributes that can degrade a soul so low that it cannot withstand the cleansing of the Holy Ghost, let alone live in the Glory of the Heavens. They fall into the lower worlds and hells.

Rape may be caused by the feeling of not being loved or wanted by another. This brain malfunction is caused by lack of love and affection, but it is not only curable by human love. If a person is not loved by humans, they should seek God directly, or learn to give love to a cause so that they radiate with more love. These humans can ask God especially for God's love. Trust me, I speak from experience. If a person is not loved by humans, and that soul wants love so badly, and that soul prays to God for love, God has more mercy on that soul than almost any other. Never resort to stealing another human being's affections.

Stealing comes from the feeling that one does not have enough and needs more. If poor people steal from the rich and greedy, then God will be the Judge of this. If rich people oppress the poor, then God will be the Judge of this crime.

War: The base of war has already been discussed, stemming from knowledge of good and evil as conflict and the birth of egotism. However, most humans look at the armies and governments as the cause of war. This is not so.

For example, in the recent United States against the Persian Gulf war in Iraq (Sadam Hussein), the war was fought over the issue of the tiny country of Kuwait. Kuwait was created by American and Europeans so that they may control the price of oil coming out of the Gulf. This would prevent the Iraqi government from raising the price of oil for Europeans and Americans. All persons who drive cars that run on oil could have protested the use of oil a long time ago and stopped driving their cars until hydrogen fuel was made available to them. This they could have done if they were serious about the environment and ending dependence on foreign oil. Every war has many unseen players. Overpopulation is one of the greatest contributors to modern war. It forces the peoples into each other in competition for resources and technology. Who makes the population? It is the people, and not the government. The same people who hold up peace signs contribute to the factors that make their military go to war. Do not be fooled by apparent passivists.

Bearing false witness to a crime is lying. Lying comes from fear of losing something that one feels one does not have enough of.

Coveting what is thy neighbor's comes from the feeling that one does not have enough. This may stem from being oppressed by the rich, or by not having love and affection for one's own. Being oppressed by the rich can force one into material poverty, but not spiritual poverty. When we put conditions on our love, such as material gain, then when we live in poverty do we not give our love? In 1994, the majority of poor people on the street are not loved enough at all. In fact, that is how most of them got there in the first place.

Evolution

Jesus' point in showing how the sins are caused by malfunctions in the brain, *is to point back to the original cause for the malfunctions of the brain and soul,* which is a lack of love. If we focus on the "cause of sin" it might better help us to undo the cause inside of us, individually, and become free. The cause of lack of love is manifest by partaking in the knowledge of good and evil, as explained previously. If you are good at math, you can witness how many other illnesses are caused by conflict.

No human being has to be perfect to enter God's Kingdom, but in order to enter, their imperfections will have to be washed away. It is true that the human body is not the paradise body that we will receive when we are reborn in Heavens. This body is prone to disease, death and even worse, suffering. However, Jesus did tell me that humans have to have love in their souls to be washed clean of sin. After being washed clean, the new body is given to us by the Lord. That is the resurrected body. If a person does really well, or a person does not do so well, but still has love, God will Judge and reward each soul according to the soul's works. This is talked about in the Book of Revelations, Chapter 22. This is God's mystery as to how this will be done.

By having partaken in the fruit of the knowledge of good and evil (conflict), the greatest tragedy was revealed to me. It is the loss of the union with God's Glory and Love. When human souls become encased in an ego, and become separate from God, they lose the daily nutrition that God shines on all beings day and night. This light cannot enter a soul with a strong barrier. The barrier is formed and looks like an egg-shaped silvery-gray force field around the soul, when looking back from the light of the First Heaven. Looking from earth's light, this same silvery-gray egg-shaped barrier appears as the human aura.

The positive electric charge of apparent good turns towards and around the negative charge of apparent evil and creates a circular or egg-shaped barrier around the soul. The greater the conflict, the greater the barrier (force field) which shields God's Glory from entering the soul.

Dissolving the inner conflict of apparent good versus evil, we are left with the eternal truth. To end the conflict means, as Jesus said, "If thine eye be single (undivided), thy whole body shall be filled with light"; the force field dissolves and the omnipresent Glory of the Lord shines in. I have actually seen this in spirit just above the earth dimension and inside the First Heaven. This is not to say that the First Heaven is just above earth, but can appear interdimensionally that way because Heaven is beyond time and space-distance.

If you notice in Genesis, Adam and Eve hid themselves from God because they judged their nudity *themselves.* God did not judge their nudity; they did it themselves. See the Book of Genesis, Chapter 3, Verses 9-11: "And the Lord God called unto

Adam, and said unto him, where art thou? And he said, I heard thy voice in the garden, and I was afraid, because I was naked; and I hid myself. And he said, who told thee that thou wast naked? Hast thou eaten of the tree, whereof I commanded thee that thou shouldest not eat?"

This ignorance was the sign that humans could not see the deep illusion of Satan. Satan provoked humans to judge for themselves, and the judgment ended unity with God amongst humans, and ended total undivided love for each other. Most importantly, it also ended the human soul's direct communion with God, and handed it over to conflict and ignorance, which made it naturally subservient to Satan. Humankind would judge each other all on their own. Religions would judge each other and kill each other. Where did Jesus say to kill one another in his name or any name? He did not say this. Neither did Moses, Enoch or God, yet Muslims, Hindus, Jews, Atheists and Christians have been at great wars with each other, even inter-religious wars since religions were born.

In their own judgments, even though their apparently separate religions had the same basic laws of loving thy neighbor and not killing, they would kill one another and break God's commandments not to kill. This is because of the great power of the illusory knowledge (conflict itself) was so great that it could corrupt even the religions. Even if fundamental laws of God are laid down which include "thou shalt not kill," humans kill each other over their own separate illusions about the issues of Jesus, God, and the perception of which religion is right or wrong about this. This is the chaos that Satan fell victim to and it even created suffering for Satan.

The kind of thinking that my religion or version of religion is right and yours is wrong is a manifestation of separatism, lack of love, and war created by this fatal knowledge in our hearts. It, itself, is violent thinking and causes sin. This is not to say that there are no false religions, but however, it is to say that a false religion can be recognized as one that does not bear the fruit of undivided love and healing to those who practice it, undivided with the outside world.

This is not to say that the saints who started God's work were not saints, it is to say that those who have made religions in the names of saints have ruined the truth, or worse, ruined the teachings and truths of the Son of God. Also, certain saints became saints and thought that because they became a saint by living in certain conditions, that others would have to do the same; because they knew no other way. Jesus has told me there are many other ways to love and Glory.

Every religion I have studied is guilty of being elitist and feeling better off than other religions. I have witnessed all of the big ones—Christianity, Judaism, Islam, Hinduism, Buddhism, Atheism, and so on—and I have not seen one that is not ego-righteous. History has shown how religious wars and inter-Christian wars have claimed the lives of millions. Even though Jesus said to love thine enemies, we did not listen. Jesus told us to love our enemies because he wanted to end separatism and the very concept of the enemy. For him there is no good and evil. He knows that this knowledge corrupts souls. Jesus told me he is very sad for humanity because of our lack of love for one another and our planet.

In many modern apparitions and miracles, we see the weeping Virgin Mary or tears coming down a Jesus' eyes in depictions of Christ. God is sad for us, not happy for us. God's compassion is so great for us, that even God's tears can heal the sick. I feel God is trying to ignite the flame of love in people by doing this. Why is it so hard to stop fighting and to love? It is certainly more fun to love.

Coming back to love, to just say "love each other" is like saying "no to drugs." It doesn't work unless you understand the spiritual physics of the cause of suffering and the physics of returning to love. If it did work, then we wouldn't have to go through this. We would already be in peace.

VII

Dissolving the knowledge of "good and evil" internally is the end of "conflict" and the return to inner peace and love.

When you sit in meditation or prayer, try meditating on this message from the Lord, even if it takes you a lifetime: When there is no knowledge of good and evil in the mind, body and soul, there is no conflict inside the mind, body and soul. Solving this, we become undivided in our love. When there is no inner conflict, the mind, body and soul are peaceful and cannot produce violence or sins that result from a lack of love. When the mind, body and soul are peaceful, thinking becomes full of wisdom and miracles of creation follow. The soul now re-emerges with God's Glory and feels the joy and peace of the Lord's natural emanation. This natural quality of God does not need to be held by belief because God's Glory "naturally reveals itself" when the inner conflict ends. In God, there naturally is no sin. It is no longer an effort to refrain.

This part of the message shows that the qualities of God reveal themselves and manifest in the soul spontaneously when the inner conflict is dissolved. It does not leave you in chaos. It also shows that there is a true "good" but it is God's true good. God's true good does not appear as some idea in the mind. It is real and unsupported by belief (the mind). It is not a quality that needs to be held together by a belief system. These qualities are natural and permeate the entire universe and every being in it without effort. Every being will feel these qualities eternally growing in them when they dissolve the barrier that was held together by individual interpretation of good and evil.

This part of the message is to say that when the mind tries to conceive of "good," not only will it be different from and perhaps opposed to another person's view of what is "good," but it also will be a product of the mind. The true "good" that comes from God will dwarf any human conception of apparent "good" as if a supernova of love were awakening within. With God's love and Glory shining in your soul, you will look back at what you previous "thought was good" and have a good laugh.

As evidence for this spiritual truth, we find a clue in the Bible, Matthew, Chapter 11, Verse 11: "Verily I say unto you, Among them that are born of women there hath not risen a greater than John the Baptist: notwithstanding he that is least in the kingdom of heaven is greater than he."

Jesus is saying that he feels John the Baptist is the greatest of souls ever to be born of a woman, alive on earth, and that Jesus acknowledges how great of a man John is. However, the point is made that God's true good dwarfs any human good (John the Baptist). As Jesus says, ". . . he that is least in the kingdom of heaven is greater than he." This is because even the least person in Heaven is living directly inside God's Glory, the Glory which dwarfs all apparent "good." This truth is so powerful—it reveals the human conflict over apparent good and evil as a deep egotistical illusion. Again this is why Jesus says, in the Gospel of Philip, "In this world there is good and evil. Its good things are not good, and its evil things not evil." This is what humankind has done: to go to war over conflicting views of apparent good versus apparent evil; thus the "cause" of war is revealed.

Belief systems are so unique and myriad, just as the number of plants and living organisms on earth are myriad. Beliefs come into existence as part of what each person experiences and shares about truth. The whole is so vast and myriad. Can we allow for each other to have so many different experiences and live in the beauty of such diversity without conflict over it all? We can simply share our experiences and see if there is any use or playfulness to them for the whole. There is no need to end shared knowledge, I think, but there is a need to end the conflict over knowledge. Because we got so serious about defining good and evil, we felt a need to defend our views even if we had to use violence.

Psychology has shown that violence stems from inner conflict. Violence is produced in the nervous system in stages: first conflict/neurosis, then psychosis resulting in violence, which is a psychotic episode. When there is no inner conflict, the mind, body and soul become peaceful and return to the inner harmony of paradise light, becoming incapable of unloving thoughts of separatism and war toward all others and the earth. When there is no knowledge of good and evil in the soul, there can be no side taking, no religion formed as a closed circle that is in opposition to another circle. Now, the true natural qualities of the spirit descend from God into the peaceful and undivided soul and they remain unsupported by belief, simple like the natural sun that shines on the forest.

In fact, from this perspective, belief has little value, other than to inspire spiritual growth. Belief is also an effort to defend something. In the peace of God, there is no need to defend anything. God just shines.

As previously explained, the barrier around the soul dissolves and the Glory shines in. There is no belief form in this. It is true enlightenment. These qualities go far beyond apparent good, yet they are true good, and evolve into higher good. The soul now rests in the natural laws of the spirit suspended in God.

Now humans become full of love and Glory again, as was the birthright of all souls. Today, humanity is a long way from this. It sounds far away, but only because we have placed ourselves far away. This is what Jesus meant in the Bible when he said: "If thine eye [soul] be *single* [no longer in division], thy whole body shall be filled with light." It means the perceiver or soul is no longer divided into inner and outer conflict. Having your body filled with God's light is the glorious reward for ending the conflict within, and Glory can begin to manifest through you.

By your inner enlightenment process, by the Grace of the Lord you may be granted spiritual visits to the Heavens, Lower Worlds, or Hells to gain experience and wisdom. Inner light is like a passport to gain access to higher and higher worlds.

VIII

Jesus shows how the inner conflict of good and evil holds the ego in place causing people to think separately from the idea of working in humanitarian togetherness.

When the inner conflict in your nervous system is over, there is peace and the light of God shines in your soul again. This is what Jesus meant by this. Jesus explained this to me as what needs to happen to get egos to come together to solve worldly problems, to dissolve the barriers between us. The division keeps us apart. With the strong ego, it couldn't work. Materially wealthy persons tend to have problems with taking the advice of poor people. It is too humiliating for them. They are outraged when a tree planter is suggesting to them to invest $50 million into Sterling Solar-Powered Hydrogen for clean-air automobiles.

Being in inner conflict makes us more attracted to outward violence than to beauty and love. You can see this in today's movies. Hollywoods of the world make violent movies because the masses keep going to them rather than to loving movies.

When a healing technology presents itself in the world such as aneutronic fusion and hydrogen fuel to run our automobiles and aircraft, masses of people are less attracted to it because they love death and violence, because it matches the conflict within them. Beauty doesn't. Humankind loves violent movies and boxing matches because it matches what is going on inside of them.

Jesus said to me that because this lack of love for each other and earth, there are few human beings willing to work with making loving choices for a healthy planet and loving life on earth. This is another reason why the company formed by myself and Ghassan failed. God's angels helped us meet all the right people, and helped other people meet the right people to do their work, but people were not getting together and making the choices happen. Mainly, money people don't want change. God can make introductions through angels but cannot force any decisions, otherwise the whole creation would be a forced dictatorship, and by this nature, there would be no soul. It would be one soul living all by itself, just painting pictures, and there is no love and life in just pictures. That is why we are free. When we reach God in our freedom and the Heavens, God evolves.

My failure had nothing to do with God not helping. It had to do with our unloving free will, which stems from conflict. It had to do with clashing views not wanting to work together. It had to do with angry people who wanted the end of the world to hurry up and get here. It had to do with people being distracted by the meaningless phenomena of the world. I was so relieved to understand that it wasn't God who did all this to me.

When fallen angels and humans wanted to decide for themselves, they gave birth to free will. This became a free will planet for the duration of the lesson to be learned. By our free will, we decided to destroy our earth. Jesus said he couldn't force humans to chose paradise for themselves. They have to do it on their own. Unfortunately, because of the lack of loving choices, very few humans have enough love in their souls to be saved and lifted to God's paradise in the Heavens. This is a crisis situation in the eyes of the Lord. Jesus is very sad for those numerous souls that he knows will not make it to Heaven or the new earth. He knows how greatly they will suffer.

I pray to all of you who are rich and powerful in this world, who previously said "no" to investing in the technologies that could allow us to live in harmony with nature, to repent and change your minds. I pray that you hear this call. It may even save your souls.

IX

By the Holy Ghost, the Perfect Knowledge that is available to all who live inside of God's light is revealed, versus the false or limited knowledge that fallen angels and humans live by.

Then Jesus showed me the power of the Holy Ghost from a new perspective: Now myself, "i," have become one-with-God and the universe. A woman in a white nightgown with long brown hair was floating by in her dreaming body. Jesus sent the Holy Ghost after her, a most holy white energy field shaped like a cross. She could not see us in the First Heaven dimension looking at her as she was absorbed in her own inner dreaming world, floating by.

I stopped and thought I made the command to send the Ghost after her, not Jesus, but I realized that I felt this because of the new momentary perspective of really being as-one with Jesus, the Universal Mother-Father, and the Holy Ghost. Everything is known in God's Kingdom. The "oneness" was incredible. There is no possibility for a lie or false testimony to exist here because each soul here is connected to God's whole nervous system. If something happens, we all have access to the exactness of the event. This would mean that, in God, there is no need for the written word, or testimony in writing, because the exactness of anything could be known to anyone by willing it. Human beings rely on the written word to store history, testimony, fact and lies. In fact, there is a danger to relying on the human written word in that it can be corrupted and misinterpreted.

People can use false testimony against one another, need lawyers and judges to try and find truth in a crime, and sometimes even commit the wrong person to jail. To rely on God's central nervous system to access accounts in exactness is a perfect system, a perfect form of the "word," and thus errors in judgment are not made. Humans do not have the power to access God's central nervous system anymore, and will not until they return to the first stage of their original creation, to evolve in the ascending Heavens. It is one of the gifts they lost by taking in good and evil. So, when you die and this life passes away, wherever you end up, it was not a mistake by the Lord. There is no paper work that gets mixed up in Heaven.

In the Book of Enoch, Richard Laurence translation, page 85-86 (Chap. LXVIII), it is written that God speaks against some of the qualities of the fallen angels in verses 9-15: "The name of the fourth [fallen angel] is Penemue: he discovered to the children of men bitterness and sweetness; And pointed out to them every secret of their wisdom. He taught men to understand writing, and the use of ink and paper. Therefore numerous have been those who have gone astray from every period of the world, even to this day. For men were not born for this, thus with pen and ink to confirm their faith; Since they were not created, except that, like the angels, they might remain righteous and pure. Nor would death, which destroys everything, have affected them."

Many translators and scholars even got mad at God when reading this, thinking God wanted us to be ignorant fools, and they inadvertently sided with the fallen angels because they did not understand these passages from the Book of Enoch. What they did not know is that when the soul lives in the Lord's emanation or Heavens, all is known in its exactness. There is no need for a written testimony, no need for a trial before a Supreme Court Judge. There is no trial and testimony because all is known.

This kind of knowledge of the word is supremely superior to what we humans call knowledge and knowing. It can take a person an entire lifetime to study ancient history even, and then find out in Heaven that such a person was mistaken by the interpretation of historical text, or that what they learned was even a lie. This is why such minds will be devastated upon discovering how little the human mind can know when they enter even the First Heaven.

Even physicists like Albert Einstein and Murray Gell-Mann will be baffled upon discovering the science that Angels know compared to what they know. It will be so devastating for them, less they drop their limited perspectives and enter and partake of God's Perfect Knowledge. Astrophysicists like Carl Sagan, Steven Hawkings and Kipp Thorne will be baffled upon seeing God's true knowledge of the stars and galaxies. However, many of them are already humbled and baffled. Perhaps they have glimpsed God's Perfect Knowledge, thus they are baffled.

From the Gospel of Thomas, Verse 2: "Jesus said, 'Let him who seeks continue seeking until he finds. When he finds, he will become troubled. When he becomes troubled, he will be astonished, and he will rule over the all.'"

Any person living in God's knowledge can access anything and know it in its exactness! From the Gospel of Thomas, Verse 5, it reads: "Jesus said, 'Recognize what is in your sight, and that which is hidden from you will become plain to you. For there is nothing hidden which will not become manifest.'" This is to reveal that direct knowledge by real transformation of the individual (ego) into the omnipresent light of God is the meaning of having access to true or highest knowledge because any event in history or in the universe could then be known in its exactness, uncorrupted by mere false testimony. From the complete perspective of highest knowledge (direct in God), all written knowledge has very little use and is seen as inferior.

This discovery does not mean that I think we should abandon studying written text. Rather, we might hold direct experience of God as the higher form of knowledge and teach people in our universities how to have a direct experience of God. If realized and manifested, this point alone could revolutionize education in the modern world. It would mean that we should put more study into actually having a direct experience of God and also study the direct experiences of other modern visionaries; even our professors at universities should do this. Further, we should examine those experiences and messages and integrate them into what humans call knowledge. After all, that is what the ancients did.

Standing near the Lord, being inside of God's central nervous system, I could now see part of what humans lost when they kicked themselves out of paradise. I thought I made the command to send the Holy Ghost after this young woman because "i" was now in God's direct nervous system. The whole system made the command to send the Holy Ghost after this young woman. Anyone living in Heaven would know, or could know, any event within their spiritual ability to know.

Jesus said his last personal words to me and said good-bye.

The Ghost chased after this young woman and she was terrified of it like death. It wrapped itself around her and she shook violently as the Ghost made her clean from her sins, and she was made clean. Jesus stood by the side and she saw him. Wow!

I could see the amazing Glory and light of Jesus dim from the light of a thousand suns to a light that was bright to this woman, but less than that of the sun. Now I really got a good look at him. He was making his presence available to her at her own spiritual ability. This was to clarify what Jesus first told me that "I have appeared to a number of people throughout history, but at different levels of their spiritual ability. . . ." This is not to say that she was in a low state of spirituality. Even to be able to meet Jesus directly is a miracle in itself. Soon her and Jesus were standing together and what he had to say to her was private and personal.

I left and immediately went back into my body. I saw myself sweeping back in. I awoke in a puddle of water, and I was soaking wet and cold. I was immensely happy. I sat in the freezing water smiling. I didn't care that I had nothing in the world now, including no money. It is important to note that I should have gotten hypothermia and perhaps died in that cold. I did not even catch a cold.

When Jesus says that the Father-Mother, the Son and the Holy Ghost are as one, he doesn't mean they are one and the same the way we perceive sameness. The Son of God manifests as the body of Christ and even Christ is multidimensional. The Holy Ghost purifies souls and washes them clean so that they may enter the presence of the Son (the emanation of Christ) and the Father-Mother (the same being but the whole).

The Father/Mother is multidimensional and omnipresent throughout the universe and is beyond any understanding of time and space; He/She is all pervading Love, Peace, Power, Ecstasy, and Graces. The Father/Mother, Son and Holy Ghost live *as one* but they cannot ever appear in any one point in time or space as an entirety to be seen by anyone. So, really it is all inconceivable Glory and will always be part of the great mystery.

The most frightening things Jesus told me are almost too terrible to mention. I don't believe I should tell them because it may cause more harm than good for people to know. It would be better to focus on healing and the emphasis on encouraging people to choose true love wherever and however it reaches them in their lives. By this people could be saved.

Now I have been set straight by my Lord and Master Jesus Christ.

I found this quote from the Bible that I wanted to share with all people who do not believe in healing the earth. It was delivered to St. John the Divine by Jesus in the Revelations. The Book of Revelations, Chapter 11, Verse 18, finishes: ". . . and those who destroy the earth shall be destroyed."

CHAPTER TWO

Second Meeting with the Lord, Jesus Christ

Easter morning, 1997

X

Meeting with three angels
two months before the second meeting with the Lord Jesus.

One lonely night a few months before Easter 1997, I had fallen to my face on the floor of my new tent and cried, begging God to give me another visit or take me out of this world forever. For me, it was a great trauma to live in this world without love. I missed God so much. I had a very hard time just being here on earth, always wanting to return to the Heavens I had visited on my first Near-Death-Like experience during Christmas of 1986. I begged God and nothing happened. I had visited the edge of the First Heaven a number of times since the first visit with Jesus. I had been visited by many ghosts who need help, which I see in the night with my physical eyes open. I had been to India, studied with the Dalai Lama there, and had many beautiful meditations, but nothing could satisfy me. I had gone to a small church near to where I live and listened to the minister. Nothing could make me feel like being in Heaven or being with Jesus.

Three nights later I was dreaming in my dreaming body, and suddenly saw the sky above the dreaming world open up with bright white light. In spirit, I traveled upwards to be greeted by three shining angels of the Lord who patiently waited for me, hovering just beyond these large gates at the edge of light. I laughed inwardly knowing that there were no real gates of Heaven, that Heaven was the light that begins just above what mystical people call the Astral World. I could see the light just above the Astral World and the gates in the light as the three brightly glowing angels waited there for me. Although they were illumined with white light, and were enlightened beings, it was immeasurably easier to gaze directly upon them for a long duration, yet not easy at all, compared to how extremely difficult it was to gaze upon the face of the Lord Jesus. This was an important observation for me, and perhaps the purpose of this visit, to distinguish between an enlightened being and the Lord. They did not have wings or human forms from the perspective of seeing them gazing from the Astral World into the periphery of the First Heaven. I knew that I could see more of their form as my own spiritual body started to vibrate with more light.

As I approached the three angels, I could clearly see that they were previously human. I even felt I knew who they were when they were on earth. I will not tell everything, but one of them was a genius scientist who died on earth in 1947.

Looking down at the beings in the Astral World below me, I could see that they were attached to the occult sciences such as the Tarot, astrology, palm reading, psychic readings, etc. I had also dabbled in those sciences myself.

I heard the fearful calls of those many people in the Astral World below me saying: "Don't go up there; you will die! You are crazy!" They trembled and shook as they tried to follow me and approach the three angels. The emanations of the First

Heaven above and the angels made it difficult for even the Astral human souls to breathe. They were as if drowning, unable to live as they tried to follow just behind me.

As I floated higher and closer to the angels, and got caught in the crossfire of the human souls in the Astral World trying to stop me from going "up there," I could clearly see that the same death of the ego, the purification of the soul by the Holy Ghost, was too difficult to bear for these many souls who still enjoyed the notion of living in the Astral World. I could clearly see that there was a smaller sense of "oneness" in the Astral World but very little "Clear Bright Light" and Glory, if any at all.

What the Astral beings did not know was that they interpreted the angels' "Clear Bright Light" above and the emanating Glory as the "wrath of an angry God" because it made them feel like they were going to die as they approached it. They thus feared the brilliant angels of "light," and even more so what was beyond them. Also what they did not know was that the "wrath" was their own impurities magnified, mirrored back to them by the light. That is what the light shows you. "Fear of love" is what those souls in the Astral World are experiencing at this time in their development. So the light shines that message in their faces and says "here is what you are and have been living": Fear.

Because I could feel the souls of the Astral beings, I also sensed that they interpreted these great beings of light as "evil," of all things, just because they felt a terrible shaking and death as they approached the angels. In fact, to the Astral beings, the angels were not even angels at all. They were evil and the Astral beings thought that with their psychic abilities they were going to save me from danger by warning me not to go near the angels. I laughed inside, knowing the spiritual physics of the soul as it approaches Heaven. I knew that meant the death and transformation of the ego, and that the process of death, cleansing and rebirth was traumatic to pass through, but Glorious on the other side.

As I moved closer and closer to the angels, it was as if an abyss was opening up beneath my feet. The closer I got to the three brilliant beings, the more light I felt and I felt less and less of anything human. This, I perceived, is what terrified the human soul the most, the loss of human feelings of earth, air, water and fire. All of those elements are necessary in order for a human to perceive the physical natural world and all of the senses in it. To not feel these elements is traumatic at first.

I moved even closer to the angels and all perception and even non-perception of human sensation ceased to exist. At that moment I remembered what the Tibetan Buddhist Dalai Lama had meant when he taught that upon approaching enlightenment, one would have to understand the meaning of realizing the emptiness of all phenomenon (earth, air, fire and water sensations)—"Perception neither non-perception," the trance-like state of consciousness that preceded "Clear Light" or enlightenment. Just approaching the angels taught me that what the ancient Buddhist masters understood was a very advanced understanding about what it means to approach "enlightenment" or the emanation of the Lord.

The Tibetan Book of the Dead was dictated by the Father of Tibetan Buddhism, Padma Sambhava the Buddha, to his consort Yeshe Tsogyal. The knowledge in it was obtained by the actual experience of Padma Sambhava Buddha in his in-the-body and out-of-body travels in the many dimensions of existence. This is where there is a serious split in Buddhism. There are those Buddhists who do not believe in the other dimensions and those who do. The reason being that teachings such as Theravada Buddhism know that enlightenment happens in the here and now, and there is no need to believe in what happens after. However, many meditators who practiced in realizing the here and now started entering other dimensions and traveling beyond time and space. Those who didn't experience that separated in view of those who did.

In *The Tibetan Book of the Dead* (Robert Thurman's commentary with a foreword by the Dalai Lama) it is said that when a person dies, they approach the "Great Clear Light" but it is usually too powerful for an average soul to withstand for more than a second or so. Most fear the light and find themselves, by their quality and virtue (or opposing qualities) choosing their next parents, and reincarnating again. The view of reincarnation is to say that Heaven is far too great for the unenlightened, and most beings have to return to earth until they evolve enough to become enlightened during life or at the time of death. The Buddhist notion is that "death is the greatest moment in life" in that it is the easiest time to become enlightened and break the chain of having to be reborn in suffering realms, such as earth or other natural worlds. The Buddha considers pleasure and pain (all duality) as suffering. The Buddha considers enlightenment (Nirvana) as the end of suffering, pleasures and pain, and the beginning of true liberation. But there are far deeper truths in Buddhism.

The Tibetan Book of the Dead is a true masterpiece and is so sophisticated that without a great education into Buddhism it is almost incomprehensible to Christians, Muslims and Jews. Yet, in a 1997 CNN interview between Larry King and the Dalai Lama, the Dalai Lama described the one great difference between religions such as Christian, Jewish and Muslim. It is that the Buddhists do not believe in a Supreme Being who is creating the universe. The Buddhists believe that a being can become supreme when they attain Nirvana "enlightenment," but their view is that "there is no one being that created the universe."

When I was in Dharamsala, India in 1996 studying with the Dalai Lama in a 7-day teaching, I was told by monks that they believe Jesus was a Bodhisattva, a great being of compassion who serves to teach others and guide others into enlightenment or Heaven, but who withholds his own enlightenment until all others are saved from suffering realms. The Dalai Lama is also considered to be an emanation of the great Bodhisattva Avaloketeshvara. Some of the monks in Dharamsala consider the Dalai Lama to be a Buddha (enlightened one). In Buddhism, a Buddha is far greater than a Bodhisattva in Buddhist spiritual evolution.

After meeting both the Dalai Lama of Tibet (he is one of the most compassionate and happy beings I have ever met), many of Tibet's great masters such as Kalu Rinpoche, child reincarnations of many great Buddhist masters, and having met Jesus Christ in person, it seems quite clear to me that Jesus is The Supreme Being that the Buddhists deny exists.

Although I will always love the Buddha, the Dalai Lama and all of the saints that attained enlightenment through the practice of Buddhist meditation, and have great respect for the teachings of the Buddha, I know from meeting Jesus that those who enter the "clear light" of God are in the Lord and saved from suffering. However, I can safely ascertain from experience that there is a great difference in the enlightenment that Buddhists attain; they are like angels who live in the same beyond-time-and-space "light" that Christian, Jewish, Muslim or Hindu angels (enlightened beings) live in, including angels of mercy who try to save beings trapped in hell realms. They know what it means to understand and experience even a fraction of who Jesus really is. The reason most Buddhists do not understand who Jesus is, is because Jesus' body "is the Heavens in their entirety." I experienced this while gazing upon the Lord. This would be as if a cell was born inside of my physical body and lives, yet denies that I exist as a Supreme Being and that the cell is inside of me debating whether or not I exist.

I know this sounds very difficult to understand how such a great phenomenon could be so. When any person is in direct communion with the Lord, "knowledge" of many great truths become crystal clear and apparent. This truth became apparent to me, and was delivered to me in such a way as I cannot describe, but I knew as I experienced the Body of Christ standing in front of me. I experienced Jesus as a magnifying glass (a larger body of Christ as the Universe) focusing light into a small point of light, which was the body I was physically seeing in front of me, shining over a thousand times brighter than earth's sun. Jesus was both of these bodies, the micro and the macro, at the same point in time and space. To see this is to know the greatest humility.

Swedenborg describes the miracle of this in *Heaven and Hell,* in that angels collectively make up the whole body of Christ, which is the heavens in an entirety. In Chapter 11, Verse 78: "... heaven as a whole and in its parts reflects a person because it stems from the Lord's Divine Human."

Swedenborg's experience concurs with what I experienced: That Jesus' whole body is the heavens (paradise planets, stars, galaxies, and all) in their entirety and more. He witnesses each angel as its own little heaven (because of their inner enlightenment), and countless angels collectively making up communities which, when seen as a whole, make up the body of Supreme Angels, of which there are countless number, which, when seen as a whole, make up the "Lord's Divine Human," meaning the Body of Christ.

This means that galaxies and stars are all inside of the body of Christ in a macro form, and each emanation of Christ or angels are inside the body of the macro form of Christ in a micro form. How great is Jesus Christ in the Lord's entirety? For the universe to be the Body of Christ and more, Jesus should radiate more energy than it took to create the whole universe and more in the Lord's entirety. Who could dare gaze upon an energy source that great in its entirety? This is a great mystery.

The most terrible irony of this is that throughout the ages, Christianity has suffered because it lacks a form of meditation practice, a real spiritual technology that can be used for transformation. Because of this, many Christians, even though they shout Jesus' name from the rooftops, still do not evolve into real and actual clear light "enlightenment." Thomas Merton, a great Catholic priest of this century, attested to this when he commented on the Hindu *Bhagavad Gita.* Merton wrote: "Swami Bhaktivedanta brings to the West a salutary reminder that our highly activistic and one-sided culture is faced with a crises that may end in self-destruction because it lacks the inner depth of an authentic metaphysical consciousness. Without such depth, our moral and political protestations are just so much verbiage."

Thomas Merton remained a Catholic priest for life, but spent much time with the Dalai Lama and other Tibetan Yogis. I have read some of Merton's work. He was very impressed with the real experience of God consciousness that the Buddhists transmitted to him through holy communion, versus the Western Christian "belief" in God that Merton calls "just so much verbiage." What he means by the Western world lacking depth in real consciousness, and our moral and political protestations being so much verbiage, is that by mere yelling up to the sky and praising God, we think we are evolving into God. Merton has witnessed that this is not causing a true spiritual evolution. Merton also found many things about the Eastern views that were also problematic. But, you will have to read Merton if you want to find out.

The terrible irony for today's Christianity is that it upholds the notion that all one has to do is "believe" and they will be "saved" regardless of their behavior and spiritual development—that they will be forgiven their sins and somehow enter Heaven. In meeting with Jesus I experienced that your sins are forgiven through a cleansing by the Holy Ghost. Not everyone will be able, Jesus told me, to withstand the cleansing by the Holy Ghost, let alone the Glory in the Heavens.

If Heaven were a place just like earth is right now, then what need would there be to enter Heaven when we are already on earth? If Heaven were not a quantum leap in actual consciousness, why all the fuss and why are the souls I was seeing and hearing in the Astral World (what Jesus calls a Lower World) so afraid of the Angels of Light? Of course, it is a quantum leap into the Heavens and the consciousness of Glory that goes with it. That is why it is a Heaven away from violence. If a quantum leap were not needed, why do people feel that something is missing inside their souls? How could that "something that is missing" be filled and overflow if the psychological and spiritual leap from living with a negative void (the missing) to Heaven's Glory was not a quantum leap? Why is there war on earth, and why has there been war for millennia? Why are women and men raped? Where will they be safe from criminals if there is not a real place called Heaven?

Why does Satan rule all the kingdoms on earth if earth is our supposed Heaven? I know for a fact that after being in Heaven, that neither Satan nor any dark angel that has taken in the knowledge of good and evil (having not dissolved it) can live in Glory in Heaven unless they transform back into an Angel of true Glory. They may flee in terror. "Flee in terror" means no thieves or murderers or rapists could live there. The fact that Satan lives on earth and has for millennia, is proof that this earth is not the actual place called Heaven. Even so, if an individual spirit became enlightened they could make it so (Heaven on earth). This is the Lord's prayer.

Satan tempted Jesus Christ, as written in Matthew, Chapter 4, Verses 8-9: "Again, the devil taketh him up unto an exceedingly high mountain, and showeth him all the kingdoms of the world, and the glory of them; And saith unto him, All these things will I give thee, if thou wilt fall down and worship me." Jesus rejects Satan's temptation, of course, because the things of this world are meaningless to anyone who has been to any of the places or planets in the Heavens.

This modern message from Jesus revealed to me that the classic notion of being "saved by just being called a Christian" does not necessarily qualify one to make it into the Heavens. It is not enough in itself. By the Grace of God and real effort, one must transform their soul to qualify.

The Gospel of Thomas is proof of this, however disturbing it is to the hierarchy of the Churches. The Gospel of Thomas, Verse 22, reveals it so: "Jesus saw infants being suckled. He said to his disciples, 'These infants being suckled are like those who will enter the kingdom.' They said to him, 'Shall we then, as children, enter the kingdom?' Jesus said to them, 'When you make the two one, and when you make the inside like the outside and the outside like the inside, and the above like the below, and when you make the male and female one and the same, so that the male not be male nor the female female; and when you fashion eyes in place of an eye, and a hand in place of a hand, and a foot in place of a foot, and likeness in place of likeness; then shall you enter the kingdom.'"

This verse reveals that one must accomplish a tremendous amount of inner and outer spiritual work before one can enter the Kingdom of Heaven. It is far apart from the mere philosophy of just being called a Christian. What I have witnessed in the Lord concurs with this excellent Gospel of Thomas.

If it were so easy, then why hasn't Jesus appeared to millions of Christians, and why does Jesus make appearances to Hindu Yogis such as Paramahansa Yogananda, the first Eastern yogi to come and reside in America?

Why does Jesus appear to such a Hindu Yogi like Yogananda in a blaze of light and not the leaders of our local churches? Could it be because the Yogi, whom had attained "real enlightenment" was actually spiritually capable of meeting Jesus? Does this mean that many Christians are not even capable of surviving a gaze from the Lord? Could Thomas

Merton have been wise in suggesting that we Christians must really and truly evolve in enlightenment before we could actually experience God, rather than just believing in God?

I realize these are very challenging questions. I know from having experienced sitting in meditation from half an hour per day to twelve hours per day for over fifteen years that real spiritual growth takes work and effort. It takes insight and practice. Even then, you will see what happened to me in this second meeting with the Lord.

I know Jesus is not appearing to the priests and leaders of our local churches because I have asked them. In 1997, after this second meeting with the Lord, I went to a large Catholic church in Santa Monica, California and approached the man who gave the Sunday sermon and told him I wanted to speak with him in private about something. He was rude and said, "I have no time. What is it?" I told him about my meeting with Jesus and the man immediately got upset with me, saying, "If you are having meetings with him, you don't need to talk to me. I have never seen him." I then said to the man, "Don't you want to know what Jesus' message is?" I was so naive. He said, "No, I don't have time." I left the church in a great sadness. I was so happy to spread the Lord's message to this man, and he didn't even want to hear about it.

Because Jesus can appear as the emanation of the body of Christ that humans and angels (enlightened beings) can see, yet is the whole (the Mother/Father), and because the Lord's emanation body lives in the highest Heavens most of the time, it is rarely possible for any being other than those supremely enlightened beings, who can live in those Highest Heavens, to catch a glimpse of the Lord in the highest. Also, unless Jesus comes down and makes appearances in lower realms and even upon earth, as Jesus did to me. Because few ever see the face of the Lord, few know who the Lord is. I know that Buddha lives in those highest Heavens, being a Supremely Enlightened Angel, but I will have to reveal more of this as the message evolves.

I believe there is a deep reason for Jesus making this appearance to me, a person who has practiced Buddhist-based meditation, and still does to this day, with Jesus as my master. The reason is unfolding slowly in this message. It has something to do with integration, and that each religion only has a piece of a giant puzzle. If we are too one-sided, and most religions are, we will never even see the "other," let alone see what happens when we all bring our pieces of the puzzle to the table of humanity. The only way you will see the whole puzzle is if you let down the barrier and integrate.

Ever since these experiences started, I have as if "gone mad" trying to find answers, even if it meant I had to cross the lines that humankind has drawn itself into. And I did cross the lines.

Since my Near-Death-Like Experience in 1986 (chapter 3), I became a member of the International Association for Near Death Studies. I had to get help with my new and serious problem. I was having a hard time adjusting to living in this world after being in the Light. In southern California, I attended meetings over several years, meeting with other experiencers. I wanted to see if I could hear other stories to obtain additional pieces of the giant puzzle.

At those meetings, I met and heard the story of a woman (whose name is confidential) who had a heart attack, floated out of her body and met Jesus, Buddha, Krishna and one other mysterious, yet-to-be-revealed being at the same time, in a blaze of Glory and light. This woman has such a beautiful innocent heart, it is no wonder this world gave her a heart attack. I really mean that.

It is so difficult for this woman to even speak about her experience and reveal her name because of the ridicule humankind gives back to people like her. She is afraid of that. She is afraid of being called a demon by Christian fundamentalists who think this is all one giant war, with Jesus on one side and Buddha, Krishna and the others on the other side.

If the Fundamentalist Christian notion of "My religion is right and yours is wrong, we are going to heaven and you are going to hell because you got it wrong"—the basic football game theory of God—is right, then what is Jesus doing with Krishna and Buddha in a blaze of "light" and appearing to this woman who just had a heart attack and died?

This sets the precedent for my second meeting with the Lord.

XI

The second face-to-face meeting with Jesus Christ on Easter Morning, 1997. Message ends at 4:46 A.M.

I, David, swear that the following is a true story about my meeting with Jesus Christ. I swear that it is true, and that if it is a lie, that I be cast into hell for telling such a lie. I am so sure that it is true, I know I will not be cast into hell, because it *is* true. This is my oath for any and all spiritual meetings with God, God's enlightened angels, and/or the Kingdom of Heavens. I will not tell a lie.

Since my last meeting with Jesus Christ, I followed most of what Jesus told me to do. I continued to carry the environmental work that Jesus told me to continue with—that which I wanted to abandon because of too much rejection, and ended up living in a tent. I still live in a tent; however, it is a very modern tent which my loving father helped me build on a sun deck, and have been in since 1994, all year round. I thought it was incredibly kind of my father and his wife to let me live on their land.

Because, here I am, a 37-year-old man, a failure in the material world, living at home. I was just above being homeless. Many nights are absolutely freezing.

Anyway, with much hesitation, I wrote and Richard Hubbard edited, and I had published the article "The Fifty Year Nuclear War—Lies, Theft And Cover-ups Over Nonradioactive Fusion." I receive calls from people and scientists who say our article is still making waves all over the world. Dr. Bogdan Maglich is an excellent fusion scientist, a Massachusetts Institute of Technology Ph.D. and applied physicist. His non-radioactive nuclear power, with 9 grams of helium-3 fuel equalling the energy equivalent of 1,000 barrels of crude oil, and no radioactive waste, could slowly transform the global ecology crisis if it was fully developed and implemented successfully. However, I have experienced the political and economic forces against it to be in a brilliant conspiracy.

I am now working for Dr. Bogdan Maglich (one who Jesus told me to serve), as Vice President of his company HiEnergy Microdevices (chemically specific detection of buried land mines). We are receiving military funding for the prototype development of a most advanced technology for finding buried land mines.

There are over 110 million land mines deployed in over 70 countries, while another 100 million are stored in national stockpiles waiting to be planted. In the U.S.-Iraq war, there were reported to be some 25,000 victims and 26,000 people are blown up by land mines each year—over 90% of them innocent civilians. In 1996, the total population of the United States was some 275 million.

This means that the silent war being set by land mines has the potential to kill or maim a population nearly the size of the United States of America. It is one of the largest problems in the military/civilian world. It is potentially the largest war in history. In Cambodia, Angola and other deprived nations, the people have extreme difficulty with farming because their oppressors have placed land mines in their fields. Many lose their lives and limbs. There are many great humanitarians working to solve this problem.

Between tree planting, photography and working closely with a brilliant scientist on de-mining, I feel I have kept up most of my deal with God. Most importantly, I made several copies of the written testimony to my first meeting with Jesus Christ, and gave them to the minister of my local Church, David Bunch, Father Ralph at the Sera Retreat House in Malibu (a Franciscan Catholic Priest), the Pope, Prince Charles, the Queen of England, my friends, family, and many, many more people who think that I am crazy.

It is fun to see the reactions from people when they think I am imagining all this. However, one of the most sincere reactions I received was from Father Ralph, a Franciscan Friar. He felt the meeting was genuine. I liked him a lot, even though one part of my first meeting with the Lord baffled him: the part where Jesus told me: "you made this agreement to carry this environmental work (burden) with me *before* you came here." You see, many Christians do not believe that any of us ever preexisted before we were born.

There is a great mystery as to what happens after death and between dimensions that I was not given the full answer for. What I do feel would cause great debates amongst scholars, but I find no reason to fight for any truth, so I will not persist. Truth does not have to follow what people think they already know. It stands on its own, and exists, undefiled by any belief waiting for us to discover and evolve in truth. It is not the other way around. Truth does not need anyone to approve of it, fight for it or defend it. It just waits in eternity for souls to recognize it.

I will start this second meeting with my final approach toward the Lord Jesus Christ, because the whole approach is extremely complex in spiritual physics and difficult to understand. It is too complex for me to write about at the beginning of this second message, but it will be understandable at the end.

It is very important, in this new message, to clearly understand what Jesus first told me in the first meeting, from October 1994: "I have appeared to a number of people throughout history, at different levels of their spiritual ability. *No one has seen me in my entirety.* Even now, you are not seeing me in my entirety. It is not possible at this time."

This is perhaps one of the most important parts of this new message, as you will see, and understand. What Jesus is saying is that when people have visitations of Christ, an Angel of the Lord or Heaven, they are only perceiving and experiencing as much Glory as they are spiritually capable of at that time. I have met those persons who also met Jesus, and felt that they were as-one or the same level as Jesus, and that they were capable of being with the Lord, and wondered why the Lord sent them back to earth or on their way, when they felt they could live in the Lord's presence so easily. To those people, what you did not know is that Jesus only revealed to you as much spiritual Glory as you were capable of at that time. Your answer is in this message.

Many are not capable of experiencing any of this at this time in their development at all; mostly those who do not know Glory and love, have chosen to stray from love, or fear love. For those, I beg you to use this message to guide you towards love and even Glory in your life. Just as people may fear love in a relationship, they will fear God's love and Glory even more, because God's love, let alone his/her full Glory, is millions and billions times greater than human love.

XII

One second in the Lord may amount to a million years of normal evolution of the spirit in time and space without the Lord.

As I approached the Lord Jesus Christ, who was and is always ablaze with light and Glory, I was accompanied in spirit this time by at least three other human souls, also in spirit. I think they had just died on earth, but I am not sure. As soon as they all saw Jesus, ablaze with light and turning towards us, they all involuntarily fell to their knees and on their faces, trembling in the extreme power and Glory of the Lord. They were instantly humbled by the greatest power in the universe. As Jesus was slowly turning and walking, he had not even gazed upon their faces, when they all collapsed down. Jesus showed them a fraction of his profile, his cheek, for a millisecond and they could not bear the sight of the Lord, so they fell down on their knees and faces to the ground. I think they must have seen Jesus' face for only a millisecond when they involuntarily collapsed; they involuntarily collapsed because the spiritual power and Glory in God's presence is so great (when the Lord wishes to reveal it), it is difficult or impossible to stand up, let alone gaze upon the face of the Lord (literally and actually so).

Why is it so difficult to even gaze upon the Lord for a millionth of a second? Why can most humans gaze at the sun for a few seconds but not even gaze upon the face of the Lord for even a millionth of a second? What were these souls so terrified of? I will tell you that it is not only that the physical light of the Lord's face is many times brighter than one thousand suns, but the Lord's Innocence is immeasurably brighter than the light. From the Lord's Innocence shines so much wisdom, it is too baffling for spiritually inexperienced souls to conceive of this so they hide their faces. I will tell you that the Lord's Love is so overwhelming, it makes the light created by a whole galaxy seem like darkness.

The Lord's Love shows them that they lied to their hearts their whole lives by chasing false loves, and seeing this they hide their faces from the Lord. I will tell you that the Lord's Ecstasy is so ultra-blazing bright, and so much wisdom about happiness shines from the Lord's Ecstasy, these souls know that they have no training in experiencing real ecstasy, because they chased false ecstasy in their lives, so they hide their faces from the Lord. I will tell you that the Lord's Peace is so immeasurable, that it stills the ecstasy and sustains it, for those who have not known how to live in peace on earth, they will hide their faces from the Lord. I will tell you that the Lord's Power and the wisdom that emanates from it is so vast, whole galaxies could be created by it, let alone a new earth. If such souls misused power while on earth, they would be ashamed to gaze upon the true Power of the Lord. I will tell you that the Grace that shines from the Lord is so Holy and pure that it defies all of the previous qualities of the Glory, resounding in Holy silence, and souls who did not allow for Grace and forgiveness, Grace and tolerance to others, will hide their faces from the Lord. I will tell you that the Lord's Beauty is so unfathomable, it is no wonder that such a beauty as this earth could be created by the same power. If such humans thought they had seen beauty on earth, in any form, they will be offended by the Beauty of the Lord and they will hide their faces.

Looking at the other souls hiding their faces from the Lord, which was somewhat how it was for me in my first meeting, I noticed that they never gazed upon the face of the Lord, not even for a millionth of a second. I wondered, what would the Lord do to them?

My God it was beautiful to watch them, to see that kind of humility. I cannot recall any one of them ever looking upon the face of the Lord, but they received their messages with their face hidden, facing the ground. I could write an entire chapter on the humility before the Lord. It is not a bowing down in respect; it is a bowing down because the energy emanations are simply far too great to bear for the human spirit (ego), so it collapses. The human will is separate from God and has to die in God's presence; otherwise no real communion is possible. Even with the ego humbled, it is still almost impossible to gaze upon the face of the Lord directly.

In many accounts I have read, many witnesses unto Jesus have seen his feet or robe only (his robe is brighter than the sun because it is a robe of Glory), and even his robe and feet are so holy that to gaze upon them is a powerful and wonderful blessing. There are accounts where a whole meeting with Jesus transpires with only contact with his feet or robe, without ever gazing upon his face, such as what I was seeing. Even so, those witnesses knew it was Jesus.

What they don't know is that they were not ready at that time to gaze upon the Lord's face, even for a second, and could not withstand it without fleeing in terror. And, even so, if they could, Jesus will still only show them as much Glory as they could withstand.

It really is extremely difficult to gaze upon the Lord's face. No matter how pure you may feel you have been in life, just to see the Lord's face for one second (even if that is possible) will show you more Holy, True Glory and Wisdom than a person can learn in a whole lifetime on their own. This shows that there is no time and space-distance in the Lord. One second in the Lord may amount to a million years of normal evolution of the spirit in time and space. This shows, that by the Grace of the Lord, just upon meeting Jesus, we can all make a quantum leap forward in our own spiritual development. This leap would only be possible if we followed the wisdom we gained by the blessing of the meeting. We will all have that chance. The purpose in revealing this is to make us aware of what we must prepare for, our own personal meeting with God.

XIII

What I was now seeing, was that Jesus is truly nameless, pure, and undefiled. But most of all, the Glory of the Lord is so great, it would be impossible for the impure in heart to even withstand or survive such a gaze. But why was I perceiving this about Jesus? If Jesus were the Son of God, at the right hand of the Lord, and fits the same description the ancients gave to the Lord God, Jehovah-Allah-Yahweh, could Jesus actually be the same as the Father?

In the Book of Exodus, Chapter 19, Verse 21: "And the Lord said unto Moses, Go down, charge the people, lest they break through unto the Lord to gaze, and many of them perish."

Many scholars interpreted this as an angry God who would try to destroy the people if they even dared to attempt to gaze upon the Lord, and it is not so in truth. The truth is the Lord and the Lord's emanations of Glory are so great, it would literally destroy a human being to even gaze upon the Lord's face if they were not ready in their spiritual development. The truth is contrary to the "angry God" perception. Rather, the Lord is so compassionate, the Lord knows that humans would be in danger. They would go insane or die just by such a gaze, by their own impurities.

This is to say that there is no wrath of God, but the wrath is felt as the impurities mirror in the mind of the perceiver as its own wrath. So, there is no wrath in God, but it can appear that way because, by the impurities of the perceiver, the perceiver will experience a shaking "like a wrath." They will fear God although there is no fear in God. The fear of God comes as the fear of real love.

Now we will see that the God of the end of times, the return of Jesus Christ in the Second Coming, fits the same description of the God in the beginning of the Bible. Could this be what Jesus meant when he said "I am the Alpha and the Omega"?

The first clue is rather mysterious. In the Book of Revelation, Jesus appears to St. John the Divine on the Island of Patmos (Greece). This book was written long after the time of the apostles. It was a vision that St. John the Divine had, an excellent example of how one man's spiritual vision (direct experience with God) became actual human knowledge. It is written in Revelation, Chapter 1, Verses 10-14: "I was in the Spirit on the Lord's day, and heard behind me a great voice, as of a trumpet, Saying, I am Alpha and Omega, the first and the last: 12, And I turned to see the voice that spake with me. And being turned, I saw seven golden candlesticks; And in the midst of the seven candlesticks one like unto the Son of man, clothed with a garment down to the foot, and girt about the paps with a golden girdle. His head and his hairs were white like wool, as white as snow; and his eyes were as a flame of fire." Verse 18 says: "I am he that liveth, and was dead; and behold, I am alive for evermore, Amen; and have the keys of hell and death." The statement, "I am he that liveth, and was dead, I am alive for evermore," is clearly a description of Jesus having lived, died on the cross and resurrected for evermore. The mystery is: why does Jesus physically look like God, the Father, with his white hair, unless Jesus "is" the Father—that very same Ancient of Days whom Enoch and Moses met? But this mystery is still greater.

Describing the end times, Revelation, Chapter 6, Verses 15-17: "And the Kings of the earth, and the great men, and the rich men, and the chief captains, and the mighty men, and every bondman, and every free man, hid themselves in the dens and in the rocks of the mountains; And said to the mountains and the rocks, Fall on us, and hide us from the face of him that sitteth on the throne, and from the wrath of the Lamb." Jesus is the Lamb, but he fits the same description as the Lord in the time of Moses.

In "The Acts of John" *(New Testament Apocrypha,* edited by Wilhelm Schneemelcher), a gospel ordered to be burned and never practiced by Pope Leo the Great (the first Catholic Church Pope), there is a story that must have baffled religious experts so greatly, it is no wonder they ordered the text to be burned. Thanks to some very concerned individuals, the manuscript has resurfaced. It reveals the mystery of Jesus' being one and the same as the Father in "The Christ of Many Forms." It reads: "For when he had chosen Peter and Andrew, who were brothers, he came to me and to my brother James, saying "I need you; come to me!" And my brother when he heard this said: "John, what does he want, this child on the shore who called us." And I said, "Which child?" And he answered me, "The one who is beckoning to us." And I replied: "Because of the long watch we have kept at sea, you are not seeing well, brother James. Do you not see the man standing there who is handsome, fair and cheerful-looking?" But he said to me, "I do not see that man, my brother. But let us go, and we shall see what this means." And when we had brought the boat to land we saw how he also helped us to beach the boat. And as we left the place, wishing to follow him, he appeared to me again as a rather bald headed but with a thick flowing beard, but to James as a young man whose beard was just beginning. So we were both puzzled about the meaning of what we had seen."

Peter, Andrew and James are all deeply troubled because, in the same moment in time and space, they all physically see Jesus in completely different forms. One sees Jesus as a small child (the child Jesus), another as a young man (the way Jesus usually appeared and always was to them all) and another as an old man, rather bald looking with a thick flowing beard (the image of the way God appeared to Moses and Enoch). But, was Jesus transfiguring himself into these three forms, baffling the disciples, showing them the mystery that Jesus is the Father, Son and Child, a further insight into Jesus' meaning of the great mystery of just who Jesus is? The mystery will baffle you more as this message evolves.

This is a clue to the meaning of Jesus' statement, "I am the Alpha and the Omega, the first and the last." He describes these particular people to St. John the Divine in the visions of the Revelations as those who will hide and tell the rocks to fall on them because the Lord and the Lord's emanations are so great, if you do not have love, innocence (an open heart) or Glory, you lied to love in your own soul all your life, and you will fear the magnitude of love and Glory of the Lord. These particular rich and corrupt kings of the earth have none or little love and that is why they will tremble and quake and try to hide.

For Jesus to be compassionless to human beings would be like sending a million volts of electricity (the Lord) into a one-watt circuit (the under-developed soul). This is not condescending. It is truth. The Lord is so great, that for a soul to gaze upon the Lord's face or even feet before being ready would destroy it. Today, in Jesus' glorious body of Light, he does not appear the same as he was when he was on earth some 2,000 years ago. On earth, Jesus took upon living in the same body as we live in. He described this body as a body of sin. The body Jesus lives in now is the same body the Lord has always lived in, the Glorious and mysterious body, the totality of which no one has ever seen.

As we approached the Lord Jesus Christ, his back was facing us, having met with some other souls coming from the other direction who he was finishing with. The Lord was ablaze with blinding light and Glory, resounding in virgin holy silence and innocence. In his shining white robe and bare feet in sandals, he slowly walked and turned to face us. Jesus is so patient, pure and holy. Again, I could write chapters on how Holy the Lord is and what I experienced in the Lord in detail, and I could never do justice. I could perceive that he was as ancient as all of time and timelessness, the Alpha and the Omega, blazing with light and Glory for eternity. The purity and innocence alone would break any heart to behold, even to witness that innocence alone, if it could be separated from the whole contents of the Glory. It is like finding out that God is billions of times more innocent than any child, and that little innocent heart is the most powerful being in the universe.

To understand that innocence corresponds to openness of the mind, body and soul, reveals that power and Glory flows into a soul who is open (innocent) in their mind, body and soul. Glory does not flow into a soul who is "closed" or rigid, and only appears wise like a scholar, in solidified knowledge alone. For if a person were "closed"—opposed to innocent and "open"—where and how would the Glory flow into them? It could not. This means that innocence is not to mean a lack of experience, or to be technically undefiled by sin. This is to mean that innocence corresponds to "openness" of the heart, mind, body and soul. For if you were not open, how could you receive?

In the Bible, the book of St. Matthew, Chapter 18, Verses 1-4 read: "AT THE same time came the disciples unto Jesus, saying, Who is the greatest in the kingdom of heaven? And Jesus called a little child unto him, and set him in the midst of them, And said, 'Verily I say unto you, Except ye be converted, and become as little children, ye shall not enter into the Kingdom of heaven. Whosoever therefore shall humble himself as this little child, the same is the greatest in the Kingdom of heaven.'" As I was seeing the Lord, this is so. The reason Jesus is Supreme in Heaven is because Jesus is supremely innocent.

In some cases, persons who are innocent feel so sensitive in today's world they feel a need to sequester themselves and make very little use of their love for humankind. God has sent many who are not doing their work because we have scared them away with our violence. Also, there are many who are being distracted. There are also a number of people who have had visitations by angels of the Lord and visitations of the Lord, but fear being ridiculed by the world, and they speak not. Today, as we move into the new millennium, I ask that you all come to the table of humanity and deliver your piece of the giant puzzle, so that humankind may partake of it and heal itself by it. With our collective vision of the whole evolving puzzle, we may project and build the New World and the new child, woman, man and ecology.

Seeing the Lord this time, I could clearly perceive that it was through the great quality of "innocence" that all the Glory flowed into and out of the Lord's emanation body. Jesus always was made of that innocence and Glory, even when he was on earth. However, while Jesus was in a body his witnesses could not see as much as people will see when they meet the Lord in spirit today, and even more so in the Heavens.

There was one recorded incident that reveals Jesus' more Glorious emanation body. The Bible book of St. Matthew, Chapter 17, Verses 1-2 read: "And after six days Jesus taketh Peter, James and John his brother, and bringeth them up unto a high mountain apart, And was transfigured before them: and his face did shine as the sun, and his raiment was white as light."

The disciples became terrified and fell to the ground. But why, if they had not already seen the Lord by being with Jesus day and night? Because, as Jesus told me, whose face did shine in the second meeting with a light brighter than 1,000 suns, "No one has seen me in my entirety." Obviously then, even when Jesus revealed himself on the mountain shining with light, the disciples still had not seen Jesus in his entirety, because Jesus told me, "No one has." That would include his disciples and Angels.

While even Jesus' disciples became very spiritually evolved, noted by the many healing miracles that they performed by the power of Christ through them, they still had incredible spiritual difficulty perceiving Jesus when the Lord revealed more of the mystery of who Jesus really is. To prove that Jesus' disciples did not, nor could they, bear the Glory of Jesus' higher vibration body of light for any great length of time, we will look at transfigurations that are aside from that written in Matthew.

From the book, *New Testament Apocrypha* (edited by Wilhelm Schneemelcher), "The Acts of John," we see an amazing account of Jesus revealing more of the mystery of who Jesus is, to John, James and Peter: "Another time he took me and James and Peter to the mountain where he used to pray, and we saw on him a light such that a man who uses mortal speech cannot describe what it was like. Again he took us three likewise up the mountain, saying "Come with me." And again we went; and we saw him at a distance praying. Then I, since he loved me, went quietly up to him as if he could not see and stood looking at his hinder parts; and I saw him not dressed in clothes at all, but stripped of those which we usually saw upon him, and not like a man at all. And I saw that his feet were whiter than snow, so that the ground there was lit up by his feet; and that his head stretched up to heaven, so that I was afraid and cried out. . . ."

From the same book in "The Acts of Peter," we hear perhaps another or the same account by Peter: "Our Lord wished me to see his majesty on the holy mountain; but when I with the sons of Zebedee saw the brilliance of his light, I feel as one dead, and closed my eyes and heard his voice, such as I cannot describe, and thought that I had been blinded by his radiance. And recovering my breath a little I said to myself, 'Perhaps my Lord wished to bring me here to deprive me of my sight.' And I said, 'If this be thy will, Lord, I do not gainsay it.' And he gave me his hand and lifted me up. And when I stood up I saw him in such a form as I was able to take in."

If Jesus appears in the long awaited "Second Coming" in this Glorious form of light body, how difficult will it be for us, if for such great disciples it was nearly unbearable, and for such a short duration in time?

If the Second Coming were to occur today, most will flee in terror from entering the emanations of the Lord's presence (due to unloving and unwise hearts), and of those who can bear to be at his feet, most will only last a few seconds or so. And of those only a few will be able to withstand to gaze directly upon Jesus' face; most will last only one second, and the pure in heart will last longer. Saints may last indefinitely longer than I did. I witnessed all this and it is tragically so.

Approaching the Lord, Jesus turned to face me directly, and when he did it was a million fold in Glory, from the point when his back was turned, or his attention was turned. The Glory was so great; it was like an earthquake of love and ecstasy in my veins. I collapsed and fell to my knees and on my face, for what I had seen and perceived was too great to bear. The leap from the human waking state to the presence of the Lord was a quantum leap in wakefulness. I was seeing even more of the Lord than I saw on the first visit.

Soon, amazingly, I was able to stand back up and gaze upon the face of the Lord without looking away, my arms open at my sides. I looked straight into Jesus. I couldn't believe what I was seeing, how beautiful and how great the crushing Glory was. Oh My God, My GOD, Lord, the Ecstasy and Love were so extreme that I was being crushed with ultra-extreme levels of Glory, and more and more dazzling, blazing light—tears of joy, yet too difficult to bear the sight of, yet somehow, magically the Lord sustained me in the Lord's sight. I was seeing so much love and wisdom it was overwhelming. It was like staring into the heart of a galaxy of Glory. Whole galaxies could be created by this

Glory! The wisdom resounded like a never-ending mathematical formula rippling through eternity just waiting to be captured for spiritual use.

The Lord is all, and everything in creation is suspended in the Lord, including the Heavens. I could see this with amazing clarity. The light in Jesus is the light in me and Jesus was a million times more than I had experienced in the first meeting (where his face was brighter than 1,000 suns). Words will never describe what I was seeing and feeling, ever, ever, and ever.

My God, who he *IS*. The galactic *Ecstasy was crushing me* as I stood gazing upon the Lord. The whole universe, the beginning of creation and the continuing creation was all and in the Lord. To see that in one point (this Body of Christ), that the whole could be contained in a point and reflected out of a point, was like seeing that the microcosm and the macrocosm were linked. Jesus really is the Alpha and the Omega. It was the sweetest ecstasy, so extremely sweet, and almost unbearable because I am used to suffering (pleasure and pain) as a human and do not know my real birthright, our real birthright, all of us, which is Glory.

From "The Acts of Peter" we see evidence of what it is like to be crushed with more Glory than Peter could bear: "And when prayer was made by all, the room in which they were shone as if with lightning, such as shines in the clouds. Yet it was not light as is seen by day, but ineffable, invisible, such as no man could describe, a light that shone on us so brightly that we were senseless with bewilderment, and called upon the Lord and said, 'Have mercy on us thy servants, Lord. Let thy gift to us, Lord, be such as we can endure; for this we can neither see nor endure.'"

Jesus opened his being and showed me even more Light, crushing me further with his Glory, more and more each second, like billions of magnitude stars of ecstasy. I lasted around one minute, and some of the others had left him because they could not bear any more Glory for their own development at that time, and a few others were on their faces still not even glimpsing his face, trembling in the Glory. It was all so beautiful to see the others, and feel what they were feeling, learning more and more. Literally, you could feel everything everyone was feeling: no separation. As I stood in the Glory of the Lord, Jesus' new message was being delivered to me and to you, in less than a minute, but that minute was an eternity beyond time and space, as all these pages reveal.

It was so bright now, all I could see was Jesus' robe and feet, and the rest of him was just light, Glory and *ecstasy crushing me, and love overwhelming me.* I perceived the serenity and silence of the Lamb. The silence was so pristine and pure, radiating from him throughout all of creation. He is so pure and full of innocent love. So much innocent love, it is breaking my heart, which is now ablaze in light. Literally breaking my heart with Jesus' Glory, I cried from deep inside my being, in Love for the Lord. The ecstasy: I love it and can't bear its increasing magnitude, with each passing second. At this point the Lord doesn't even really have a face. It's all too bright. I am blinded in the Glory now. All I see is light and the Lord's feet.

XIV

I am here now for everyone to meet with.

Jesus' whole message is like silent waters and is telepathic. There is no voice, but I understood everything: **"I am here now for everyone to meet with. I am not hidden. I am more available now than I was for some time. Anyone can come and meet me now, but it will not be easy for them."**

There is a deep meaning to this—cross reference from the first meeting where we know that for a time he was not allowed to intervene directly with all humanity, and cross into the realm of free will. The meaning of this is vast. The Lord doesn't turn anyone away, but as their own impurities reflect in the Glory, most will flee in terror of the Lord's Glory (Love, Peace, Ecstasy, Power, Grace and Beauty millions and billions of fold over human), even from miles away. Others will receive their spiritual nutrition and messages for their own development in seconds or perhaps minutes.

The Glory is telling me that the Lord Jesus has gone through an amazing preparation to make himself more available to humans at this time. That preparation involves lowering the spiritual light vibration rate of his body, having come down from the Highest Heavens, to a point where humans can perceive the Lord. This involves a great task. It is long and complicated to tell. I do not know how easily the Lord can make preparations like this. Is Jesus making these preparations for the foretold event?

Imagine atoms vibrating at billions of times the speed or vibration rate of light, and that it would be necessary to lower that rate below or equal to one thousand times the rate of light for humans to be able to possibly glimpse the Lord. Can you imagine how great Jesus must be? The Lord had to lower his vibration rate to get ready to meet with humans, but even then they would only be able to last a few seconds or minutes (depending on their ability to love and perceive spiritual Glory) in the Lord's presence because of the great power of the Glory. At a higher rate of vibration, it would not be possible at all for most humans to even catch a glimpse of Jesus.

It is not because humans are incapable of reaching a higher state of vibration, or spiritual development. It is because most humans have *not evolved enough* in love and thus have not reached a higher state of vibration and Glory to be able to see the Lord in a higher vibration.

That is and has been within their own free will to choose ignorance over love in their individual lives. Only experience in love and divine spirituality can prepare a soul to withstand a meeting with the Lord, even in Jesus' lowered vibration body. Nothing, nor anyone, can fool the Lord because fools will tremble and quake even a million miles away from the Lord, and flee in terror before they can even catch a glimpse of the Lord.

I witnessed this. The Lord's Glorious emanations, which pervade the entire spiritual Heavens and universe in omniscience, know as a complete intelligence when someone is fooling their heart and thinks they can enter. Such persons will tremble and quake even at the Gates of Heaven (the borders) and fear to enter, let alone catch a glimpse of the Lord Jesus Christ.

Can you imagine the great compassion the Lord Jesus Christ has? Some 2,000 years ago, Jesus came to earth with love, Glory and healing, got rejected and even murdered by us, and today, he is making special preparations to lower his vibration rate so that humans can barely glimpse the Lord for a few seconds or minutes each. For most humans, one second will be enough to teach them everything they need to know about how to evolve more. In that "one second," there is an "eternity" for each soul who gazes upon the Lord. You will understand this more as this message gets clearer, and even more so when you are taken yourself to gaze upon the Lord.

I could perceive that even saints or angels last very little time in his presence because of how great the Glory in Jesus is. Even for saints and angels to gaze upon the Lord is part of their continuing spiritual development. It is also unbearably bright for them to bear a meeting any longer than seconds or a few minutes depending on how much is revealed to them. Only the highest enlightened beings could withstand a long visit or life at the side of the Lord.

I am not one of those angels or saints yet, for I only lasted a small duration, but that was enough to deliver this message. I am still on my path of spiritual service, meditation, prayer and attempts at love.

Jesus gives people so much Glory and wisdom that they simply cannot bear to withstand any more and leave when they are overflowing with the divine. They are immensely happy when they leave, knowing they can take no more ecstasy, Glory and Love, lest they burst. This shows the Lord to be generous and full of immeasurable abundance.

Can you imagine what this means? It means that in Heaven, angels can come and meet the Lord directly but even they don't last very long in the presence of the Lord. The Lord fills them with more ecstasy than they can bear and they leave when they are overflowing. It may be quite a while before they attempt to gaze upon the Lord again, yet they live in Heaven. A day or a year later, they try to come before the Lord again and see how much Glory they can bear. What a supreme blessing it is to have the Lord available to all of us like this. I thank you Lord!

XV

Understanding the true freedom that exists for all beings in the Heavens versus the "conflict" slavery, control and suffering that exists when a soul lives separate from God and the Heavens.

It is as though the spirits—enlightened ones and ones evolving in deeper enlightenment—come to see the Lord from the Heavens to receive more of the Spiritual Glory, as nourishment, than they could perceive during their last visit. Jesus told me: **"They go out and create the Heavens on their own, as a spontaneous reaction to the Glory (Love, Ecstasy, Peace, Grace, Power, etc.) that is here and everywhere in Heaven,**

and that which they receive with each visit. The Heavens are suspended in the Glory and it is spontaneous the way those who live here create their lives in the Heavens and create the very Heavens themselves by it all. Because everything is suspended in Love and Glory, all is created from it and by it, so nothing unholy can manifest here. Because of this, there is no need for any kind of enforcement. There are no strict rules here (no one orders people around—everything is done out of spontaneous love). This is real freedom, opposed to the ideal the fallen ones have using control and oppression."

As I mentioned at the beginning of these messages that, when the Lord speaks in total silence, there are the "words" Jesus actually speaks and there is all that is "implied" by the words, the "implied" being as real as the words. The "implied" radiates out from each word like a great mathematical expanding formula of resounding wisdom. When you see the resounding wisdom radiating off of each word, all you have to do is catch it and remember it. That is what follows from these powerful statements of the Lord in these messages.

The True Freedom and Abundance in the Heavens

This message is to show that when a soul lives in the Lord, that soul has access to the greatest true abundance and power in the universe, and "they go out and create their lives in the Heavens and create the very Heavens themselves by it all" as a spontaneous reaction to the Glory. Because the angels "create with love" (because love is the power of creation), all things created in the Heavens are emanations of love and Glory. Imagine angels creating whole paradises, planets and galaxies (depending on their level of enlightenment) "in total freedom," as they wish, without anyone telling them what to do and what they can't do. That is what the Lord is telling us. Can you imagine how much abundance and prosperity this gives those enlightened angels who live in Heaven? Of course, the power to create is evolutionary. Because everyone and everything in Heaven are suspended in love and Glory, it is impossible to create anything unholy, not because a being will be punished if they do, but because creation only happens by love and Glory. It is the natural spontaneous law of Heaven. This is so perfect. What a great system.

Seen from this heavenly perspective, the notion of being materially wealthy on earth, or having to wait until you get rich before you can create what you want in your life, appears as true poverty. That is because the greedy hoard the money supply and most others don't have enough on earth. In Heaven, all will have as much abundance as they can handle. Even so, the abundance in Heaven for a single angel far surpasses the qualities and abilities of all the treasures on earth. Material treasures have no value when seen as objects.

When Jesus said in the New Testament to "seek not for yourselves treasures upon earth where moth and rust do corrupt, but seek for yourselves the Kingdom of Heaven and all else shall be added unto you," he was talking about how real the wealth and freedom are in Heaven. It is not that in Heaven everyone is poor and in rags. In fact, all of the things that humans regard as true prosperity and wealth on earth will seem like garbage in comparison to the quality of the same in the Heavens.

Why then have spiritual devotees lived in such poverty on earth as if the Lord were against wealth and prosperity? The answer comes to me by the wisdom I have seen in the Lord and the Heavens. If you worship wealth on earth, and the greedy hoard the wealth of the earth, which is money and treasures, who will you be a slave to? Who will you serve? Will you serve love or will you serve fool's gold? I have seen that on earth there is more money in fools' banks than there is in the wise. The scientists for the ecology are starving and poor, the tree planters live in shacks, the protesters against humankind's destruction live desolately, the revealers of the banking conspiracy hide in friends' closets, while fools make themselves available for any amount to the masters of the money supply. If there were more money with the spiritually wise than with the fools, there would be so few martyrs living in poverty. This is because if there was more money in the banks of the wise, they would have invested in new ideas to heal our world. They have not done this.

If you want to be wealthy in this world, and if you are not fortunate enough to find a wise person with money to work for, you will have to serve the corrupt masters of money. They will make fools, and have made fools out of you. They have asked you to sell your soul so that you would have money and fame and earthly power. They will bring you to starvation so that they may be master over you. Then they will get you to do whatever they desire, making you dance like puppets, lie and steal for the almighty dollar, take your clothes off to the world, sell your own mother's and father's pride, your very own self.

If you want to live in real prosperity in Heaven and free yourselves from the slavery of the fools, it is better to either serve a brilliant man or woman and work for less, create a brilliant work yourself, or live in rags until you are made free and enter the Heavens. There, we will all be truly rich.

The Conflict, Slavery and Control that Exist Outside of the Heavens

Now what happens to the "fallen ones" and to those under the spell of subservience to them? True freedom, prosperity, Heaven and Glory are opposite the "fallen angels" view of the perfect world, which has to maintain itself by total control. This involves purposefully limiting resources so that abundance is not available to all, thus the slaves will gather. If abundance was available to all, how could the fallen ones and their servants control? There must be "control" because of the many conflicts, disagreements and wars that are caused by the "knowledge of good and evil." And, unfortunately for the "fallen angels" and their slaves, they go mad trying to agree on anything, fight amongst themselves, and have no real prosperity or freedom at all. The ones who are subservient to the "fallen angels" live as slaves to material wealth, manipulation, control and the never ending idea that they will one day create the perfect world all on their own, such as the earthly planners of the coming "New World Order."

Total control is necessary in a world where dual-natured (good and evil) egos are always in inner and outer conflict. Because of this mind-body-soul state of conflict, there is very little love and a great need for control and imposed order to give balance to the chaos of "conflicting views." Because of each group's innate desire to be in control, there is always a competition for power to be the chief controller. Even when the fallen angels create an order, there is always inside fighting and competition amongst themselves to gain higher political power. This is not to say that humankind cannot live in peace, it is to say that humankind cannot do it without spiritual love and wisdom as its guide. Luke, Chapter 11, Verse 18: "If Satan also be divided against himself, how shall his kingdom stand?"

We can notice that there will be signs of control with respect to discovering who and where the fallen angels are operating on earth. The idea of a computer chip implant to give clear identification and satellite tracking of human beings, is an example of how the coming New World Order plans to bring order and control to a chaotic society. Was it introduced to humans through the modern day UFO-aliens called the "Grays," as revealed to us by human abduction cases? Incident reports show that silicon-like computer chips were found under many of the abductees' skin. The implants allow the aliens to track or find that person wherever they may try to hide. It can also be used to manipulate their brain waves for more mind control. Mind control is terrifying. The idea of using it is, again, to control and to create a supposedly orderly society. CNN News reported on January 14, 1999, by Sam Witt, "Is Human Chip Implant Wave of Future?"

Such a technology to control, locate and track persons is very primitive compared to what angels have to do. This is obviously a sign, by what has been revealed in this new message, of the fallen angels. Now, by this sign, we know who they are and where they are operating in our societies.

To compare how primitive this fallen angel technology is, in 1987 I was visited by my Aunt Patsy, the sister of my stepfather, on the very night she died. She appeared to me while I was sleeping on a friend's sofa, glowing with blue and violet light floating a foot off the ground. She was a Buddhist who studied with the Dalai Lama of Tibet. Her body was youthful and beautiful again, as if she was 24 years old. She was not "see through" but solid as we are—but glowing with real light. The question of "how did she find me," not knowing where I was staying, shows that angels can track someone with total ease, using no control or manipulation devices such as a computer chip implant. Obviously I was not implanted by a tracking device. When I was finished with our visit, she floated right through the fireplace wall and was gone. I am sure the angels or the Glory (which is supremely intelligent and omnipresent) guided her to me and to anyone else in the family she wanted to visit before she moved on into the higher realms.

The point in showing this is to demonstrate how much wealth, power and freedom angels have over the poverty of those who have to track and control people with a mere "computer chip implant." Could this computer chip implant be evidence as to where the notion of "control" comes from? We can now see in the Lord that there is no control in Heaven, but total freedom and abundance. So, who and where does the idea of controlling humanity come from? And so it is written in the

Book of Revelation, Chapter 13, Verses 16-17: "And he causeth all, both small and great, rich and poor, free and bond, to receive a mark in their right hand, or in their foreheads: and that no man might buy or sell, save he that had the mark, or the name of the beast, or the number of his name."

To understand if an extraterrestrial being or group of beings is benevolent, we can now use this spiritual knowledge as our guidepost. If such beings are full of love and do not use "control" consciousness and technology to show us how to create supposed order, but showed us how to evolve in Love and Glory instead, we would know them to be benevolent. However, if such extraterrestrials introduce more control methods to humankind, we would know they are of the order of the fallen angels.

If we could educate our children into evolving in real love, they would naturally respond to their own love and make loving choices in their lives without being told what to do. Love is so powerful that if it is established first and foremost in our children through their growing years, they will spontaneously grow and respond to love in their lives. In today's world, such a loving person (for example, Martin Luther King, Jr.) will face many hardships because the world does not respond well to loving people. The world assassinates such loving and nonviolent people. The Dalai Lama and the people of Tibet live a religion of Buddhism that is firmly rooted in nonviolence. The Chinese knew well that it would be easy to massacre 700,000 Tibetans with little resistance.

They did massacre that many and more still today. To walk in true nonviolence and love in today's world makes one appear as a martyr. It makes outsiders think that to be spiritual is to be pathetic and weak. I have been to Heaven and I know that nonviolent and loving human beings end up there very easily and the outsiders live as slaves to money and fall even lower at death unless they too repent and return to true love themselves.

The return is difficult. I speak from experience. To live a life that is devoted to healing the ecology, because so few wealthy persons support it, one may have to live in poverty. To be poor is to be an outcast in many ways. Such a person is not wanted by others. It is very difficult.

Who are the servants to the masters of money and the very masters of money subservient to? Who are the fallen angels?

Ancient Sumerian cosmology shows depictions on cylinder seals of small, large headed, big eyed android/robots who did scouting for a race of gods/goddesses. The goddesses/gods are the same beings who are referred to as the Annunaki in ancient Sumerian cosmology (according to author Zechariah Sitchin's "Earth Chronicles").

One of the most astounding accounts of extraterrestrials visiting the earth is the story of Eduard Meir, the Swiss farmer who took amazingly clear photographs of flying saucers in the 1970s. He claimed to be visited by the beings inside the ships. They were human looking, just like the gods and goddesses of antiquity and the leader was a beautiful looking blonde woman named Samjasee (pronounced Samyaza). She told Meir that "our forefathers were your forefathers." If this account is true and did actually happen, then there is an amazing resemblance to a story from the most ancient civilization of earth, the Sumerian tale of creation. The Sumerian tale says that the first civilized humans were created by these gods and goddesses in test tubes, the Adama and the Eve. This is outrageous to modern day Christians, for they believe that the very Lord God created human beings. But deep in scripture, there are clues that concur with the Sumerian tale of creation. However, it reveals something terrifying. Don't worry, your soul has nothing to do with who created or re-engineered our bodies. Your soul is free of the body, but bound by its limitations while living within it.

Enoch was the first saint in biblical history, although the Book of Enoch was not accepted into the Bible. The Book of

Enoch, Chap. LXVIII, reads: "After this judgment, they shall be astonished and irritated; for it shall be exhibited to the inhabitants of the earth. Behold the names of those angels [fallen angels at this point]. These are their names. The first of them is *Samyaza . . ."* and it goes on to name a whole list. Continuing: "and causing them to descend on earth, led astray the offspring of men. The name of the second is *Kesabel* [could be the biblical Jezebel] who pointed out evil council to the sons of the holy angels, and induced them to *corrupt their bodies by generating mankind."*

This is to first show that, contrary to biblical belief, the first humans were co-created by the fallen angels, and thus we inherited a body of sin (a limited body and brain). Could this be what Jesus meant when he said in the Bible, "we inherited a body of sin," and that Jesus too partook of a body of sin to show us the way back to Heaven by his life example?

In the Book of Enoch, Chap. VII. [Sect. II. 2], it reads: "It happened after the sons of men had multiplied in those days, that daughters were born to them, elegant and beautiful. And when the angels, the sons of heaven, beheld them, they became enamored of them, saying to each other, Come, let us select for ourselves wives from the progeny of men, and let us beget children. Then their leader *Samyaza* [the same fallen angel who visited Eduard Meir in the 1970s?] said to them; I fear that you may perhaps be indisposed to the performance of this enterprise: And that I alone shall suffer for so grievous a crime."

In Sumerian and Buddhist scripture, it is revealed that these gods, goddesses and the Buddhist anti-gods (fallen ones) have bodies that live for over 50,000 earth years, so if this is true, Samyaza could still be alive today.

If this is not enough evidence for you, take a look at the Gospel of Thomas, Verse 85: "Jesus said, 'Adam came from a great power and a great wealth, but he did not become worthy of you. For had he been worthy, he would not have experienced death.'" Jesus does not say here that Adam came directly from God, but by a great power. Jesus derides the human creation again in the Gospel of Thomas, Verse 29: "Jesus said, 'If the flesh came into being because of spirit, it is a wonder. But if spirit came into being because of the body, it is a wonder of wonders. Indeed, I am amazed at how this great wealth has made its home in this poverty.'" Jesus is deriding the fact that the wealth of the soul made its home in the poverty of the human-created body. If our bodies were created directly by the Supreme Lord, then how could Jesus call the work of the Lord a body of poverty, unless that long-held belief were not true?

The Book of Enoch and the Sumerian tale concurs with the Gospel of Thomas, thus giving testimony to what I experienced directly in the Lord: That God did not directly create the bodies we have. Jesus' Glory will create our resurrected bodies, if we evolve and choose the life in the Heavens he has in store for us.

Today's modern Human Genome Project is being called the "Biologists' Manhattan Project." The plan of the project is to map the entire human genome by the year 2020. Already scientists have discovered many of the genes that cause cellular aging and have found that aging doesn't really make any sense. They have already found ways to stop cellular aging in single-cell tissue. Will we be next? Could we regain what the fallen ones took from our DNA: 50,000-year lifespans? Would we want to live that long on earth while Heaven awaits us?

After the gods/goddesses made the first humans, the gods took wives of the first humans, and made children who were half-god/half-human who later became leaders in ancient Egyptian dynasties. They taught men and women corrupt things like war, sorcery and astrology, writing, and so on.

Even though Enoch was the first great saint and prophet in the Bible, there are a number of reasons the Books of Enoch were not admitted by the Church into the Bible. This is one of them: The Bible teaches us that Adam and Eve were created directly by God, the Supreme Lord, whereas I deduct that the Sumerian tale of creation and the Book of Enoch (Enoch, by the way, was taken through many Heavens by the Lord) must be correct. After being in Heaven, I can clearly see that the Supreme Lord could not have created us by direct means.

The body we will inherit in the First Heaven is our original body created directly by God. It is so much more perfect in all ways than the human body—sight, sound, feeling, beauty and happiness all being a million times sharper—it makes the human body seem like a mutant. God could not directly create a body that suffers so much. This aging, disease prone, inefficient (I could go on and on) human body could only be the work of a much less intelligent and evolved group of beings. Because biblical scholars did not know this (being too one-sided), they did not accept the Books of Enoch as part of the Bible. From the experience of being in Heaven, I would have to agree with the Book of Enoch which says we were created by the fallen angels (who created the body of sin), the body of sin in both physical limitations and internal conflict from which Jesus is trying to free us.

The Sumerian tale of creation tells of a human-looking race of gods and goddesses who came to earth 400,000 years ago, after they sent their alien probes (androids who look just like modern day gray aliens) and found earth to be habitable. They found the ape species evolving here and, needing gold dust to save their planet's failing atmosphere, they tried to get the ape-humans to work the mines. It was impossible to communicate with the ape-like species (Neanderthals) so they mixed their own DNA with the DNA of the apes, mutated it and created the Adama and the Eve in test tubes.

Once the Adama and Eve were created, the Supreme Being (God) spoke to them in the Garden of Eden and warned them not to take in the "Knowledge of Good and Evil" like the fallen ones did. It was the Supreme Being's (Alpha-Jehovah/Omega-Jesus) first attempt to save us from this fatal knowledge. It didn't work because we did not listen. Now the drama unfolds. If both creation and evolution stories are integrated, this reveals the creationist versus evolutionist theories as both correct, but each only part of a giant puzzle (another example of the limitation of being one-sided). It also corrects the theory that the Supreme God created humans versus what is revealed in the Book of Enoch: that we were co-created by the fallen gods/angels and inherited their DNA (a body of sin).

To give more evidence to what I was seeing in the Lord—that we were not the direct creation of the Supreme Being—I feel the Nag Hammadi Library gives the most sophisticated tale of the creation of humankind, even better than the Book of Enoch and the ancient Sumerian tales combined. While it is more sophisticated than these other discoveries, it is also supported by them.

To give a basic description of creation of the spiritual hierarchy in the Nag Hammadi Library, without recounting every page of it, I will summarize it with much greater simplicity.

First, there existed and always existed the Father-Mother being who is Jesus Christ in its entirety. This Supreme Being is both male and female yet divides into two which are as "one," being united by the Glory of it, the male being Jesus as the Father and the female being the Sophia of Christ. In total harmony they create all the angels and the first clear light Heaven and all the beings and planets in it. All angels are created perfectly and with equal opportunity to evolve in God. They always co-create everything together as nothing is created egotistically. No angel decides good and evil for itself alone, and at this point there is no good and evil because all is perfect and in love. There is no conflict.

Second, the Sophia of Jesus Christ decides to create the first being, having egotistically taken in knowledge of good and evil for herself alone. As soon as she sees her creation, she recognizes that it is terribly imperfect and awful in that it is egotistical (separate from God's Glory) yet very powerful. She repents but goes down with the whole creation. The being she created becomes known as the Chief Archon. His name is Yaltabaoth. This Archon creates many demi-archons who are all egotistical yet worship the Chief Archon Yaltabaoth as the supreme being, all unable to see the higher order of angels and the Lord above all.

The Archons then create humankind (the Adam and Eve) to worship and serve them, while the Supreme Father-Mother co-creates humankind by secretly implanting the Spirit of God in each human soul without the Archons knowing. This implant of God's Glory in each human is known as the Epinoia-Mother. This shows God to be extending itself to all creation. The Feminine part of Christ falls down with the egotistical part of creation to save it because it was responsible for its creation, while the Father remains mostly with the harmony and abundance of angels who do not live as egos but always in togetherness. By the Feminine part of Christ implanting human beings with the Spirit of God, humans have the potential spiritual power to evolve past and above all the Archons, their very egotistical creators.

Nag Hammadi texts appear to show this emanation of the Feminine part of the Lord as a fall from grace; from a more complete perspective, my own insight into it is different. I feel that God is showing that of all possibilities, there can exist a harmonious and egoless spiritual being who always works in togetherness with others and an ego-centered one who always creates and acts in a dictatorial fashion regardless of others. This way, all participants in the life of the universe can learn the consequences of both possibilities. When the Sophia of Christ goes down with the ego-centered part of creation she suffers greatly because the Glory of God, because of ego, no longer exists for her. She weeps for herself and all creation. But it is not for eternity. She will eventually rejoin Christ as she was always Christ's other half. In this sense, God exists in all creation, in the dark void of Glory and in the light of Glory. One part of God and all beings in it suffer while the other part is in Glory and all beings in it know that to live as an ego only leads to suffering. Then they will return to the highest aspect of God and evolve in it, as God evolves. In this sense, God evolves as each created being, directly or indirectly, either evolves without falling into the ego (angels who do not fall) or evolves while living in the ego (Archons and humans), suffering to evolve exponentially when they return to the Glory in the angelic realms.

In the Nag Hammadi Library, Apocryphon of John, pages 115-116, we see part of the mysterious tale of human creation: "And all the angels and demons worked until they had constructed the natural body. . . . And in that moment [when the human was finished] the rest of the powers became jealous, because he had come into being through all of them and they had given their power to the man, and his intelligence was greater than that of those who made him, and greater than that of the chief archon. And when they recognized that he was luminous, and that he could think better than they, and that he was free from wickedness, they took him and threw him into the lowest region of all matter. . . . But the blessed one, the Mother-Father, the beneficent and merciful One, had mercy on the power of the mother which had been brought forth out of the chief archon, for they the archons might gain power over the natural and perceptible body. And he sent, through his beneficent Spirit and his great mercy, a helper to Adam, luminous Epinoia which comes out of him, who is called life. And she assists the whole creature, by toiling with him and by restoring him to fullness and by teaching him about the descent of his seed and by teaching him about the way of ascent, [which is] the way he came down. And the luminous Epinoia was hidden in the Adam, in order that the archons might not know her, but that the Epinoia might be a correction of the deficiency of the mother."

Again, this shows the feminine part of the Lord to be so compassionate as to come down and help the human beings evolve higher than those who created them.

Are these beings modern-day UFO "greys" (aliens) that people claim to be abducted by the same android robots that the ancient Sumerians revealed to be their own creation? Are the greys abducting humans to observe our biological evolution for the fallen angels who created our bodies thousands of years ago? Are the greys introducing the computer chip implant to our militaries—the biblical "Mark of the Beast"—for their leaders, the fallen angels? Are they doing this because, as Jesus revealed in this message, the larger a chaotic global population gets, the more need there is for mind control-devices?

By the signs that Jesus is telling us, there is no control in Heaven. This leaves the greatest possibility that any being trying to create perfect societies by control must be under the spell of the "Knowledge of Good and Evil," and thus fallen ones.

What causes the fallen ones to be "fallen"? Many persons are under the illusion that God actually has a war and kicks certain angels out of Heaven for being bad. I have even heard that certain humans (Satan worshipers) are mad at God for kicking anyone, mainly Satan, out of Heaven. By unwise compassion for this incorrect interpretation, such persons hate God (in their illusory mind only) and join satanic cults. The mind is very powerful because it actually makes decisions and acts on mere interpretations. I am so sad that people join Satan cults just because they think God kicked Satan out of Heaven for being bad. They do not understand the spiritual physics of Heaven and self-created hell.

The truth about this will become more clear as we evolve in this message. From the wisdom of this message by the Lord, it is clear that no one kicks anyone out of Heaven. Because all the

Heavens are suspended in Love and Glory, when Satan or Samyaza partakes of the knowledge of good and evil, they become a conflict internally. Because a conflict is a lower vibration than Love, the soul in conflict cannot stand the vibrations of Love and falls down to the next dimension, or even actually creates a lower dimension in order to evolve through its need to experience conflict. God is very generous in this way. If you need to understand or experience conflict, God gives you the experience and the place to work that out. God actually allows you to create more suffering. You can suffer in the lower realms all you want. If you want to do that, just remember you wanted to live like that.

Hence, the fallen angel then falls all on their own, with no real effort on the part of God. They then live out the drama of having an ego and living with internal conflict. Conflict becomes so real to each soul "in conflict," that they react out of conflict and create problems, such as war, which they then have to solve to bring about some kind of sustainable life. There are huge organizations to solve the problems that the organization creates. Then, the notion of "control" is born to create order out of the chaos of the so called "organization" which they created. This is where the real trouble begins. People who like to be in control always go mad, really mad, because nothing goes the way they want it to. It goes the way each and every other person wants it to go (who are also trying to be in control) unless they can control the others to do what they want the others to do. If they can coerce or oppress the others to do what they want, the others all become miserable. The controller becomes miserable because everyone is miserable. How do you get out of this trap?

Imagine yourself floating above one hundred million movie theaters, each one playing a different movie. Each of those theaters is a person and the movie is their version of how the world should be to make them happy. Most of them are opposed to each other, and they create barriers around each other (the walls to their own movie theater) to protect themselves from everyone else's movie. Naturally, they have to interact to get anything done, but problems arise with interaction.

This is how the fallen angels see the world, and the only way they see fit to create order is by a certain amount of control. In most cases, a lot of control. Have you ever heard the saying "nothing ever seems to go my way"? That's because everyone is trying to make the world go according to their own movie, and it cannot do that because everyone else has their own movie too. At this point the fallen angels go mad because they cannot control people unless they create another strategy. This is where the notion of "oppression" comes in. The fallen angels and those under their service, even those who are inadvertently under their service, now realize that if you can create suffering, more suffering for these humans by making them work like slaves, just barely surviving, they will be far from freedom and they will suffer. Once they suffer, they will be easier to control. So, the notion of creating poverty for the masses seems to be an answer.

Children are the best place to witness the phenomenon of control and freedom. Try walking into a room of children who are insanely happy, going mad with excitement, and try to control them. You will give yourself a headache even trying. Now try and control a bunch of kids who you have made miserable. It is much easier to control the miserable kids.

The nature of suffering is such that it is much easier to control people when you manipulate them to the point that their very survival is at stake. They have to serve you or else they will not be clothed, housed or fed. You then hoard the money supply, and become lords of control and earthly power. Now you can dictate to the world, and they eventually rebel. More wars result. This is humankind today.

Jesus revealed to me that the purpose of showing this model is to reveal the nature of true freedom in Heaven, versus the pseudo-freedom and the terrible suffering, war and control on earth that is the result of the knowledge of the fallen angels. How many persons strayed from God because they thought that giving up their soul to God meant that they would just be subservient slaves to an unloving God? How many persons joined satanic cults because they thought Heaven would be boring and you would be a slave to God?

There is no innocence, no freedom, no abundance, no health, no beauty (even physically), no clear bright ecstasy, no peace at all, no Love, no freedom and no power to create when you are subservient to the fallen angels. This is true for the fallen angels themselves, as a measure of one grain of sand (representing the fallen ones) compared to all the grains of sand on earth (representing the Lord and the Lord's Heavens).

XVI

The dichotomies of living in the Heavens versus living in the lower worlds and hells.

What happens to fallen ones and those subservient to them as they try to approach the Lord? Jesus was so full of light and Glory now, I could barely even see the Lord's face. I was being crushed with Ecstasy. Jesus: **"In Heaven and me (all the same) there are only natural laws that are spontaneous reactions from living in the Glory, and there are spontaneous reactions from those who fear the Glory and have to go away, not because I send them away but because they are afraid of love and ecstasy (Glory). They do not know it yet and must go away and learn love in the lower worlds, before they could bear living in Glory. If they do not learn at least love, let alone Glory, they will not enter until they do, even if it takes a million or billions of years.**

Jesus was talking about the souls to my right who were still hiding their faces from the Lord. This reveals the notion of reincarnation. Perhaps the Lord is showing this because Jesus did not say anything about it in the first message. Perhaps after the first message Jesus heard me ask the question about reincarnation and wanted me to see this. The Glory in Heaven is that Great. It may take many souls a long time to evolve to the point that they can enter Heaven, or it may only take one loving and wise lifetime. The choice is yours.

There is one small clue still left in the Bible that suggests the possibility of reincarnation. In the Book of Revelation, Chapter 3, Verse 12, it reads: "He who overcomes, I will make him a pillar in the temple of my God, and he shall go out no more."

Think about this logically for a moment. First, this message was delivered to St. John the Divine on the Island of Patmos, biblical scholars say, long after the resurrection. Perhaps Jesus wanted to make a point clear that was not previously made: "He who overcomes . . . shall go out no more." To "go out no more" implies that we normally do "go out" more than once. For if we only went out once and were judged on that one lifetime, and that was final, the Lord would never have said this, but if we overcome we go out no more. The basic Christian notion is that we were created by God almighty; we live one life and are judged based on that one life. If we pass "go" we make it to Heaven. Everyone else goes to hell.

When the Lord said to me "They do not know it yet, but must go away and learn love in the lower worlds before they can bear the Glory in the Heavens," Jesus was implying the same thing he told St. John the Divine: they must "overcome" *(become enlightened before or at the time of death)* before they will be living permanently in Heaven, and "go out no more."

The Buddhists and Hindus have this same notion, that we reincarnate until we evolve to the point of "enlightenment," then we may graduate to higher worlds (actual planets). Some of those higher worlds are temporary and allow us very long lives in Lower Heavens of great pleasure. After these long lives expire in the pleasure realms, a few move higher, but most have to take another human birth to try and reach enlightenment. The Tibetan Buddhists feel that reaching enlightenment is easier on earth than in the lower heavenly planets, so those in a hurry to be enlightened avoid reincarnation in the Lower Heavens and take another human birth amongst their own religious kind.

The Buddhists have another experience of saving souls from reincarnation, but the saving is mostly only temporary. The Bodhisattva can actually help carry souls into the first Heavens and those souls may live there in the Bodhisattva's heaven for an extremely long lifetime, around fifty- to seventy-five-thousand years. Then, after that, hopefully life is not so terrible down here on earth, or other earths, and they reincarnate again until they either reach enlightenment in the body or at the hour of their death.

The Hindu "Bible," the *Bhagavad-Gita,* says the same thing although it is much more clear about the distinction between "heavenly" planets of great pleasure, which are lower in vibration than the Heaven planets where the truly "enlightened" live. The Buddhists do not speak of planets for the enlightened. The reason being cannot be made clear until the last part of this message.

Written in the Hindu *Bhagavad-Gita As It Is,* page 431, Text 15: "Since this temporary material world is full of the miseries of birth, old age, disease and death, naturally he who achieves the highest perfection and attains the supreme planet, Krishnaloka, Golka Vrndavana, does not wish to return. The supreme planet is described in Vedic literature as avyakta and aksara and parama gati; in other words, that planet is beyond our material vision, and it is inexplicable, but it is the highest goal, the destination for the mahatmas (great souls)."

Could this be similar to what St. John the Divine realized when Jesus told him that "He who overcomes, I will make him a pillar in the temple of my God and he shall go out no more?"

The Hindu model reveals that upon attaining full enlightenment, that soul will have access to life on the supreme planet or planets. The *Bhagavad-Gita* reveals three basic levels of spiritual worlds within the universe: The Hell planets (planets of war), the Heavenly planets (great material and spiritual pleasures for people who did good works but could not reach complete enlightenment) and the higher ascending planets for the enlightened. All of these planets have an ascending and descending order. In other words, there are Hell planets that are not so bad and there are Hell planets that are terrible. There are Heavenly planets that are mostly material in pleasures and there are Heavenly planets that have actual spiritual pleasures. There are clear light planets filled with the Glory of God that ascend into higher and higher levels of enlightenment and higher and higher planets culminating in that supreme planet where Lord Krishna resides, Krishnaloka.

The basic Christian view is also of three levels of spiritual worlds: Hell, Purgatory and Heaven. Could we all have found the same truth but express it in different words?

When Jesus told me that the souls who were also in the presence of the Lord with me, those who hid their faces, could not enter the Heavens—that they must go back to the lower worlds to learn how to evolve in love—Jesus was speaking from the Supremely Enlightened perspective. Jesus includes all worlds below the clear light (enlightened) Heavens as lower worlds, including earth.

In his book *Heaven and Hell,* Emanuel Swedenborg, the 18th-century Christian saint, notes three basic levels of spiritual worlds of which there is a hierarchy: Hell, the World of Spirits and Heaven. Swedenborg ascended through Hell, the World of Spirits and through Three ascending Heavens.

Imagine that each of these religions has a piece of a giant puzzle. The Hindu Bhagavad-Gita, the most ancient of the three religions (approximately 3,100–5,000 BC) reveals that there are actual planets in each of the ascending and descending realms. Buddhism reveals some of the same, but gives even more clearly defined ascensions and descensions. Prince Sidhartha who became Lord Buddha is estimated to have lived circa 623 BC. Jesus lived in the turning point.

Emanuel Swedenborg lived between 1688 and 1772 AD. Although Swedenborg did not have access to the Hubble Space Telescope, what he discovered by spirit travel through the Hell worlds, the World of Spirits and the Heavens might resemble the model of the galaxy. Get ready for a discovery that may seem alarming to us earth-bound souls. Swedenborg says that the highest Heavens are the innermost (closest to the center) without saying what the center is, but that there is light and Glory in those Heavens. He says that the World of Spirits is further out from the center than the Heavens and the war planets and hells are even further out. Guess where earth is in relation to the model of our Mily Way galaxy? We are right where the war planets should be, near the outermost point of the galaxy. And, in fact, we are a planet that has a long-standing history of war. The most stunning part of the galaxy model is that the inner most point of any galaxy is where there is the most light. Could the Heavens actually be inside the galaxy, closer to its center? Would this mean that Heaven is not in some far away other-worldly dimension?

I feel there is yet another insight from Jesus hidden in the Nag Hammadi Library, Gospel of Philip, page 149. Jesus reveals this mystery in a great parable once more: "In this world there is good and evil. Its good things are not good, and its evil things not evil. But there is evil after this world which is truly evil—what is called 'the middle.' It is death. While we are in this world it is fitting for us to acquire the resurrection, so that when we strip off the flesh we may be found in rest and not walk in the middle."

The key point here is first that once again human conception of "good things are not good, and its evil things not evil" to reveal that the Lord's Glory dwarfs all human concepts about good and evil and that it is beyond it. To give evidence for the mystery of realms that exist after this world, or after death, Jesus points out that "there is evil after this world which is truly evil—what is called 'the middle.'" Jesus also warns us, "While we are in this world it is fitting for us to acquire the resurrection, so that when we strip off the flesh we may be found in rest and not walk in the middle."

What is the "middle" and where is there truly rest but Heaven? What is Jesus talking about here? By my own experience, I can safely assume that the "middle" Jesus is talking about is what Catholics would call "Purgatory," the mid-way between hell and Heaven. Hindus would call it the "Astral" or "demi-god planetary realms," and Buddhists would call it the realm of the "anti-gods and demi-gods," but it is even more than that. This is a vast subject which we will summarize.

The middle is such an evil to Jesus because Jesus knows that real salvation from all suffering starts with the clear light or real inner "enlightenment"—the inner resurrection of our corrupted spirit into a body of light. This inner transformation that resurrects us into a spiritual body of light gives us access, after death, to the clear light planetary Heavens which are above the hell or war planets and the purgatory (middle) planets.

But there is more meaning to what Jesus is saying about the "middle" that is such an evil. By my own experience, having traveled out of body to the middle, it is as though the dreaming world we all experience every night when we dream, where we all dream our fears and desires, is where we experience part of the meaning of the "middle." When you are in the middle state out of your body, everything you fear and desire will manifest before your very eyes—everything. That means fantasies, demons and monsters. Even beautiful paintings of your imaginations can trap you for a seeming eternity. There are myriad illusions that may keep you prisoner by your own fascination with them.

When you travel out of body in the "middle" you will look at a person inside their body and see pictures hovering around them every time they think a thought, and with better clarity than a person inside their mind sees pictures in their imagination. You will then know what people are really thinking because you will see actual pictures every time that person has a thought or feeling. However, so many illusions and dreams mixing in and out of each other create the greatest illusion possible for the human spirit to become ensnared in. You will see one person's "good and evil" thoughts clashing with another person's "good and evil" thoughts and the clash will create demons and wars and arguments and suffering. These "middle" or astral beings are caught in the illusion of mind-created "good and evil" views. They think that their good thoughts "manifest" real objects. They create many things with their minds, and fool themselves as though they are creators. Because they create with their minds, they think they are like gods, thus they are known as the demi-gods.

Many of today's psychics are in communication with these spirits living in the out-of-body state who are between actual incarnations (bodies), living in the middle regions. Because they can see the actual thoughts and ideas and plans of any person on earth, they sometimes give living human beings known as psychics warnings of disasters or wars to come because they see persons planning wars or disasters as though they were realities about to happen. However, there is one problem: nothing is fixed. People do not always, and in fact rarely, act out every thought or idea they have. For example, if a spirit from the middle region were observing military generals from any country playing or thinking of taking over another country or starting a war, that spirit might warn the psychic who then predicts the disaster or war on earth and we find it does not happen because the generals were merely "thinking" of having a war but decided not to "actually" have a war. How many of your thoughts do you actually act on and manifest? I know for myself, that of hundreds of thoughts, I may only act on one of them. The psychic is not really wrong about making the predictions. They were just obscured by the paranoia of the spirits because those spirits live in the "middle" region, trapped by the illusions created by the minds they live in and by those they observe.

In this middle region, the creations of human minds are sometimes (and, ultimately, always) in opposition to another's. So wars in this middle region result the same way as they do on earth. Eventually beings in this "middle" region, or what Tibetan Buddhists call the "in between state" (in between bodies or incarnations), find where they will reincarnate in a body.

The "middle" that Jesus is talking about, in its totality, really consists of a spirit between incarnations, all of the hell or war planets, and the astral or demi-god planets in each of which are many ascending and descending levels. The lowest hells are for those who egotistically hold their position against others so strongly that they burn inside with severe anger. These beings incarnate in low hells or war planets where there is almost always war going on. Those whose egotistical views of human "good" are more beautiful and vibrate with more love and harmony, but are still egotistical, live and incarnate in higher and higher Astral planets which are below the vibration of the clear light Heavens. Even they will sometimes have wars, but this is rare.

The first clear light inner enlightenment or the actual first clear light planetary Heaven is for the truly enlightened, and it literally dwarfs even the highest Astral planets egotistical views of "perfect good" so much so that it will baffle the supremely egotistical in the highest Astral or "middle" region planets when they finally transcend the highest of their middle region planets. They will transcend when they finally admit to themselves that all of their beautiful creations are void of real lasting fulfillment. This is because they are created out of ego instead of God's love and Glory. When they can admit this to themselves, they will see that all of their goodness is really boring in the end. When they end the inner conflict of good and evil in its entirety, they will enter God's true Glory dwarfed and filled with a seemingly eternal supernova of inner and outer Love, Peace and Ecstasy which was and always will be absolutely inconceivable to any mind, no matter how great that mind may be. Because God's Glory is inconceivable, the soul experiences true humility for the first time. All those millennia of lifetimes holding tightly to one's own inner views of goodness, clashing against others' views of goodness, was all meaningless in comparison to God. This becomes true humility.

To give more evidence from the Nag Hammadi Library to support that the demi-gods living in the high Astral planets are disturbed and eventually dwarfed and humbled by beings from the clear light Heavens above them, we look in Zostrianos, page 405: "When he had said this to me, I very quickly and very gladly went up with him to a great light-cloud. I cast my body upon the earth to be guarded by glories. I was rescued from the whole world and the thirteen aeons and in it their angelic beings. They did not see us, but their archon was disturbed at our passage, for the light-cloud is better than every worldly one. Its beauty is ineffable." Archons in the Nag Hammadi writings are equivalent to demi-gods in Buddhist and Hindu scriptures. They are below the clear light realms. The archon is disturbed by Zostriano's passing beyond them into the light because it dwarfs their egos to see such a greater spiritual enlightenment than they have attained.

To give cross-religious evidence to this statement, that the demi-gods or archons are disturbed by the passage of any lower living being, such as a human, into realms higher than they, we look at the Buddhist *Lotus Sutra.* In this Sutra, it tells of the demi-gods being very disturbed when a human becomes enlightened. They are disturbed because they thought they were the highest beings in the universe. When they see an enlightened human come to visit them on its way to the higher realms, they are humiliated, first because they thought they were above humans. Secondly, they are humiliated because they now know that there is a much brighter spiritual enlightenment to attain to. In this *Lotus Sutra,* the enlightened Buddha teaches the demi-gods to meditate and become free from their realm of great pleasures, although it is said in Buddhism that rarely do demi-gods actually attain to enlightenment. Both Gnostic Christianity and Buddhism concur on this very elaborate point.

Finally, this clarifies a more complete view of the possibilities of what Jesus has revealed both in this message and in the many gospels. To recapitulate, the most evil beings can move from severe war planets to other war planets where life is not so severe. The ultimately good human beings who are short of real inner enlightenment (the true resurrection) can end up living on higher Astral planets. Many who visit these planets may think they are in the Highest Heaven, but are deluded. There is still some light in these higher Astral planets as they border the first level of clear light planets whose light and Glory shines down on them. In fact, the light and Glory of the first level shines equally on all planets, even the hells, but those who live there rarely feel the light. Those who attain to real enlightenment, while here on earth or after death, are dwarfed in God's Glory of Innocence, Love, Ecstasy, Peace, Power, Graces and Beauties and are actually filled with the Glory of God, entering and evolving in the clear light heavens. Because they are free from all suffering, they can incarnate and visit beings in any suffering realm without actually experiencing the suffering that their body may display.

XVII

The Lord reveals the possibility of a great tragedy for humankind that is to be avoided at any cost.

Then the Lord showed me a great possible tragedy for humankind. If human beings remain stubborn and do not evolve in love towards each other and the earth they live on, too few of them will become "enlightened" and make it into Heaven and they will make the earth a "living hell" by polluting it and creating wars, causing the future human beings who are to grow up there (their own reincarnated selves) to curse the sky above. They would shout at God thinking God is cruel and did this to them, when the cruelty had nothing to do with God but with humankind's own ignorance. Out of this hate, the souls of humans spiral downwards farther and farther such that for any soul to come to love or "enlightenment" becomes more and more difficult. Earth could become a living hell, created by ignorance, with no way to freedom or escape until such beings repel the destructive force and learn to live in love. This terrible cycle could last for a long time. It could reach entropy.

What will happen if we lose our atmosphere by destruction to the ozone layer? What will happen to us if we have to keep reincarnating here until we evolve? Will we live underground or in biodomes? How terrible this would be. Do not rely on the Lord to make a new earth just yet. We do not know when that may be. If the Lord feels it necessary, he may watch us wallow in ignorance, to see if we will evolve. For the many loving souls on earth, some of whom have not yet evolved enough to live permanently in the Heavens, I hope the Book of Revelation is correct in saying there will be a New Heaven and a New Earth. I certainly know from seeing Jesus that the Lord has that kind of power, with absolute ease, and Jesus told me in the first message that he could make a new earth with ease. I just don't know when the Lord may do it. If that moment is still a long time off, then we may be in for more self-created suffering than we have ever known. This message is a call to all materially wealthy persons on earth to skillfully invest in technologies, and implement them, so that we may live in harmony with our earth.

The physics of Heaven reveal a terrible truth here, that may be difficult to bear. This is that Heaven is so evolved in Love and Glory, and there are many good people who are simply not ready to permanently live in the Glory—they will be able to withstand a visit at the time of their death but will be unevolved enough to permanently live there. They will need more time to evolve. But where? The physics of Heaven reveal that if a soul cannot withstand the cleansing of the Holy Ghost, let alone living in the clear bright light and Glory in the ascending Heavens, yet they are still a good person, they must, as Jesus said to me, "go away and learn love in the lower worlds."

If we destroy our own Earth and make it a living hell, guess who comes back here to live in it? We do. What are we going to do about that? To this, there are those who will say that God would be cruel for not saving us. This is not true. Jesus came here 2,000 years ago and we killed him while asking him to leave. There are many others sent by the Lord who were killed by us emotionally, financially, mentally and physically. I have also almost been emotionally destroyed by terribly uncompassionate and unloving women in my life, almost all of whom have left me because of my earthly devotion to causes and lack of devotion to financial gain. It is amazing to me that I still care about humankind so much. Perhaps I am relentless in believing that there are good people out there.

When I was in India, I witnessed so much material suffering, so much mental suffering, so much emotional suffering; it is no wonder why yogis fled into caves to seek enlightenment. This is one way to seek enlightenment, but there are many examples of people who reach God while living in civilization. But, what is civilization? As a North American, I witnessed many physical illnesses in the Indian people, and I could see them praying to God to save them from their suffering. They could not see that they had been urinating, dumping human feces, bathing in and polluting the water supply, which was a direct cause of their suffering. Yet when Europeans try and introduce technology and modern sewage treatment facilities to India, they are too proud and one-sided. They do not accept that every nation on earth each caries a piece of a giant puzzle, a gift to give each other. Some profess that they do not have modern plumbing because they are poor. Who owns the patent on steel, pipe manufacturing, water pumps, inventiveness and energy? We all do.

This was an example, and the case of India's material suffering is more involved than I am aware of. Humankind rejects the servants of the Lord who come to answer the prayers of those who suffer. In this example, the sick in India reject modern plumbing. They pray to their gods, their gods send plumbers from the Western world, and they reject them.

If suffering beings with no love in their hearts call for God to come and the emanation of God or the angels from the First Heaven approaches, the unloving and suffering beings fear them so greatly that they hide and scream in agony for the angels to leave lest they die. You can see how terrible an irony this is. With this possible outcome for humankind as a model, it becomes more and more difficult to save us and deliver us into Heaven. This is the entropy that Jesus was warning me about: those who have come to love their suffering, thinking God loves suffering, reject real love and real solutions. These souls live in a closed system that accepts no energy from an outside source and they thus spiral endlessly downwards.

Jesus showed me this in the first message, about how the souls in hells keep "themselves" in eternal hell by living in a closed system of too much suffering, cursing God while rejecting love and solutions that God actually sent them. There is no way out. In the first message, Jesus was so sad to watch, and he showed me this model, and how he would love to save the many souls in the hell realms, but they hold themselves in a downward spiral by self-created entropy. As we both stood on the precipice of the hell realms, Jesus desperately wanted to know "why so many souls were ending up there and were unwilling to come out of their terrible suffering." I felt the deepest sadness and compassion I have ever witnessed in all eternity as the Lord spoke very difficult things about the hell realms, what Jesus and the high Angels wanted to do about the hell, all of which are too terrible to mention.

Knowing this, try and understand what happens when the Lord sends angels down into those worlds to try to help. Of course they live like apparent martyrs and get rejected, just like Jesus did when he came here some 2,000 years ago. They get trampled on, lied to, poisoned, have their teachings polluted, and so on. Imagine we are the souls living in entropy, and when God sends healers to earth, we reject them and even assassinate them. We then suffer more, call out to God for more help. God hears the calls of suffering, sends another angel down and the angel lives in poverty, gets rejected by nearly all, stands holding a "will work for food" sign by the highway while a Mercedes drives by and splashes mud all over her clothes, and she eventually dies of starvation on the streets. We then suffer more, move into biodomes because we lost our ozone layer, and curse God thinking God is cruel for not sending help.

When I was standing with the Lord on the precipice of hell and witnessed true entropy in hell, and saw no way out, all of this was revealed to me. The Lord really does want to save souls from hell, but they insist on rejecting love and compassion; thus they keep themselves in a terrible downward spiral into worse and worse suffering.

When the Lord sends apparent martyrs to incarnate in such extreme suffering realms to help, they are treated poorly and most of them are assassinated. You can see this has already happened on earth by examining history. Most martyrs were assassinated. See if you can count how many have been just in your lifetime. They are assassinated mentally, spiritually, emotionally, and physically.

XVIII

Earth is like a school where souls evolve to the point that they may graduate into the Heavens. If we destroy it, the school doesn't work well.

Jesus: **"The world as we know it appears like a Disneyland from this perspective: a place of trial and error where souls learn to love or perceive Glory. If they evolve enough, they may make it into Heaven and evolve without having to be separate from God. Sometimes, when human beings suffer, it causes compassion and love to ignite in their hearts. This is very strange. It is not necessary to suffer to experience love, but it is one way that humans seem to feel love, and thus grow in love. It is terrible that it takes this to make humans feel. There are more evolved ways that most humans have not learned yet."** Then the Lord showed me the other ways.

This is a very important subject. Most forms of human compassion manifest on earth where there is suffering, especially after a war or crime. Most Christian saints helped those who were suffering the most, such as the late Mother Theresa. This is still a wonderful expression of compassion, but the Lord is saying there are many more ways to express compassion that we have not learned yet. In a strange way, our subconscious minds might attract suffering and violence because of our great need to feel compassion, and we know few other ways.

What about having compassion for the brilliant thinkers whose ideas could make life better on earth? What about having compassion and giving our time, service, and energy forms (money, labor, skills, time) to serve the evolvement of the brilliant? To serve and have compassion for the brilliant will bring forth great fruits for humankind. Very little of this is being done.

A case example of this in the modern world is the environmental foundation Greenpeace, which has so much compassion for the suffering in the environment. The organization is alleged to raise some $300 million per year to perpetuate eco-awareness of these problems. Many protesters risk their lives. An organization like the American Hydrogen Association, which educates and finances developing real solutions to oil spills, water shortages, toxic pollution and air pollution (clean burning hydrogen fuel for our cars and homes), survives on some $50,000 per year. This case example shows how much we focus on the problems with our compassion, and how little on the real solutions.

Could we even have compassion for those who are rich in material wealth but who are poor in spirit? Could you have compassion for the materially wealthy who are rich in spirit also, or would you be jealous and spite them? Could you have compassion for the poor in material wealth who are also poor in spirit? The Lord knows many have compassion for the poor.

These are all forms of compassion which the Lord feels need attention. If all humans of mercy were to only help the poor, what cure for the cause of their poverty would we have, unless we also helped and served the brilliant thinkers, who could raise the level of poverty to cleanliness and develop good technology for a better ecology and humanity? The poor would no longer be poor.

And I saw that those spirits kneeling next to me, who came before the Lord, Jesus Christ, had strong attachments to the elements of heat, water, air and earth. I saw them flee in terror from the Lord's emanations, fleeing through the doors (tunnels, actually portals in time) that lead back to the earthly worlds, where they will need to learn how to love and choose love over material gain, greed, corrupted lusts, murder, and so on. I actually chased them to see where they were going, but spiritual forces did not let me in those tunnels.

Those who choose to covet material wealth, power, fame and corrupted lusts over love, will never be happy. This is because unless life itself is suspended in love, there can be no real happiness and peace. This is why so many rich, famous and powerful people fall into corrupted lusts, drug abuse, relationship abuse, and so on. Even poor people who do not value love over the quest for material gain will experience the same failings and unhappiness. This is because the natural laws of life do not allow energy to come from inanimate objects like objects of desire.

There is energy in inanimate objects, but when Glory or Love is perceived, there is no desire for coveting them because the energy emanating from inanimate objects is uniform and perceived as "sameness," therefore no special attraction to a diamond over a rock is perceived. So many humans resist growing in love. They like money and earthly power so much, they feel that if they do not gain it they are missing something. So everyone goes rushing towards it like flies towards manure. This is terribly agonizing to see.

Those who feel that God has failed them because they are not wealthy in this world, obviously are those who value material gain over Love and Glory. It is really the other way around:

those who experience Love or perceive Glory on earth, rich or poor, are on their way to God's Kingdom, and perhaps a meeting with the Lord, the Lord's self.

Jesus said in the Bible, St. Matthew, Chapter 6, Verses 19-21 : "Lay not up for yourselves treasures upon earth, where moth and rust doth corrupt, and where thieves break through and steal: But lay up for yourselves treasures in heaven, where neither moth nor rust doth corrupt, and where thieves do not break through nor steal: For where your treasure is, there will your heart be also." It is easy to see this when you are bathed in Glory and light in a new body in the Kingdom of the Heavens.

There is no question that miserable rich people and famous people who do not know love or Glory are fools. What this means is best described in an ugly simile like this: When you look at horse manure and you see all the flies that just love to eat and live inside the manure, would you want to live in the manure? Most people say "no," but it is not true. They actually are living in manure, but think they are better off than these flies, but I tell you not. For example, try and convince one of those flies that they are living in stink and filth and that there is a Heaven of beautiful flowers and bliss and love waiting for them only if they abandon their intense desire to smell and eat the manure, and learn to love. How many flies do you think will have faith and abandon the manure? Probably not one. So it is when you have been even in the First Heaven, when you look back at anything that the most materially wealthy person on earth may offer you: a billion dollars, a yacht, a sports car, a huge mansion, and so on.

The millionaires and billionaires all look like flies on manure and what if you tell them that you can help them learn to know love and lead them unto God's Kingdom if they sell their fortune and come use their money to heal the environment, watch the flowers grow, and fall in love? The materially wealthy people will tell you to forget it, just as the rich man did some

2,000 years ago when Jesus told him to give his money to the poor and seek the Kingdom of Heaven. They love their manure so much, that they don't know what real love, let alone the billion folds of Glory and life in the Kingdom of Heavens, is like or will be like. This is not to say that all rich people do not know love. Some of them do. There are rich people who are full of love and there are poor people who are filled with suffering and anger and resentment, with no love.

So I say unto you who live like flies on manure: abandon your ridiculous quest for material gain and seek for yourselves love and Spiritual Glory so that by it you may enter in through the loving gates of love, "here and now." And when you enter the Kingdom of God, you will receive a million, and even billion fold, at least. If you become materially wealthy on earth by a good livelihood, and not by oppressing your workers or the poor, and you have love, then share and enjoy and you will enter also. For without love you will need a miracle to enter. The qualification is not being rich or poor, Muslim, Christian, Buddhist, Jewish or Hindu. Love or Glory is the qualification.

XIX

How God, angels, or the emanation can read the holographic blueprint of the soul—this is the blueprint for the Lord and the Lord's angels to read our lives and memories and the terrible ironies revealed by them.

Now, in the presence of the Lord: My whole life opened up like a giant holographic folding of thousands of pictures, persons and memories all suspended in my attachments to the elements heat, water, air and earth. It is amazing to see how the Glory itself actually illuminates an element-based human being's whole body of thought with its Glory. Jesus knew everything about me. You should see what this looks like. You will eventually see it take place. Wow!

There you are with your mind engrossed in thoughts, feelings and memories all stored in the elements. Imagine a drop of water with the coding of your whole life and memories stored in it like a computer chip and then a beam of light strikes it and all the information illuminates from it like a giant hologram.

We live inside the hologram of our memories and act out of these memories and are engrossed in thought, sensation and emotion that are suspended in the elements. When you are in the hologram of your mind, body and emotions, attachment to the elements is so thick and entrancing you can't see that you are in a maze, a real maze, and cannot get out. But, in the Glory, it all opens up and you can step out of your life and see the whole thing objectively. It doesn't take Jesus to have this done. The Glory emanation (The Lord's Body, or Body of Christ), an Angel, or a Saint could do it as well.

Jesus saw all of me as a hologram and I saw it all, including my first love Sue Smith and my dear brother Todd, for whom I prayed to Jesus months before for his illness. Perceiving Todd's hologram, from my memory, Jesus showed me the true cause of his illness, which was deeply spiritual. Todd's body was having a hard time with the breaking of the small self in the presence of the Lord's emanations, but he would be able to make it through and deal with it eventually. Even so, he would be trembling in the Ecstasy-Glory also. Jesus knew all about him and everything. He knew that Todd feared the emanations of the Lord, like most, but that he also knew how to feel the Glory. In fact, it will be possible for Todd to be in fear and also be peaceful in the emanation of the Lord's Glory. It is amazing to live in fear of God and be filled with Glory at the same time. Todd will be able to do that. It is strange to witness that the fear of God is the most positive fear I have ever experienced.

I perceived the elements that human senses are made up of and are attached to—earth, water and air (fire exists but I didn't see it)—and why that attachment made us human and unable to live in pure enlightenment/Glory. In this sense, I hate to say it to many Christians, but the Buddhist meditation technology is very advanced. They understand and experience detachment from the elements and experience the First and higher ascending emanations of the Lord's Glory even if they do not know who Jesus is. If Buddha became enlightened into the Lord's Glory, then trust me Buddha lives in the Lord's Glory and has become one with it (as all saints do), and is a Saint, and is loved by the Lord. For the Lord is not contained in the written word "Jesus, Jehovah, Ala, Yahweh," but in the word as truth. This means that it does not matter to the Lord if you call out the name of God, but what is in your heart (your intention) is always known by the Lord. This is to say that the real name of the Lord is a silent secret and the Lord cannot be fooled by mere recitation of the written word. This means that to "ask and you shall receive" requires a pure heart. This is also why it is written "Hallowed be thy name"—we should not enunciate the name of God because we may get caught up in mere vowels and syllables.

This is another terrible irony for righteous Christians, Muslims, Jews, Buddhists, Hindus, or any ego-righteous spiritual teachers: It doesn't matter one bit to God if you sit around and debate God and existence all day long. If you are having fun doing it, have fun and evolve in creative debate. But if you are so serious about it that you separate over your views and instigate conflicts and even holy wars, watch out. If you know every scripture of every religion on earth backwards and forwards, but do not know love, you will have difficulty at the time of death and will need a miracle to enter into the Glory and live in Heaven. This is because by the wisdom written in those scriptures, you should have been guided to love, and to experience and choose love over ignorance. However, if you do not feel love and are instigating so-called holy wars, it will be better for you to abandon all scriptures and learn to love and be like a small child in love than to pursue your religious studies any further.

Jesus said in the Book of Mark, Chapter 12, Verses 38-40: "Beware of the scribes, which love to go in long clothing, and love salutations in the marketplaces, And the Chief seats in the synagogues, and the uppermost rooms at feasts, Which devour widows' houses, and for a pretence make long prayers: these shall receive greater damnation." This is to show you not to be fooled by those priests and people high in the church who do not know love, Glory, or the Lord in truth. If they do not know how to feel love, to give it and receive it, then they are worthless no matter how great the walls of their churches appear.

A person who is unknown in the world, who is innocent and full of love, is far greater in the Lord than they. The Lord said that they shall receive greater damnation because they are the shapers of the world. They have power only because we give it to them, and by misrepresenting the Lord they lead many astray. These are the people who think they do not want to go to Heaven because Hell is going to be more fun. This is a common modern social behavior. It is, in part, caused by the people in robes giving the wrong impression of the Lord. This is why the Lord has delivered this new message unto the world, because the Lord feels that the Lord and Heaven have been, in many cases and in parts of the world, misrepresented by the pawns in churches and synagogues.

In the presence of the Lord, the holographic pictures were suspended in one or all of the elements. If you look inside yourself right now, you can see that your mind is absorbed in sensations based upon and fluctuating from these elements. Taste sensations consist of air, water, earth, and fire elements. We need heat or a lack thereof in our bodies to sense emotions, or anything. We need the water to moisten our lips and mouth, to taste and sense food, and for sensuality. Heat is mixed in with the other elements at all times. Smell and taste are based in the air element. Our minds are almost always absorbed in the elements.

Love is the one miracle that can deliver us from being a slave to the elements. I could see this so clearly standing in front of the Lord, as the Lord gazed upon my history, the good, the bad, and the ugly.

When he or she arrives in your life, and you feel that bright shine in your heart, even if only for a moment, at least embrace them with your heart. Too many people reject the one they truly feel real love with because conditions do not match up for them. If you have too many conditions, such as material wealth, before you allow yourself to enter a relationship, you will never know real love. If you reject it because God put challenges between you and that person (and God always does this to test faith in Love), you will be poor in spirit here and now and after death.

I could see a terrible irony for a basic (but not secret) Hindu and Buddhist philosophy, that you must be a recluse and be celibate to come unto God. It is by Love and evolution in Glory that you come to God. I was deeply fooled by the Hindu notion of such ideals, and practiced it with my first true love. It caused our relationship great trouble and it was my entire fault. It was the notion of removing one's attachments, inner and outer, by force.

I could now see the Lord was viewing my holographic image of my first love Sue. That was a long time ago, when I was eighteen to twenty-one. It was three years. I knew the Lord loved her. She loved me when we were dirt poor, and still we were in Heaven together. In the fourteen years since then, I haven't found a single woman who could love me despite my poverty the way she could.

We would plant trees together and we even bought fruit trees and planted them in the City Park in Vancouver, Canada, so that the birds would have something to eat. The park service dug them up. So, we protested and went marching into their offices. Angels visited Sue when she was a child. They would come to her when she was sick and heal her. I still haven't had an angel make me better when I am sick. I lost her due to this ignorant Hindu and Buddhist notion of strict celibacy. Perhaps it is because marriages are pre-arranged in India, and because love operates under the natural laws of freedom in the Lord's emanation, that pre-arranged versus freedom of choice makes real love more possible in a free society. Maybe the yogis, in their illumined state, could not see so many people genuinely in love and deducted that enlightenment was not possible in such sense-oriented relationships. They were right, but only for the society they created. They did not know what the Lord was revealing to me here, that Love is universal truth. Love is evolving or already beyond the senses if it is real love. If two people really fall deeply in love, they are maturing in God's Light. There is no need to ruin it with ideals. However, relationships, even marriages, that are not based in true love can be destructive to real spiritual growth.

I embraced the Hindu notion of celibacy because of peer pressure, for trying to reach God was my real goal. Now I was seeing that what I fell for was a grave mistake and I lost my true love. It was mostly my fault. Today you may notice that many modern day visionaries, such as Danion Brinkley, Betty Eady, and others, have all had relationships. Perhaps the Lord is sending us a message? We do not need to be celibates.

Love can be experienced by living in the senses or elements, but it is delivering us out of them and into Glory. That spark of light we feel when we are in love or the moments we are feeling love or Glory in relationships is the tip of the emanation of the Lord's omniscient Glory. Love can begin to deliver us out of living just in the senses (sin). Senses are not sin if they are also feeling love. The Glory is so threatening to this attachment to the elements; it causes those who do not know love, when they try to approach the Lord, to flee in terror of the Glory. Notice also how many people run from someone who loves them in this world. This is not to say that just because someone loves you that you owe them your life, but it is to say that there is nothing to fear in them if they are feeling love for you.

If we flee from a loving relationship and seek a relationship that is not based in love, even though we know someone who we feel love with, then we are most likely to flee in terror of the Lord regardless of how many days we spend in church.

Those who are still partly attached to the elements, but know love, will be divided at death from those who are capable of letting that attachment go. It is amazing to see that the holographic images of our lives are suspended in these elements, and us in them before the Glory of the Lord.

This is how the Lord, the Glory, the Angels and Saints advise us and use our own holographic blueprint to really show us and educate us about our individual spiritual evolution. The Glory can do it alone, with not one soul present, because the Glory is the extended Body of the Lord, the Lord's self.

Imagine light illuminating a glass of water, but without the light the fish do not know they live in water. This is how an Angel or the Lord can see all of our life at once, and know everything about us: they live in Glory and Glory is pure energy and the elements are energy trapped in geometry, which cannot get out. Glory causes the holographic elements to unfold and open up in an amazing way, revealing the entire history of a soul.

Because the geometry opens up, the soul can begin to be cleansed in the Glory and gain entrance to true freedom and Glory. The Glory has no sensation of elements in it, so it is free from the sensation and attachments to elements, and thus is free from sin (attachment to elements). Love can begin to deliver a soul from sensation. Sensation alone is sin or ignorance. Sensation with love is the beginning of the soul's deliverance from sin.

Perception or absorption in Glory is a very evolved state for a human. When the soul is filled with Glory, there is little desire for just sensation any more. It fades away until a soul merges in Glory more and more, and then partakes in a body of Glory, by the Grace of the Lord, the Glory, or any of the Lord's assistants.

Oh my God, could the ancient Eastern teachers have known this? Even if so, there is still much that they do not know. Does this mean that righteous Christians should put away their swords and love their enemies, even if they are Buddhist?

The Lord is showing us that if you are converted to a life of love, you are already converted and you need no label or religion, but you may receive greater blessings to acknowledge and pray to the Lord. When Jesus tried to convert sinners, it was not to be a business of making labels called "Christians." It is great in virtue to love the Lord above all, but that cannot be done until living in love, perception of Glory, or absorption in Glory evolve in the soul. Loving a statue or image of the Lord has good intent, but little virtue. It is much better to fall in love with another real human being, feel love, and perceive Glory, and evolve to the point where we feel God's presence all around us. The purpose of conversion was to convert people from living without love to living in love. Since love is a "union" and not a "separation," we would have to end our pursuit of packaging people in churches and giving them labels that do not match up with other labels, which causes separation. We would need to learn to love and unify without destroying diversity.

Now, I will reveal another terrible irony in this new message. This is the irony of love over ideology, religiousness, and unfeeling charity. It is an ideology that if you are good and do right things in your life you will go to Heaven and meet God, and those who are bad will be punished. Much of this was discussed in the first meeting. However, for example, if you go to Church every Sunday, feel incredibly guilty for your sins, give money away out of guilt for the crimes you commit, do not drink or take intoxicants, do not have sex, but have not felt any or little love, you will have trouble at the time of death, and while you are living. This is because it must be understood that you have to actually be able to feel the giving and receiving of love. This does not mean that if you do an act that is technically good, you will go to Heaven. You have to do a kind thing and actually feel the love. Feeling love is key. These are terrible ironies because the truth will not match ideology, religious belief, or concepts. You will be better off having made some errors but eventually learn how to feel love and even more Glory, than to hold to a human concept of perfection and feel none or little love.

If you have not felt love, it is most likely because you are afraid of it, or were taught to value money, material gain, and worldly power and fame over love, meaning that you should get security before you open your heart. The truth is there is no security unless you open your heart first. If you prioritized this in reverse, then if you have material things taken away or you do not receive them, your heart will not open and you will fall by your own ignorance. If your mother, father or television set taught you this, they are not worth listening to any more unless they too convert to love.

If you go to church every Sunday, donate money to the poor, but seek material gain, fame, worldly power, and so on, you will not notice the delicateness of your lover, your father or mother, your brother or sister, the earth, its animals and mammals, and all beings who are more precious than that which you desperately seek in this world (money and jewels). Then you are already suffering, and will suffer more at the hour of death unless at that moment you can see how foolish you have been. To not love is the biggest crime in the world, to yourself and to the others who are missing it. Love is not a self-centered phenomenon. The magic of love is only ignited when you share it, then it multiplies. It can never be sequestered. God designed it that way, and it is perfect.

It is better to give one cent to a starving woman than a million dollars to the Pews Charitable Trust if, when you give the penny to the woman you feel something in her heart—the receiving, the thankfulness, the suffering turning to joy—just for that one second. That is worth more than an aloof rich person giving a million dollars to the Pews Charitable Trust, because the rich person remains aloof, feels spiritual pride from having given so much, but did not take the time to go out and meet the people and give of their heart. This aloof rich person will have trouble at the time of death unless at that moment they can see the truth, that for their whole life they have been hiding from love and their own interconnectedness to all beings. This is the terrible irony: you are missing out if you do not give and receive love, in some way, in God's whole creation.

Love is everywhere, and there is every reason to notice the igniting of love somewhere in God's creation. There are no excuses before the Lord. If you cannot feel love, you will be one of the ones who flee in terror, unless you can tremble and quake for a long time and be purified to the point that you can feel love. God will try to save all souls, but God cannot save you if you flee in terror, and it will be terrifying anyway, but overwhelmingly terrifying to those who do not know how to feel love. There is a great secret here. If you cannot feel love on earth, but can bear a long and arduous purification and tremble and quake and writhe in pain and spiritual agony until your heart opens, then you too can be saved. If you flee in terror, you will live in one of the lower realms where life is difficult until you do learn to love or perceive Glory. To perceive Glory is greater than love, but much more difficult to learn how to do. I could write a whole book on just this one subject, but there are many good meditation teachers out there, and there is no one meditation technique that is fit for all. You have to find the meditation that works best for you. That is part of your own journey to explore.

If you are afraid of love and trust no one because your mother and father told you all people are bad, you will tremble and quake before the Lord and the Glorious emanation, and you will flee in terror. Come out of your shell now and experience love before it is too late. If you were raped, still give your love. If you were an only child and no one loved you, stop and smell the roses, or pick up a cat, or notice something that makes you feel love, because without love, you are committing a crime. If your husband was murdered, still find reason to continue to love. God may have not given you the best parents but God gave you the best planet to learn how to love on because there are so many expressions of love on earth. If you miss it, you are blind.

If you are too busy with your career today and reject love for a later date, it may not arrive at a later date, not because God did not send it again and again, but because you valued fame, financial gain, or anything over and above love. Your heart will become less sensitive to love and will walk right past love when it is right under your nose. There will be no excuses at that great moment when you come to try and meet the Lord.

Remember, Jesus is now saying: **"I am here to meet anyone, and I am more available now than I have been for some time. Anyone can come and meet me, but it will be difficult for them (most humans)."**

For most humans, even those millions of Christians who say they love Jesus but slay their neighbors, oppress their workers, and have felt no love but ego-centered righteousness, it will be difficult because without love as your preparedness, you may tremble and quake and go running from the Lord's emanations before you ever catch sight of the Lord. This is because the Lord is love and Glory and too many persons have been running away from love their whole life. And even though you may have gone to church, you will miss the chance of your life, and may have to wait thousands of years or more to get another chance to meet the Lord. Get ready "now" because something inconceivably great is about to happen in our history.

To all men and women: stop waiting for Superman or Wonderwoman to arrive at your doorstep before you let your heart feel the beginning of love. Too many conditions and not enough tolerance and compassion is the way to strict thinking, limited love, and eventually the death of the heart. This leads to a sequestered, elitist kind of thinking, and an aloofness that makes it less possible for the miracle of love to be discovered. When Jesus said in the Bible that if you remember just one thing above all others, love thy Lord thy God with all thine heart and love thy neighbor as thine own self, he was showing the example of love. Love only happens in giving and receiving, it cannot be owned. Stop looking at the TV that says you have to own this car or that house before I will love you. Love does not belong to any one person. No one can hold it. It always has to be moving like a river. Try and catch it and it will die in your hands. Live without it and you will miss the great moment that may be your way out of the manure.

It is written in the Book of Revelations that after the Lord and Jesus' saints come for the final Revelation and Judgment, there will be those who live in the New Heaven and those who live on the New Earth.

It is important to know that humans who are at least loving, but who are incapable of withstanding the emanations of the Glory in the Heavens for a long time, will be able to inherit life again on the New Earth. There they will have 1,000 years of peace (as it is written) to evolve towards more love. And those who live in the New Heavens will also evolve over thousands of years into each ascending Heaven (see first message), depending on how much of the Glory they can live in and withstand. No one could possibly ever get bored, accept those who refuse to have any love and simply cannot make it into either the New

Heaven or the New Earth. They will suffer a terrible tragedy by their own creation (see first message). They are the most stubborn ones who avoid love and manifesting love too much for their own good.

As I was being crushed with ecstasy, I could take no more and I fell to my knees and face and was soon sitting on a sandy shore of a lake outside a city of light (perhaps a city in the First of the Heavens). I was shaking, and crying in ecstasy, trembling in his love and message that had overwhelmed me. I now understood that even though we could evolve towards God, the Lord was too great for humans to withstand for any long duration of time. It was humiliating in the most positive way, but still a great blow to being human. Jesus is so great that stars and galaxies would bow to him.

I knew that Jesus had prepared himself and lowered his vibration level so that humans could intervene and meet with him, and that even that was far too great for me to bear for more than one minute, in direct contact with him.

Fifteen years of meditation every day, trying to love another human with no real success in reciprocity, working to help heal this beautiful earth with no real success, and after all that I last only a minute or so looking directly into the face of the Lord Jesus Christ, for now. That is humiliation in the most positive way. I love him so much it is inconceivable, yet I now know that I have a natural responsibility to create more love and spread his message to all beings in the universe, because that is my spontaneous reaction to what I perceive in creation, and the kind of a world I want to co-create.

I knew when I was made humble, and was in the Seventh Heaven years ago, that the Lord's emanation body (even though the Seventh was the body of the Lord) was still further up above even the Seventh Heaven. I looked up there listening to the Highest Angels singing (volumes could be written on the Angels' music and what it does to you alone) and knew that the

Lord was still higher up, maybe at the top of the Seventh or higher. I do not know how much higher it goes. It may be thousands or millions of years before I can withstand the Glory up there.

I know now that Jesus can appear to souls, angels and/or saints anywhere they live inside of the creation, and that Jesus lives in the Highest Heavens much of the time. I know that as much as I have evolved, I am not ready to withstand the Glory in any Heavens above my own capability. That is what Jesus meant when he said to me in October 1994: **"No one has seen me in my entirety. Even you are not seeing me in my entirety. It is not possible at this time."** In each ascending Heaven, the Glory multiplies another million to billion times. I understood in part what I perceived about Jesus having to lower his vibration rate to allow humans to interact with him. There are very few who could possibly withstand the levels of Glory in the Highest and evolving Heavens. Only the supremely enlightened could go up there, and live there.

At least I know now that Jesus can appear anywhere inside of all creation and meet with souls and help them evolve in the Glory and the creation. I knew that I would see him somewhere in creation again.

God, this is so shattering to me as I sit here, stumbling over these opulent thoughts, crying and shaking in ecstasy/Glory. I had seen so much of the Lord and "i" am even more humble before the Lord than I was before. First the Lord showed me that he had the power and Glory of the whole universe at his command, and now he showed me he could crush me with so much love and ecstasy it would break me to the point that I could take no more. I cried saying the words "Who you *are*" over and over again. I was baffled and humbled to no end, as I sat on the sandy shore of this apparent lake in the Heavens.

I knew as much of the truth as I could possibly see for now, so much that no one could ever stand to live in all his Glory except for the highest enlightened angels and saints. I remember hearing the Highest Angels singing above the Seventh Heavens years ago. They can withstand that Glory all day and even they cannot gaze upon the face of the Lord in all the Lord's Glory. I am baffled beyond any human's possible belief, including my own.

"The mystery is so great," my father told me, "no one will ever know it all or any of it because it is all ever changing and always will be."

Although Jesus did not tell me directly about his own Second Coming, see if you can translate this: If Jesus is now lowering his vibration rate to the point where humans will be able to meet him face-to-face, how long would he want to live in such a lowered vibration body and state? Does this preparation suggest the Lord is making way for the great foretold event?

If Jesus said to us in the first meeting in 1994 that he really was not allowed, at this time, to cross over and meet us directly in this free-will zone, but had to out of compassion and emergency, and now, over three years later, he is lowering his vibration rate to meet with many humans for the first time in millennia, what might this mean? Could Jesus be preparing for the Second Coming? I do not know. However, I do know that he said in the Bible that even he does not know the hour of his own Second Coming, so neither does anybody. Perhaps it is not a planned date, but rather free and spontaneous as the Lord perceives the time to be right. The Lord definitely did not say to me directly that he is preparing for the Second Coming, but perhaps he left it in the form of a mysterious clue, and wants it to remain a surprise or mystery. If I get a definite answer from Jesus, I will tell anyone who is humble enough to listen.

I returned to my body crying my eyes out and having convulsions for hours. The Glory was inside my body now. I could feel the blood flow to my heart like never before. It seemed as though he was helping me heal my broken heart.

Finding love with humans has been difficult for me. But, even so, I feel incredible love with humans during great moments, and also with the earth and its myriad beauties, in creatures, the creation, and even, as incredibly lucky as I am, with the Lord Jesus, the Lord's self.

May we all learn to appreciate a love higher than anything on earth, and honor those who live in love over those who live as oppressors and warriors and conquerors and in corrupted lusts. For every person who takes this step, the world will become the Lord's Prayer: "Thy Kingdom Come, Thy Will Be Done, on Earth as It Is in Heaven."

If I shall ever be so lucky to meet the Lord again, I will always vow to share the message with anyone who wishes to obtain it.

CHAPTER THREE

The First Two Meetings in the Heavens & Resolutions

December 1986

XX

My first near-death experience two days in a row, December 22 and 23, 1986.

Another day back in time, three days before Christmas in 1986: It was about four in the afternoon and it was cloudy outside; again, nothing new for weather in the Pacific Northwest of Canada. I went into my small bedroom with pink walls and sat down on my bed which took up most of the room.

Paralyzed with the pain I was feeling, I felt it was as though I was suddenly ninety years old, and now was to be my time to die. Something was terribly wrong with me. When I finally lied down on the bed, feelings of fear that my heart was so weak, that it would stop beating swept over me like the brooding clouds outside. Somehow inside of that feeling of dying, I thought about all my lost loves. The loss of love endured with me until it smothered me.

I remained aware of the subtle feelings inside my own body. It felt like it was now my time to die. Every feeling wanted to come to its end. I was tired of them all. I was tired of the feeling of desire, nagging at me. This was not the same as a bad case of depression. This was different. My body felt like it was actually, physically dying, tremoring.

Feelings of pride and vanity always bored me. Self-exhilaration was another feeling that had the same side effects: pressure build-up in the head, expectation, exasperation, and so on. Somehow, all of these feelings gave me a sense of isolation. What I was feeling was going to destroy all of this, to feel more liberated and free from the bondage of isolated awareness. The ominous dark emperor of death beckoned me even further.

It was about 4:15 P.M. The feeling of dying drew me down with a very powerful sense of gravity. I have never felt my body that weak in my whole life. Lying down, I started to drift away very quickly until I found myself in a very vivid, crystal clear vision. I was now in the first out-of-body state as previously mentioned. It is the Astral world, just below in vibration and apparent distance to the First Heaven. There was a very old man lying on a bed in a worn down old wooden home. His surroundings were very poor. He had two elderly women in old cotton clothes praying over his body.

I thought the man looked like he already passed away. As I stared at his pale expressionless face, I couldn't believe the level of severe poverty I was seeing. Bed sheets of yellowed cotton and old wooden furniture that was badly in need of repair, curtains aged in dust and dried by harsh sunlight and walls covered with hundred-year-old wall paper were all most noticeable to me. This was the beginning of showing me how things are rarely the way they seem.

Surprisingly, the old man got up and approached me as though he were a youthful boy with vitality in his bones again. His eyes appeared very happy and quite unique when he said to me: “Do you want to see an angel?” My answer was a quick “yes.”

The moment I said yes, he walked into a kitchen through an old wooden door and I followed him. Like magic, he had vanished into thin air. This was the beginning of showing me how things are never the way they seem. The meaning of his worldly poverty would show its truth to me now.

The whole vision and sensation of the room was flooded by a rumbling downpour of fluttering wind and thunderous sounding white light. Like a spring rain in sparkling sunlight, the powerful light was so intensely beautiful and bright, I thought, that no dream could cast such a lovely, almighty power upon this lifelessness. I was now immersed in a sensational feeling a million or billion times more sovereign than the human waking state of consciousness.

A world of powerful Godly light above me sends a deep rumbling, fluttering, pulsating wind into the very core of my body. It was so loud, a nuclear bomb would seem quiet, yet my spiritual ears had no problem with this level of Glorious sound. As I was soon struck with a feeling of far too much love to bear, I noticed that whatever I sensed coming from above was moving its way into my being, slowly and yet feverishly sent to destroy the boundaries and barriers between me and my surroundings. I would soon become what the light itself possessed: drowning, overwhelming winds of peace, love and ecstasy. Somehow I was terrified of losing the feeling of control over my thoughts and my singular identity. Soon, the remainders of a small personality (ego) would dissolve into an eternity of Godly power of which I had no control of. The sound was deafening and the power of God was terrifyingly gargantuan.

I could hear the sounds of the most beautiful angelic voices of far greater resplendence than human ears could ever have dreamed. Perception of these new sounds came as though every atom of my whole being were as sensitive as the ear itself and the angelic sound vibrations moved like musical forms of pure energy. The angels' voices were not human at all. Yes, there really were angels' voices! I couldn't believe it. Their awesome power and reach was greater than I had ever imagined God to be in his or her very self, and yet I knew that these angels were only a part of God. The beauty was unimaginable. The power was awesome. The sounds moved within the winds of my soul with the ease of a gentle hand but with the strength of menacing thunder. The source of the blinding light was high above.

Imagine that it would take the most powerful force in the universe to break down the barrier of knowledge in the human condition that truly separates man and woman from God's omniscient pure ecstasy and its overwhelming beauty and love. Imagine that the same force made every human being and would always be waiting to reunite our awareness with this true and dazzling power of light.

Inside the light was a feeling of so much love, if you can imagine "a universe of love" breaking its way into your veins asking you to let go, to be taken away by a feeling with the magnitude of an ocean of stars, this would be a small comparison. The experience became very frightening because I had no control over the most powerful, overwhelming feeling of death and dying that the love from God brought on.

That was exactly what it was, a feeling of being shattered by love into a million pieces and being destroyed by a tremendously powerful force of light energy to the point of non-existence. Can you imagine non-existence? Can you imagine that it only means the non-existence of all that is false in you? Can you imagine that this means almost every single part of us? The rumbling force was drawing me towards a greater death than the death of my body. This was the death of "me" as a small self.

The two women, now standing beside me, fell onto the floor, having been absorbed by this same feeling. In the presence of this light, beauty and humble surrender were almost spontaneous emotions.

My knees and body became weak as I was now feeling the sensation of immobility and death completing itself over me. The loss of control of my bodily movements and, even worse, mental movements, was the most terrifying feeling of all time. It was the worst claustrophobia, yet it was hopeless to try and resist the power and magnitude of this God-like force. Where will you take me, dear God? What is happening to me now? I was going mad with Love.

I wanted to resist the whole experience as more fear rushed through my veins, but my own inner voice said, "trust and let it do to you what it wishes; what have you got to lose but your own limitations and suffering?" I felt like I was dying when I fell, paralyzed and helpless, onto the floor next to the two women who were praying. We lost all control over our selves. It was absolutely terrifying to be in the presence of God. What have I done? I had asked to meet God, and now it was really happening, not just a dream. God is inconceivably greater than all imaginations of the mind.

All I could feel was humility in the fright of the most awesome power, even greater than my comprehensible universe, and I wondered how it must have been created. Humility before this great presence was all there was. As much power as it took to create the universe, did not even compare to the source of this power I was in the presence of. In sight of its power ever more, I lost all sense of a personal self. I no longer had any control over my body or the expanding wave of sensation. The rumbling, fluttering wind and resounding angelic voices became so powerful that I knew I was in the presence of God and the Angels.

David, as I once knew myself to be, was no longer the one who had any control over anything, not even thoughts, not even feelings, and yet God's essence was the one exploding in the new waking rise of this ever wonder of powerful love. God was not an "it" or a "he" or a "she." There was nothing in the energy that said the source was single pointed. Omnipresence was the only obvious solution to the riddle. Resplendent, the angelic singing was like no choir or group of voices ever to sing upon this lovely and yet tragic earth. The beauty was glorious and superbly magnificent. Intensifying every passing moment, the light was so bright I could not see a thing accept for my limp body starting to become luminous as the force of light awakened a universe that had been separate from me until now. Somehow I perceived that the luminosity would have an unbearable surprise for me. The feeling of dying swept over me like an ocean wave and seemed to swallow me whole. I would no longer be. David was no longer going to exist. The rumbling force was all of God above.

At this moment, the great hand of death transformed my being. My body burst forth with an explosion of thunderous, glorious white light. Unbearable beauty of ecstasy and love were the only sensations I knew as the feeling of the divine mother's hands picked me up and began to carry me upwards, twisting and turning into this splendid shower of brilliant, blazing light. There was no desire in me that carried me, like the bird that does not desire its own path of flight. Desire was now seen as limited because it was controlled by an isolated little mind. That limitation and desire to be free and in control is what was causing the duality of pleasure and pain, good and evil, to hold the small self together.

Both pleasure and pain are perceived as suffering entirely from this perspective. It was effortless, desireless, knowing and trusting that infinite power of ecstasy to carry me with its own love. My will would now be one with God.

I went up and up and could now see the city of Vancouver, Canada in clouds below me. My body was becoming more luminous and I was feeling innocent, pure and like this: "I'm really going home now. You're on your way back home David." I was feeling so much love and freedom, my grateful "is-ness" released tremendous currents of joy. I was twisting and turning upwards becoming more and more luminous and feeling expansion and space around me. Angels were singing louder and louder.

The intelligence of the whole light told me there were millions of paradise planets suspended in this enormous Heaven. Soon, the density of the atmosphere I was in became too dense for me to contain this ever-growing feeling of unbearable amounts of happiness. The light and Glory was so bright here, I couldn't imagine more was possible. The ecstasy was crushing me to no end.

It is important for the reader to note, from this point on in the experience, when I use the term "I" it is not in duality, nor to be understood in the singular or plural sense. There is only "isness."

Being absolutely crushed with joy, I was leaving the First Heaven going into the Second. The atmosphere changes drastically. It is a million times more crystal clear than the first. I could see forever. I would then be taken higher and explode silently with even more white light as my body became even more luminous and a billion times more ecstatic; now, like that of a bright white sun. I could feel the sense of a less dense atmosphere, with more room for new feelings. It was incredible to even sense this.

I could still see my arms and legs, but they were not the same; they were so light and free of all the suffering and pain that I had accumulated in my physical life. I couldn't believe the miracle of it all. It was the best day of my life, but I thought I must have already died. Will my dear brothers find my body no longer living? Will they understand? The intelligence told me again that this Second Heaven was full of millions of paradise planets, of a higher spirituality than the first.

Being absorbed by a multidimensional presence, I was being cared for and taken yet higher where even this atmosphere was too dense for the happiness I was feeling. Ecstasy here is not possible for a human mind to even fathom one percent of. That would mean all paintings of Heaven were false, misleading and even damaging. Again, the point of transformation was being crushed with ecstasy.

Another silent explosion of a million times more light within my being and I was entering the Third Heaven. I could actually perceive this feeling of pressure in the ecstasy, knowing I had to be taken even higher in order to release and be able to exist with the extreme intensity of ecstasy that was now within all of me and unto a limitless awareness field. I had never before imagined enlightenment or God to be really this powerful—not even one percent. Again, the Third Heaven is full of millions of paradise planets suspended in this higher spirituality. My Third level paradise body was now being crushed with ecstasy, as I was moving at remarkable speed through this enormous Heaven, upwards towards the source of this spiritual light. The Angels' singing above was so loud and thunderous, yet so serene at the same time.

Entering the Fourth Heaven, billions of times more ecstatic than the Third, there was love, power, peace and light, and the singing got louder while the rumbling, fluttering wind pulsed with greater intensity as I exploded in brighter light into an even more beautiful feeling and dimension.

My body was now like that of a small Asian boy of about five years old, and was extremely bright; explosions of ecstasy, power, love and peace, all silent peace beyond all measures. Suddenly, like a hologram I could see a high mountain Buddhist temple below me (perhaps a past life). I perceived the very miracle that allowed my being to actually be able to bear these extreme levels of ecstasy. Surely, ecstasy this extreme would frighten and destroy anyone who was not ready. It was not possible for me to handle any more ecstasy. I had hit my limit. Something in me wanted to say to God "enough, I can't take it any more." But then a miracle.

The miraculous feeling descended like countless millions of leaves all falling from the sky at the same time, in perfect harmony. It was defined as Grace. This amazing Grace now stilled the intensity of the ecstasy, making it possible to bear being so unbelievably light. It was a miracle because I didn't feel it would be possible for me to exist in these extreme levels of ecstasy for very long. With Grace, it was now possible and it was happening.

Entering the Fifth Heaven, a state of this kind of happiness would certainly be almost impossible to bear while living in a physical body. It would be like living in a heart with the light and magnitude of a hundred billion suns. I even doubted great gurus at this point. How could they walk around like this all day in a body?

Now I was being carried up even higher. They weren't finished with me yet. Where would I get dropped off? Who would I get to talk to? I was still being taken upwards. I didn't ask any questions because there was no one to talk to and I was just so happy to be up here. I didn't care. The man had said, "do you want to see an angel?"

If the very light of the brightest star known to humankind could be shadowed in the presence of a brighter source of light, what power would that source hold for us? What power would it be that would cast the shadow of the sun? The answer was clear to me now. Relative to this Light of God, the light of the human aura appears as darkness now. The answer to that observation would come to me tomorrow.

Vibrating billions of times higher with all the qualities, ecstasy billions and billions of times brighter than the orgasms of stars, even brighter light was so intensely alive above me now, and the ecstasy was so extreme. There was little remaining of what was once known as "David," but a feeling of identity and individuality subtly remained in my body of light. It is not that the little man became all of this and contained it in his ego, it was just the opposite: the little man's barrier dissolved and came unto what is and always has been happening in the universe. How do you like that? And slowly, even this feeling of subtle identity was dissolving. I felt a tremendous new blessing of grace and peace come over me as I moved higher up into this even brighter dimension of light which I recollected as the Sixth Heaven. I don't think there are any planets in this Heaven. I don't even appear to have a spiritual body anymore.

Each level had a very unique quality of Grace. Grace was now an even newer sensation. It descended downwards and made it possible to bear all of this even more than the first Grace before it. It was like no other feeling I had ever known. Supernovas would pale in comparison to what I was seeing and feeling. The happiness exploded forth and out of my being, given in abundance from everywhere around me, dissolving all my senses of desire. The singing was so powerful, I didn't doubt for a second that the power of this source could create whole galaxies and planets in days.

I didn't doubt for a second that God and its Kingdom of Heaven was, is and ever will be real. Even the word "it" to describe God was too one-pointed and defined and could only come from a single point of awareness, not the whole of existence. A mind could never spawn forth so much love and power beyond all comprehensible thought. A mind could never enter in through these gates. The more stable I became in the ecstasy and power, the more I could perceive the universe around me.

The atmospheric changes were so clear and obvious, it was easy to know when what was left of David was moving into another Heaven. Entering the Seventh Heaven, the light enveloped me so intensely and the ecstasy took up so much of my awareness that there was now very little remaining of "David." It was at this precise moment that the light became so overwhelming that it was now going to remove the very subtle feeling of "David" from existence. I could feel it extinguishing my identity with its tremendous force of love and power. There was only many billions of times greater pure peace, ecstasy, love, power, and grace for the moment and I could no longer bear to pass. I could sense something so inconceivable here, as if my small observation point (by body and being) was about to become enormous in size, not as a vantage-point, but the body itself. My physical body told me that if I crossed this point it would terminate its life force below. I chose to come back just because of my intense desire to communicate how real the Kingdoms of Heavens, the reality of God and the beauty of Angels to others. I awoke on my bed with a sudden pull to my furiously beating heart.

My body was vibrating with tremendous energy but I was no longer up there in the celestial sun of the Holy God. I was so excited, I ran downstairs and told my brother Tim, my father Lynn and my stepmother Trish what had happened. The response I got from them was genuine, but not one that told me they really believed me. Believing me was not the kind of respect I wished to receive. I just wanted them to know that God is real, the Kingdom of Heaven is real, and so are God's Angels. How was anybody going to believe me? What could I say to get people to redeem themselves from despair?

For the remainder of the night I walked in a daze. I couldn't believe what had happened. My normal waking state now felt like a dark shadow passing through darkness once again, and forever again. All of the money and riches in the world seemed like pale expressions of false delight. I know what Jesus meant when he said that for a rich man to pass into the Kingdom of Heaven would be like a camel passing through the eye of a needle. I was suddenly struck with an altered expression and sensation of what reality might be. Not even the greatest of the world's treasures could ever entice me now. Not even the greatest physical pleasure could ever permanently satisfy my sense of delight. How was I going to live the rest of my life as a normal person, having known the likeness of being in God's celestial existence?

Suddenly, the darkness of the world I lived in swept into me, leaving me standing on the edge of an emotional, bottomless abyss. I would not fall into the abyss, but I would have to walk along its razor's edge, caring for the vision that I would later understand and tell.

The next day was December 23, 1986. 4:15 pm rolled around again and the same feeling of dying came over me. It was interesting to note this time because my mother Linda said I was born at 4:15 in the afternoon, August 21, 1961. I laid down in my pink room just as I had done the day before. In a very short time, without any trauma, I was moving out and beyond my body again. But this time, what I saw was not of pure delight, at least not yet anyway.

Taken out of my body very swiftly and effortlessly to the edge of the First Heaven, I was in a realm where hundreds of thousands of people were still stuck inside of their limited dualistic small selves, seen from my perspective in the First Heaven as oval, silvery gray luminous energy fields of physical matter.

I could see the energies of duality, good and evil, holding the oval energy field of a single small self (ego) together and holding the barrier in place, shielding the soul from the very bright luminous energy of God's vibration of the First Heaven. The multidimensional light (God) literally kept the human aura-energy fields alive as it shined into them without destroying them. They were perceived as separate from the universal consciousness of the First Heaven. Separate, only because they wanted the freedom to choose for themselves where to go, what to do, and what is good and what is evil. From their isolated dualistic perspective, this was seen as freedom. From the perspective of the First Heaven, it was seen as slavery to the limited self-ego and suffering. Real freedom was in Heaven.

I knew that from the human perspective of darkness, even the light of the human aura appeared as a glow, but from the perspective of the First Heaven, that light was faint and actually silvery gray (note that on earth all colors appear grayish when there is no light on it). Also, if you held a candle that dispelled the darkness of the night, the candle would be seen as bright, until the sun shone upon it. Then the candlelight would seem like a shadow.

Some of the humans were agitated and trying to get out of their limited energy fields as they sensed me and another bright glow off to my left, which I perceived to be an enlightened being. The being was waiting for me. I was trying to help the suffering ones. I could see that they were blind; they could not even see out past their barriers. However, they could dream within them. They might have even been absorbed in visions of suffering or pleasure (still a duality), reviewing their past life experiences projected against the silvery gray energy field of their awareness like a movie on a screen. None of them could see me and I felt so much compassion for them.

It was amazing to perceive that each separate soul, encased in the dualistic small self (ego), was capable of perceiving a separate reality of their own, and actually live and appear in pictures in that dreaming reality that reflected against the screen of their own gray-luminous barrier. Billions of these separate realities could not only individually be experienced, they could interact with each other. Hence, they could appear to one another in separate realities.

One of them sensed me. It was a male. He almost broke away from the other cocoon-shaped energy fields, but when he did, he started to tremor and shake. This was amazing to witness because I was looking back at the process I had gone through myself when my small self (ego) was dissolved by the light. I had the same symptoms of shaking and fear of being destroyed, but now I was witnessing it from the other side.

This is an important state of consciousness to observe for me. If the barrier (silvery-gray luminous energy field) held by illusion dwellers was very weak, the soul could much more easily perceive the light and dissolve their barrier, although it would still be very powerful, awakening and even frightening. But only at first, and only because of residual impurities. Once the impurities of the small self dissolve in the light, love and ecstasy would carry the soul to the supreme state of beingness.

Because of iniquities and illusions in those souls with thicker barriers, when the vibrations of God in the First Heaven struck the outside of their barrier, they would feel so terrified that the dreamings and illusions produced by their own imaginations would be of a terrifying and even demonic nature. If they could see that the demons and terror were being created by the emanations of God striking against their barrier, trying to dissolve it, and that it is only their impurities that feel death, terror, and demons, they would let those terrors and inner demons die in humility. If they could surrender their ego or small self to the thundering and trembling, and fall down and become humble, the emanations of God in the First Heaven might even be able to wash a corrupt soul clean and take it to Heaven. This, however, is very rare, because those souls rarely have the awareness to know what is happening when they approach this kind of terror, let alone do they know what to do about it.

Souls with little or no residual impurities, like saints, would feel little or no terror upon dissolving a barrier in God's presence in the First Heaven, because their barrier is either very weak, or does not exist. From this point of non-duality on, the only test to move closer to God, is "how much ecstasy, love, power and peace can your selfless self withstand?" Now, supremely bright ecstasy will dissolve the subtle remainders of self, perhaps over millennia, so that life in the super realms evolves.

From the First Heaven, pleasure and pain both appeared as suffering to me now as I observed this man trying to break free. The whole duality had to dissolve in this man and he would be happy. He pulled back and went back with the others. He, as an isolated ego, was too afraid to die in God's power. Most likely, he would reincarnate somewhere in the dual universe.

Strangely, I feel that the often experienced "tunnel going into the light" (experienced in other NDEs) might even be the walls of the small self in its own energy field, with the light of the First Heaven just beyond that. Danion Brinkley, author and experiencer in *Saved By the Light,* described the walls of the tunnel before going into the light as silvery gray. I could see that it would be possible at this point to collectively visit, in anyone's energy field, relatives, friends or even saints. Also, the small self could still be held together here, just a perception in the light.

A few souls had seen me for a moment but they had not the strength to believe in a way out of their suffering. Some were in bodies of gray amorphous matter and could not sense anything other than being stuck and not being able to get out. Perhaps they would have to wait until they were called upon, I didn't know. Perhaps they were waiting to be replaced or incarnated somewhere in the Universe.

I drifted above these suffering beings that had already passed away from their earthly lives. My being was soon greeted by the same light and experience of going through all the six Heavens and up into the Seventh Heaven as I had the day before.

The happiness and the glorious presence of light was just as wonderful to be in as it was the day before.

The happiness was not like the emotional feeling of being high and happy that would soon beg for a calm relaxation from the effort of sustaining emotion. I could see what emotion was now, the very tension in it, the very duality of it all. I could see the very personal effort there was to sustain or control emotion. I could see it all so clear now that I was free, even from the growing emotions of human life.

The angelic voices were of sounds so pure and of such sensational feeling, there is absolutely no way that I could describe what existence was like here, but I will try: Walk without feet and fly without wings and enjoy the mystery of things. Imagine a world where sensing everything is sound, pleasure, ecstasy, grace and mystery greeting you through every dimension of sight, touch, sensation and even more. Imagine being lifted up, unbearably light. Trust and you will no longer be the person who lived before. Bow to the graceful delight as it warms your insides with the gift of eternal bright.

I was lifted higher and higher in effortless, expanding brightness to the same place where, if I crossed, I would no longer be able to come back and write. The identity of the self as an individual does not have to be protected here in this realm of white. There is a sense of trust that one's placement will be right. Ever expanding and ever dissolving, the mind that dreams its life back down where gravity made its isolated world of fright, would now be gone.

Is freedom the flight of being gifted with wings of desire like the dove? Is this true freedom I ask? Or, does the bird who has flown the greatness of blue sky and passing clouds become free from a sense of having flown? Does the bird retire from having known the freedom of having flown? As the desire to be free to fly is one day fulfilled, the wings of all desire must at some time bow in thanks to the great one who gave this very blue sky above the clouds and falling rain.

What then happens when desire has known that this bird has already flown? What else is there? When the wings bow down and surrender to the ground, when stillness becomes the greatest prayer ever known, this is the greatest time that no mind can know. But, it is through the beating heart that we can know time. What else is there? Be still thy mind. When the question disappears, the mystery of the eternal inner sun has just begun.

After a blaze of overwhelming joy and light, I woke up on my bed again in my room. It was now coming into the evening. I had been a practicing meditator of Buddha's Vipassana meditation for many years, and now, as I have known, I was obviously in the company of Jesus' Angels and it was two days before his celebrated birthday.

Having been a Buddhist who studied Hinduism, practiced yoga and meditation, wouldn't Christianity disagree that I could have been let in through the gates of Heaven? The questions came upon me now. I knew that I was going to have to understand what had happened as I now had to face the shadow of the world and its torturous, righteous minds. Why did Jesus choose a Buddhist meditator to deliver this message? The answer is more clear now than it was at the beginning of this journey, but it will evolve more.

I had always loved Jesus as a child. In fact, my first and foremost memory as a child was being baptized at the age of four months, as my father had told me that was when it was. I remember being carried over to the priest in the arms of someone and then the man had poured water all over my head. My thoughts were so clear: "You idiot, what do you think you are doing? Do you really think that you are performing an act of God as some holy man?" I coughed and cried after being doused with water. I thought the man was spiritually blind. I knew that God did not require that such an act be performed by an empty heart and mind and that it would truly make people instantly spiritual. I was carried back to my parents. I knew that Jesus was not the man that most Christians thought he was. But I did not have my answer then.

There I was, Christmas Eve of 1986, sitting in a large Catholic Church, and there was all this singing. Although I appreciated the voices of the choir, I knew they were not capable of sensing the sounds that came from the Angels in Heaven that I heard, not even close.

I walked out of the place knowing from direct experience that the masses were being deceived. It was asked of me in the light to express, in any way I could, that Heaven is not at all boring, not at all like people have envisioned it to be and that God has the most wonderful and beautiful mystery to show us all—something so wonderful, no mind should even imagine how wonderful it is really going to be. My task is going to be enormous. My own desire to return to the Kingdom of Heavenly mystery and beauty would beckon me with every passing day of my life and yet I would have to stay here and learn patience.

The darkness of each passing day seemed like an eternity in hell. Somehow I had to find a way to live in my body and contact that light at the same time. I know I had done it before and I know how fervent my practice of stillness and prayer must be. I know that nothing that I had ever experienced before even compared to the experience of being taken up there, into that realm of light. I knew that I couldn't just fly up there with some will of my own. It is purely a blessing and a gift to have been taken up into that light and have my sense of singular identity dissolve.

XXI

Integrating the experiences of others into the giant puzzle.

This is the story of Gwyneth Thomas. I think this is an incredible example of the consistency of the Lord's messages to humankind, regardless of where or who the recipient of the vision is. Her story is written in first person and is in the exact form that it was in when she sent it to me.

When I was about 12 years old, I met a new friend at school. Her mother was Catholic, and her father was Jewish. I thought that she was really lucky because she got to celebrate both Hanukkah and Christmas. Despite her tall stature and strength, she was also an especially kind and gentle person. I liked and respected her a great deal. To this day, we remain close friends.

In our senior year of high school, her parents thought that she was getting a bit rowdy, and that California's public educational system was not offering her the discipline that they felt she needed. So, they sent her off to a Christian boarding school somewhere near the Russian River, deep in the California wine country. Although she always saw herself as being both Catholic as well as Jewish, according to the school, she became the first "Jewish" student to attend.

We didn't see each other much that year, or the next, because her school was several hours away. But, as luck would have it, we ran into each other a year or so later, in 1983, after we had both begun college. Of course, we picked up our friendship where it had left off.

Since we were close, we often openly discussed topics such as religion and ethics. It was then that she related to me a series of events that took place during her senior year at the Christian high school. Although what she told me greatly disturbed me, it served only to deepen my respect for the strength of her soul.

Since it was a boarding school, and she was a student, she was required to attend each and every religious service. She had grown up with an open-minded religious background, so this, in and of itself, did not particularly bother her. However, what took place during these services did.

The preachers would begin their services in the usual manner, and then midway into the service would begin to preach that: "Jesus was put to death by the Jews." They would go on in this vein, until my friend was nearly in tears. They even went so far as to place the blame of many modern day worldly ills upon the heads of those of Jewish faith today, and even hinted that Jewish prayers weren't heard by God but rather by Satan.

My friend, who in many ways was a typical teenager, was afraid to tell her parents of this. Instead, she tolerated it for many weeks. Finally, she simply couldn't put up with it any longer. Having grown up with an open-minded faith in God, she knew she had to take a stand against such unfounded and prejudicial nonsense.

One day, as the preacher started up with his usual Jew Bashing, as she termed it, my friend stood up in the middle of the service. She rose to her full height, and marched down the center aisle of the school's chapel. She grabbed the Bible from the hands of the small-minded preacher and slammed it down on the pulpit, while shouting, "You show me where, in this book, any where in this book, that it says that!"

She demanded an apology, and stated that she would not return to another service until they either apologized for their slurs or could show her where in the Bible these remarks could be found. Then she stormed out of the chapel.

Needless to say, she got her apology, and an opportunity to explain what Judaism was. She was not again forced to tolerate that kind of behavior, which so clearly had been directed towards her.

Although several years had passed from the time these events took place and the time my friend told me of them, it was quite clear to me that the events still were upsetting to her. She told me that she probably never would understand why it was that people didn't seem to realize that the God that those of the Jewish faith prayed to was the same God who was the father of Christ, and therefore the same God that Christians prayed to. I told her that I didn't think that I would ever understand why people were such idiots either.

After our conversation, I began to wonder if I would have the strength of character to stand up for my beliefs the way that she had. I wondered if I was capable of facing such ridicule and rising above it.

Several weeks passed, and I still found my mind drifting to how she must have felt. She had been alone as she walked, tall and proud, up what must have seemed such a long aisle, to take a stand for her faith and beliefs. I know I was in awe that a teenager had possessed such strength.

About a month later I had a dream, or perhaps, what was truly a vision. I am sure that this dream, or vision, was representative of my own personal realization of the struggle she must have faced having had to stand up for her religious background. My concern for what had happened to her must have worked its way into my subconscious, or, perhaps, empathy for what she had endured worked its way into my soul.

As I look back and remember my dream, I cannot say that it would have occurred without the knowledge of what someone whom I loved and admired had endured. Perhaps I would have dreamt it anyway, but it would not have held the same personal meaning for me. It remains the single most significant dream that I have ever had. I suspect that I may never again have such a dream.

Each detail of that dream remains crystalline and frozen in my memory, like the way the inside of the modern cathedral where we were sitting looked. I can still see the way the sunlight dimmed as it filtered through the deep blue of the stained glass and over the heads of the people crowded inside for the Revival.

The audience was hushed listening to the hypnotic voice of the animated preacher at the pulpit.

The dark figure at the pulpit spoke of Jesus, and of His miracles. As the figure rambled on, the audience became ever more mesmerized. They began to sway slightly at the rise and fall in the pitch of speaker's voice. The dark figure spoke of how Jesus died at the cross for our sins. Then the timbre of the speaker's voice began to grow coarse. Suddenly, the figure paused and flatly stated that it was the Jews who had put Jesus to death. Then the figure paused again and looked around.

"Did you know," the figure said, "these same Jews dare to come here today." The figure looked around again, and focused its attention in my direction. I looked to my side, and the same friend who had suffered at the ignorant hands of the preachers at her "Christian" boarding school was seated next to me. She looked back at me nervously, and then we both quickly looked forward as the figure continued. "Jews," the figure stated, "have no place in heaven."

I don't know what motivated me to stand just then, but I stood. My friend tried to stop me. She pulled hard on my arm in a futile attempt to yank me back into my seat. "No, there's too many here," she whispered. But I was not to be silenced. I shook off her grip and reached out my arm. Then I pointed my finger at the dark, and now obscured by my rage, figure. "You HYPOCRITE!" I shouted over the deathly quiet audience.

To my horror, the figure didn't back down. It didn't apologize. It simply smiled, and I knew then why it had been so hypnotic.

It looked back at me, with glowering eyes, and then at the audience who seemed unaware of the two reddish pinpoints that danced from behind the pulpit. Then it shouted, "Look, there's the Jews. Get em," as it pointed back at us.

I tried to shout back, "You're wrong; I'm a Christian." But the audience was in an uproar. My friend grabbed me and pulled me hard by the arm. "We have to get out of here. We have to run." Those sitting nearest us seemed to know us. They tried to help us by acting as human shields as we climbed over the makeshift seating at the back of the cathedral and headed for the nearest exit.

We headed out the door of the cathedral and into the hot sun. The rest of the congregation, or what now seemed to be a mob, chased us. Somehow I realized, as we ran through the streets, that we were in a very old city, perhaps even Bethlehem or Jerusalem. Although we ran as fast as we could over the narrow cobbled streets away from the modern cathedral, the crowd chasing us kept pace. It seemed that they became angrier and angrier as they pursued us. They began to shout, "Kill them. They are Jews. They worship the devil."

Within several minutes we realized we could not outrun the crowd. After rounding another corner, we quickly discovered that we had become trapped in a dead-end alley. There was a brick wall of the back of a building on one side, while on the other side, there was a low white plastered railing which ran along a sheer cliff overlooking the valley. At the end of the alley was an old crumbling whitewashed wall. There was nowhere left to run, and nowhere to hide. We were terrified.

It was then that my friend realized that the crumbling wall at the end of the alley was no ordinary wall. It was, in fact, a wall that for long centuries had been used by those of the Jewish faith for prayer. I don't know how she knew that, but she did, and I knew she was right. Having no other hope, she immediately knelt in front of the sacred wall. The hot afternoon sun beat down on her back as she began to pray.

For some reason, I didn't then join her. I hoped that perhaps the crowd would somehow not follow us into that alley. But they did. Seconds later, the crowd rounded that same corner. I noticed that many of its members had small rocks clenched in their fists that they had found time to pick up along the way.

When they got within about twenty feet of me I shouted at them, "You must stop. You call yourselves Christians, but this is not what Christ would want. We all pray to the same God. What you are doing is wrong." For some reason this caused the mob to momentarily pause. I noticed that the dark figure at the pulpit was now nowhere to be seen.

As my friend prayed fervently for God's help at the wall behind me, someone in the crowd shouted at me, "If you're so sure that we all pray to the same God, then you go pray at that Wailing Wall next to your Jew buddy!"

I looked over at the wall where my friend knelt. I didn't know if it was a "Wailing Wall" or just some other sacred site. I didn't care either. She looked so small and helpless. Yet I knew, somehow, that she was full of hope. I turned back to the crowd and faced them.

I was afraid. What if they were right? What if I prayed with her, and I condemned my soul to hell? What if those dancing red eyes wanted nothing more than to tempt me to do exactly that? Still, I could not join them. I had to stand on my faith alone. I had to risk everything to do what I truly believed was the right thing. The angry crowd was quiet as they awaited my reply.

"I will pray with her," I said. I turned and faced the wall. My steps echoed in the silence of the hushed crowd. Perhaps they, too, were curious as to what would become of me? With each step I took, I grew ever more fearful that someone would break the silence and hurl one of the stones that so many had tightly gripped in their hands, but no one did. The ten or so feet to the wall seemed liked miles. As I knelt beside my friend, I again wondered what would become of my soul if they were right. But, I knew what I had to do.

I held my shaking hands above my head and open to the sky. "Heavenly Father and Son of God, if what I do now is a sin then I ask for you to cast my soul forever into darkness," I said, choking back my frightened tears. Then I clasped and folded my hands. I bent my head in prayer. "Lord," I whispered, "please forgive me if this is a sin." Some part of me hoped that nothing at all would come of it.

As the tears began to well up in my eyes, I began to pray. I thought that I saw the wall turning to liquid. I started to close my eyes, thinking that my frightened tears were blurring my vision. Then, I heard the now silent members of the crowd draw in their breaths. Several people screamed in terror, while others fled. Both my friend and I opened our eyes. To our horror, the wall in front of me was, indeed, turning to liquid. This was no illusion from my tears.

She and I both stood up. We began to back away from the wall. Neither of us now cared that there was an angry mob behind us. The mob backed away too. More of its members screamed and fled as a figure began to emerge from the wall. My friend flattened herself against the bricked back of the building that ran along the alley as the figure walked past her and headed towards me. I just kept backing up. For a moment, I was completely terrified. I had no idea what shape the figure would take. As the figure approached, it became clearly recognizable to all those who dared to remain. It was Jesus Christ.

As I looked at the now perfectly formed figure of Jesus Christ, I knew what love was. I knew that no human, especially me, was worthy to look upon that face. As He approached, I fell, sobbing uncontrollably with relief, to my knees. As I stared downward, I looked at His perfect feet. His feet were as if chiseled from ivory, with small circular scars on his arches. I was too afraid to look up. How could I have dared to risk what I had just done? I knew I could never be worthy to stand in His presence.

Then I felt the soft touch of His index finger touch under my chin. Gently, He raised my head, and stood me up. I heard Him tell me not to be afraid, though I don't think He actually spoke. Never have I since felt such peace.

He supported me with His right hand and turned me to face the cliff. I knew the crowd could see us, but they were silent. No one dared to speak.

We looked over the low crumbling railing at the dusty old city that sprawled below us. With His left hand, He reached forward to the right and then made a sweeping gesture from right to left. Again He spoke. "Behold!" It was a word I knew all could hear with their minds. But I knew what I was to see would not be shared with the others then present.

The ancient city below disappeared. It was replaced by a battlefield, the likes of which no one can possibly imagine.

I could see all the great religions fighting with each other. Many smaller sects rose and fell by the wayside. I could see all the "Holy" wars. I could see the Greeks fighting and the Romans fighting. The Crusaders were there fighting with Muslims. I could see Christians fighting Catholics, Jews, Muslims, Hindus, and even Buddhists. It was just one giant battle. All religions seemed to be represented in the fight with one another. They were even so busy fighting that they fought amongst themselves. They were so engrossed with hatred that rarely did anyone even bothered to look up.

At the center of the battlefield, the atrocities were horrendous. Parents were killing children. Children killed parents. There were rapes and mutilations. There were innocents being burnt and there were hangings. It was chaos, and it was sickening. I longed to look away, but I could not.

At the core of the battlefield, where the fighting was by far the most vicious and intense, there was a repulsive black vortex sucking away at the oblivious would-be warriors. Some of the cruelest even seemed to vanish into this churning pool of venom.

Still, amid the utter chaos, He showed me that there was hope. Whenever one of those lost souls glanced up towards where we stood overlooking the battle; the fighting immediately around that soul eased up just a bit and that soul was given hope.

If that soul tried to help others to see that above the valley there was peace, the fighting around that soul would begin to cease, and that soul would begin to move away from the core where the vortex seemed strongest. When a soul laid down all of his or her weapons, no matter how close to the vortex that soul was at that time, a pathway cleared so to allow that soul to walk out of that valley.

Despite the horrors of that chaotic place, there were some souls who had already been shown the way out, yet they voluntarily remained to help others to look up, and to lay down their weapons. There were others, too, already out of the valley. They often seemed to choose to return to help others to look up. Some of those souls hovered over the battle like gentle birds hoping to be noticed and hoping to urge those below to look up and find in them some meager measure of hope and grace. The only fighting any these souls seemed to do was to wrestle the weapons away from others long enough to turn their heads to look beyond that wasteland.

Those souls that escaped the valley were of every background. They weren't just Christians. Nor were they just Muslims, Hindus, or Jews. They were of every faith, of every sect, and of every background. Some were of faiths or traditions long past, while others were of those faiths we know today.

Those who returned to help were also of every faith and of every background. Once in a while, it seemed, one of those courageous souls would pick up a weapon, for some reason, and begin, once more, to fight. Then, a truly vicious battle would break out around them. But that soul would not go unnoticed by those on the hill. Help for that soul was always sent. Always those who remained or returned to help were able to leave again. Those souls were never forgotten. The vortex was never able to engulf a single one who had offered another help.

As I looked out over this battlefield, I knew that somehow, I was looking at eternity. It seemed like forever that I watched.

Yet it was only moments. It was so terrible, yet so inspiring. It was beauty, and self-sacrificing love, and horror and anguish all at once. Finally, it overwhelmed me. I turned my head away. Shamelessly, I buried my face in His robe and silently wept.

When I again opened my eyes, the battlefield was gone. Once again, the old city lay below. The reflection of the afternoon sun glistened from distant rooftops. I knew the crowd still stood behind me. Only moments had passed, yet I had known the passing of ages. I didn't understand why I, alone, had been shown this. Nor did I understand why those on the battlefield continued to fight. There was so much I didn't understand.

I finally raised my eyes and looked into His. To this day, I can't remember what color they were. I only know that they were full of such love that I was filled with courage and hope.

There was so much I wanted to ask. There was so much I didn't understand, and so much I wanted to know. I knew I had but a glimpse of eternity, and I was speechless. I looked down at His right hand. With it, He still held my left arm. The strength of His gentle hold was still that which supported me. Finally, I mustered the courage to say one word to Him. I asked Him, "Why?"

I raised my head and looked again at His face. I hoped His eyes would somehow help me to comprehend. He looked back at me. As He let go of my arm, I felt Him give me the strength to stand on my own. He said to me, in a voice that I this time felt others could hear, "Try to understand." Then He began to fade. There was a kind of stillness to the air. I knew that someday, I would understand. I tried to say to Him, "Wait, don't go yet." But, I couldn't make a sound.

Where He had just stood was, once again, a dusty dead-end alley overlooking an old city. There was a breeze, but only a slight one. It was a hot afternoon. The sun was still where it had been moments earlier, before an eternity had passed, beating down on the peeling paint of the wall where I had dared to pray along side someone not of my faith. My friend stood quietly leaning against the brick of the building that backed the alley. I knew she was no longer afraid. It seems God had heard her prayer too. Those of the mob that hadn't initially fled as the figure began to emerge from the wall still remained, with one difference. They had laid down their stones.

Though that is when I woke up from the dream, I knew that I would never again view the world the way I had always seen it. I cried frequently in the days and weeks following that dream, as I felt that, quite possibly, it was more than just another dream.

I didn't tell many people about that dream, only just a handful. At the time I wasn't ready to openly discuss my thoughts and dreams.

Now, even as the new millennium begins, wars over ethnic and religious backgrounds continue to plague humanity. It is my hope that by sharing this dream with others, perhaps what I was shown might help to inspire someone, somewhere to seek peace and to lay down arms.

I hope that someday I really will understand what that dream meant. For now, I can only hope that what I saw might help inspire even one soul to learn tolerance and forgiveness.

I don't even pretend to understand the meaning or message of this dream that I had so many years ago. As time has passed, I have come to believe that one possible message might be that when we are lost, there are many roads that we can follow to lead us home again, and that when we love, we help others to find their way home. Perhaps, now, two thousand years after the first message of love was given, one more such message may be recognized and heard.

Kindness gives others hope. Charity sheds light. Caring stirs hearts. But it is love that awakens the soul.

Perhaps as the dawn of this new millennium rises, we can turn our love to those areas of this world where there is no peace. Perhaps our love will help those on distant shores to look beyond their battles and thus find love and peace waiting for them at home.

With our love, we might dare to hope that those restless souls closer to our home also find their way to peace.

Perhaps we could begin by sharing more of our love with our own families and hope that the love we share with those closest to us grows.

May peace and love be with you wherever you find yourself.

Gwyneth Lois Thomas

Imagine that as we approach the millennium, many of us are being called to receive a piece of a giant puzzle, and we bring that piece before the giant table that is called humankind. When all the pieces are brought to the table, we can see the puzzle coming together. What will we find?

In the Book of Genesis, Chapter 5, Verse 24, it is written "And Enoch walked with God; and he was not; for God took him." In the Book of Enoch, which was taken out of the Bible for reasons that confused scholars (see the Richard Laurence translation) it is written that when Enoch flew in spirit up into the Heavens and approached the Lord, a terror and trembling overwhelmed him and he fell upon his face. Page 19 (Chap. XIV), Verses 19-23: "From underneath this mighty throne rivers of flaming fire issued [they used fire as a metaphor for light in those days because they didn't have light bulbs], To look upon it was impossible, One great in glory sat upon it Whose robe was brighter than the sun, and whiter than snow. No Angel was capable of penetrating to view the face of Him, the Glorious and Effulgent; nor could any mortal behold him. A fire was flaming around him."

Elsewhere in the Book of Enoch it is written that even the Angels Gabriel and Michael could not gaze directly upon the face of the Lord because it was too Glorious even for them to bear the sight of. Eventually, after a number of meetings with the

Lord, the Lord tells Enoch to stand up and gaze upon his face, and gain eternal life. This shows that it is possible to gaze upon the face of the Lord, but only for a short moment, and only if the Lord allows it.

From 1945 to 1959, a simple office worker from Amsterdam named Ida Pederman received visitations from the Blessed Virgin Mary who shined with the brilliant and beautiful Light and Glory of God. Mary gave her many powerful messages. But, on her last visitation on May 31, 1959, Ida was about to encounter the Lord for the first time. For what she was about to encounter, all she had previously seen by Mary would be dwarfed. This is an excerpt from the book *Messages of the Lady of All Nations* (the stories of Ida Pederman's visions of Mary and Jesus): "Then the scene changed and all of it became a brilliant, dazzling Sacred Host. It shone so brightly that I shaded my eyes so as not to get blinded, but I was forced to keep looking at it. The Host seemed to be made of white fire. In the center of it was a little opening or hollow; I cannot describe it any better. Then all of a sudden, the Host seemed to burst open, and exposed to my view was a figure, soaring in mid air, a person, exceedingly mighty and strong. Forgive me, please, I cannot convey the strength and majesty this person embodied, it was so overwhelming! I hardly dared look."

"I dared not look upon him" is the point I am trying to make. This is the same as many who have experienced a direct gaze upon the Lord. It is nearly impossible unless the Lord allows it, just as I had previously said. But, again, why does Jesus fit the same description as the Lord whom Enoch visited thousands of years before Jesus was born on earth, unless it is true that Jesus was the Lord God incarnate on earth, the very Lord's self?

It was Emanuel Swedenborg, the 18th-century Christian saint in Sweden, who had met Jesus in person and wrote that Jesus is the Son of God, but not a son like an earthly father gives birth to a child. Swedenborg said that Jesus was the physical incarnation of the Lord, and that is why he was called the Son of God. Before Jesus, the Lord appeared to Enoch, Moses and others as a living spirit, not yet incarnate on Earth. When Jesus incarnated on Earth, he was that same ancient of days, the Lord, but in a body, the so-called Son of God, as Swedenborg wrote.

I feel that Jesus referred to the Father being greater than he because humans could see the body of Christ and his aura but could not perceive how much greater the Lord is, so he extended the term to include the Father, meaning the whole greater mystery of the creation. This is so correct of him because the Jesus-body humans see is not the whole at all, so he must extend himself to his Father, the greater creation which he is "as one with" and is suspended in. And when Jesus returned to spirit in the resurrection, he was that same Lord, the Ancient of Days that Moses and Enoch knew, newly Glorified. I witnessed the same when I gazed upon Jesus both times.

Swedenborg wrote in his book *Heaven and Hell,* page 28, Chapter One: "We need first to know who the God of Heaven is, since the rest depends on this. Throughout the whole of Heaven, no one is recognized as God except the Lord [meaning Jesus]. They say there, just as He Himself taught that: 'He is one with the Father, that the Father is in him, and He in the Father; that anyone who sees Him sees the Father; and that everything Holy comes from him'" (John 10:30, 38: 14:9-11; 16:13-15).

This is a theory from a witnesses unto the Lord, Emanuel Swedenborg. I am not going to argue over it, but I now think it might be true. This would mean that Muslims, Jews, Christians, Native Americans, Buddhists, and the rest, are all right, but each only carries a part of the giant puzzle. This does not mean that everything about each of them is right. Each one is imperfect still and will probably be arguing about God and fighting over it until the end of time. One day they may realize that to love is greater than all debates.

I don't know the answer to this mystery, if there is an actual Father of Jesus. All I know is that when I met Jesus both times, he fits the same description and emanation that Enoch gave when he met the Lord God, and that St. John the Divine gave after meeting Jesus before the Revelations were delivered unto him. I believe Emanuel Swedenborg might be right.

Swedenborg describes that the Angels are really humans who have evolved and earned a life in Heaven where they continue to evolve. He describes an Angel as having the same body as a human, with not one part missing, but in utter supreme perfection and beauty, not only physically, but also with senses far more perceptive and perfect than humans'. I can attest to this also, in that seeing with eyes in the First Heaven is a million times more crystal clear than on earth, and hearing a million time more acute. But seeing and hearing are not limited to the eyes but expanded into every atom in the spiritual body all at once. Swedenborg writes on pages 71-72 of *Heaven and Hell:* "I have seen them in their own light [Angels], many times brighter than earth's moon, and everything about their faces was crisper and clearer in that light than faces of people on earth appear. I have even been given to see an angel of the inmost [Third] heaven. He had a more brilliant and radiant face than the angels of the lower heavens. I looked at him carefully, and he had a human form in all perfection."

Swedenborg writes on page 138 of *Heaven and Hell:* "The reason angels in the inmost heaven are naked is that they are in a state of innocence, and innocence corresponds to nakedness." It is amazing to see that in the highest Heaven Swedenborg visited, angels have returned to the paradise state that Adam and Eve were in when they lived in the Garden of Eden (naked and innocent again), but now it is the Third Heaven. Innocence does not mean ignorance, but it means being "open" to receive the Lord's Glory; thus it is truly wise.

Swedenborg describes the lower Heavens as places where angels are seen wearing beautiful radiant clothes, yet in the highest Heaven he visited, the Third, the Angels were seen living in paradise naked. Could this mean that God's paradise is so liberated? Of course, from my own experience, the ecstasy and Glory in the Third Heaven is incomprehensible to any human, so whatever they are experiencing there is beyond the ecstasy of human sexual lusts. But, perhaps they experience a supreme form of love and communion with each other which helps them evolve in higher ultra-bright ecstasy in the Lord and each other. I do not know because when I was moving through the Third Heaven, I was told there are millions of paradise planets there, but I did not stop on any of them because it was not the will of the Lord for me to stop. Perhaps the Lord wanted me to share the message of spiritual evolution even for the enlightened, that even they will evolve over millions of years into higher spirituality.

In Book II of Corinthians, Chapter 12, Verse 1-5, it reads: "It is expedient for me doubtless to glory. I will come to visions and revelations in the Lord. I knew a man in Christ above 14 years ago, (whether in the body, I cannot tell: or whether out of the body I cannot tell: God knoweth;) such an one caught *up to the third heaven*. And I knew such a man, (whether in the body, or out of the body, I cannot tell: God knoweth;) How that he was caught up unto *paradise,* and heard unspeakable words, which it is not lawful for a man to utter."

This is to show that according to the Bible, a human could first be taken up to Heaven out of body before the Judgment, and secondly could be taken up to paradise. We know that Adam and Eve were living in paradise (the Garden of Eden), and that they were naked before they took in the knowledge of good and evil (the sign of this to God being that they hid their naked bodies with fig leaves) and were kicked out of paradise for doing so. Could the nudity of the angels in the Third Heaven be the unspeakable things that this disciple of Jesus is afraid to utter? Could Swedenborg have discovered a terrible irony, that God is more liberated and full of love than modern humans would ever believe?

The Gospel of Thomas, Verse 37, reveals: "His disciples said, 'When will you become revealed to us and when shall we see you?' Jesus said, 'When you disrobe without being ashamed and take up your garments and place them under your feet like little children and tread on them, then you will see the son of the living one, and you will not be afraid.'" Could Jesus have been speaking about the return to Paradise, the Garden of Eden in the Heavens?

This is by no means to say that what is going on in the Third Heaven is obscene in any way. First, the ecstasy alone, which permeates omnisciently (only a small part of the Glory), is multiples of billions of times greater than the human capacity for physical pleasure. The ability to see with the eyes is multiples of billions of times more crystal clear than the best of human eyes, hearing and feeling are the same, as well as senses humans will not know until they evolve. But, with these supreme senses, the ability to share Glory with each other must be supreme.

No one will enter even the First Heaven and be able to continue in corrupted lusts, greed, selfishness, manipulation, and so on. They will all be washed away. The sacredness of communion between beings (Angels) in any of these Heavens is so full of love and Glory, it will be only for the innocent. Remember, Swedenborg said that nakedness corresponds to innocence. In perfect innocence, there is no violence and there is Glory.

On page 71 of Swedenborg's *Heaven and Hell,* he writes: "On the basis of all my experience, covering to date many years, I can say, I can insist that angels are completely people in form. They do have faces, eyes, ears, chests, arms, hands, and feet. They do see each other, hear each other, and talk with each other.

In short, nothing proper to man whatever is missing, except that they are not clothed with a material body. I have seen them in their own light, many times brighter than earth's moon, and everything about their faces was crisper and clearer in that light than the faces of people on earth appear. I have been given to see an angel of the inmost heaven [Third Heaven, where they live naked]. He had a more brilliant and radiant face than the angels of the lower heavens. I looked at him carefully, and he had a human form in all perfection."

I feel it should be added that "human form in all perfection" includes physical beauty, touch, feeling, seeing, hearing, perceiving, and living in Glory, all a million fold over human qualities in the First Heaven alone. Human beings do not compare in the slightest to the beauty Swedenborg is speaking of, even for those who only notice physical form.

In December, 1997, I had the experience of going to meet such a being, again in my out-of-body state. I was dreaming the usual dreams in the boring Astral world. The Astral world is even more of an illusion than any I have ever experienced. It is experienced by anyone who remembers their dreams. The problem with the Astral world is that all our fears, desires, fantasies, and more, manifest right before our eyes there. Landscapes can change just by turning around, whereas on earth they are consistent. The Hindus call this state "Maya" or illusion of the world. Seeing the terrible illusion of my dream state, I let my Astral body fall to the ground and die. Soon I was in the bright light, and before me stood a total goddess of absolute beauty. Her face and body shined like a full moon, with more clarity than the human eye could reveal by at least one million times. Her eyes sparkled with light and life. Her body and hair were flawless.

Many years ago, long before any of these visitations in the Lord, I was at a ten-day Buddhist Vipassana meditation retreat in British Columbia, led by a monk named Munindra. One night, he told us a story of how one of Buddha's proposed followers, who was obsessed with physical beauty, wanted to marry this most beautiful Indian woman. Buddha advised him that this would be an obstacle to enlightenment, to be so obsessed with this beautiful woman. The man married the woman and was very happy. Later, the man kept noticing how blessed the Buddha's presence was and still wanted to meditate and become enlightened. Later, the Buddha somehow made the Heavens open, and the man was taken up to meet some of the gods and goddesses (probably out-of-body) in the Heaven realms. When the man returned he said to Buddha, "My wife looks like a monkey now." It would be the same for women who have seen men in Heaven.

This is to support what Swedenborg saw in the Heavens also, how much more beautiful and magnificent what Jesus calls "the Resurrected Body" will be, which we will inherit in the Heavens. Of course the beauty and qualities increase with each ascending Heaven.

For years after my visits through six of the Lord's Heavens and just into the edge of the Seventh Heaven, I searched for answers in ancient scriptures as to where I had been. When I was in Lucknow, India, in 1996, I asked a Hindu Guru named Poonjaji about two things. First, Poonjaji had claimed to reach enlightenment and had many face-to-face visits with the Hindu saint Krishna. Krishna is regarded by the *Bhagavad Gita* as the Supreme Being of the universe. Poonjaji never described Krishna as having a face brighter than 1,000 suns, nor did he describe any difficulty at all in gazing upon Krishna. He did however feel a lot of light and love around Krishna. I told him about my first meeting with Jesus and how his face shined brighter than 1,000 suns and Poonjaji got upset at me, frowning.

The *Bhagavad Gita* does reveal that Krishna also has many spiritual levels to his manifested body. When Krishna is made manifest in his universal form, he is described as being ablaze with the light of many suns. In the *Bhagavad-Gita As It Is,* page

563, Text 12 reveals: "If hundreds of thousands of suns were to rise at once into the sky, their radiance might resemble the effulgence of the Supreme Person in that universal form." Perhaps this man Poonjaji did not meet Krishna in Krishna's higher universal body?

I then asked Poonjaji a very difficult question. While in India, I said that I had just read the Buddhist Lankavattara VIII Sutra. In it, a particular Buddha (enlightened one) described the many lifetimes that the Buddha was first enlightened all the way up to the lifetime that the Buddha became the fully enlightened Buddha, called a "Tathagata." That was Gautama the Buddha, also known as Sidhartha or Shakyamuni. It is written in that Sutra that there are many yogis in India and abroad who attain samadhis (enlightenment) from one up to the level of the sixth and think that they have attained full enlightenment. Each of these inward levels of enlightenment corresponds to having access to the same level of Heaven or paradise. Many of them live in these enlightened states and teach that they have attained enlightenment. But this is not the enlightenment of the Tathagatas (full Buddhas).

Later in the Sutra, the Buddha describes that in order to cross from the Sixth into the Seventh enlightenment (samadhi), one has to come out of their extreme bliss and help raise the level of consciousness or healing of other suffering beings in the lower realms. This appears as a sacrifice, and has led many Buddhists to believe that to do so makes one a Bodhisattva, a being of compassion, who helps all other beings into enlightenment before the Bodhisattva goes into Nirvana and becomes a Buddha. The Sutra shows that there are two alternatives at this point, first to go into Nirvana (total cessation) and disappear into the formless Glory of God completely, which is the Seventh Heaven or final enlightenment, never to have your own body again. The second option is to become a Bodhisattva and vow to help all other sentient (sense-oriented) beings to reach full enlightenment. The second option is greater, to become a Bodhisattva. In it, the Sutra says, Nirvana is total enlightenment, but such a being will not evolve past the Seventh Heaven.

To become a Bodhisattva at this level means that such a one will enter the truth body (Body of the Father/Mother or the whole) and maintain an emanation body that can appear to other sentient beings and help them. The person who does this, the Sutra says, will eventually attain to levels of God that are higher than Nirvana, called the Eighth and Ninth samadhis (Heavens). By this, there is evidence of a spiritual evolution higher than Nirvana. Nirvana means to go into total extinction in God. To become a true Bodhisattva at this level means to still have an emanation body and achieve even higher levels of God. For these Bodhisattvas, Buddha is saying, there is no Nirvana or extinction in God.

This is so evolved that to understand what the Buddha attained here means that he, or those who became enlightened by his teachings, could teach souls in all the lower Heavens, and guide them with wisdom to reach the higher Heavens. Even the angels in Swedenborg's highest Third Heaven do not qualify for the Buddhist true meaning of "Full Enlightenment," so they are still evolving in their enlightenment and need guidance and teachings. In this case example, neither do those who are saved and live in the Heavens as ascended gods and goddesses qualify as fully enlightened. However, they are still shining with light and Glory and have supremely wonderful lives. In their own right, they are enlightened, but still evolving in God. The Buddha has very high standards before he calls one "Fully Enlightened." There is certainly no hurry because most of us will have difficulty being full of the Glory in the First Heaven alone. We have millions of years in front of us and even eternity.

If I am any good at math, the Seventh is at least a billion times greater in ecstasy and Glory than the Sixth. Many may not be able to become a Bodhisattva just because of the inability to deal with billions times billions of fold Glory in their being beyond the ability in the Seventh. The Eighth must be billions of times greater in Glory than the Seventh and the Ninth even more so.

After asking this complicated question to Poonjaji in India, I asked why he so easily called persons enlightened. He said "still these Seven levels to go," got upset, and left the gathering. I knew from visiting the entrance of the Seventh Heaven so many years ago that if any person had attained such a level of God's enlightenment "permanently" and was walking around like that, such a being would be so powerful, radiant and capable of great miracles, that it would "knock everyone's lights out" for hundreds of miles. I do not believe any of the great gurus I have met are anywhere near that level of enlightenment. However, they are still great teachers.

After just visiting the edge of the Seventh, there is so much power inside the Glory of the Lord there that I understood when Jesus said, "They go out and create the Heavens all on their own"—such Supremely Enlightened beings could create whole galaxies on their own. Of course there is that much Power and Glory up there. Who else is making all of those galaxies that the Hubble Space Telescope keeps finding in our universe? God and the enlightened Angels are still creating in total freedom. They are not finished yet, nor ever will be.

In the Buddhist *Lotus Sutra* there are clear descriptions of Buddhas creating universes. I see the universe as the whole thing, so they must mean galaxies. Galaxies themselves are a universe in size. I hope this is humiliating and exciting to all of us in the most positive way. We have a lot of room for growth; each of us have billions of years worth.

Could we be heading towards a paradise that is not in some far away imaginary universe, but in our own galaxy, moving closer, evolving towards the center of our own galaxy, and then to higher galaxies? Could the brighter and brighter light and

Glory that I and others experienced when we were taken up have really been the inmost light of the central super sun of the galaxy? I was told by the light that there were millions of paradise planets inside of each ascending Heaven I went through.

To protect the identity of certain persons, I will give case examples of other near death experiencers, without revealing their names. From my meetings at the Institute for Near Death Studies, I will always remember that woman who had a heart attack, died and met Jesus, Krishna, Buddha and some mysterious one she is afraid to tell the name of, all at the same time in the "light." How incredibly blessed she is to have met all of them. I feel certain that Krishna and Buddha can withstand the Glory and are Supremely enlightened far beyond my capabilities to understand, and can live in the Highest Heavens in the Lord.

Whoever came up with the notion that Heaven is a small place, as if only one planet, and that only the people of their little religion get to go there and everyone else goes to hell, is absurd. For such persons, I suggest looking at astronomy and the photos of the myriad galaxies in our universe.

To back up my experience that there are millions of paradise planets in the ascending Heavens, I met an American man last summer who is a Buddhist. He was running in a track and field meet when he had a heart attack and collapsed, dead. The paramedics came and started working on him as he noticed he was no longer in his body, but floating just above it. Suddenly his body turned into a ball of light and started speeding out of and beyond our solar system so fast that he said stars were going by as fast as the posts on a picket fence when you are driving. He then came upon a very bright star-like planet that was shining with spiritual light. He knew he could have gone there and that he would live in paradise. However, he thought about how he had wanted to serve humankind more on earth and soon awoke in his body as the paramedics revived him. Could he have gained the Buddhist notion of having compassion for those who are less fortunate than him and wished to help them, meaning us on earth?

If we should choose to welcome those who are here to help make our world a better place to evolve in, and welcome the healing technologies such as hydrogen fuel, natural gas, aneutronic fusion, sterling solar power, and hundreds more, we will surely evolve and co-create a stable humanity as we move into the millennium.

I hereby ask that every gas station in the world at least make natural gas or hydrogen available at the service station so that we may convert our gasoline engines to run on these clean burning fuels. I hope and pray that we legislate this into action by the year 2010 at the latest.

I also ask that the many persons who have been visited by the Lord or Angels, and have a piece of the giant puzzle, to please bring it to the table of humanity. That way, when we have the pieces together, we may see the new vision of how we will co-create and live in our new world.

We have so much to look forward to in our universe. How will we ever get bored? Impossible!

XXII

The Alpha and the Omega.

The purpose of this section is to first express, with evidentiary support, some meaning to the Lord having said, "I am the Alpha and the Omega" to many witnesses unto him. When I gazed upon the Lord in both meetings, it was very clear to me that Jesus never "did not exist," and is the Supreme Being, which is a definition for Alpha and Omega all in one. The physical body Jesus lived in on earth was born, lived, died on the cross and was resurrected. Jesus was only resurrected back into what Jesus always was, and that is the Lord. The Lord has always been and always will be for eternity.

Because the human brain is born and dies, it is very difficult for the human brain to even conceive of that which always was, that which has no beginning and no end; thus defying the logic of the brain. This is because the brain is locked in time and space and the Lord is not. So, when a person can exit their body, by the Grace of the Lord, and come into their own Spirit, it is much easier, although still tremendously difficult, to gaze upon the experience of the "Alpha and the Omega," which is the eternal experience in the Supreme Being.

The Book of Revelation was delivered to St. John the Divine by the Lord Jesus, the Lord's self, in such a manner. How did John see the Lord? There is an incredible similarity to the many accounts of persons who have seen the Lord. That is, they see the Lord while they are in the "Spirit" or projected out of the body. In the Book of Revelation, Chapter 1, Verse 9-10: "I John, who also am your brother, and companion in tribulation, and in the kingdom and patience of Jesus Christ, was in the isle that is called Patmos, for the word of God, and for the testimony of Jesus Christ. I was in the Spirit on the Lord's day, and heard behind me a great voice, as of a trumpet."

This is first to show that St. John the Divine was in the "Spirit," which means he was not in the body when he met the Lord and received the Revelations. It also says that John had this visitation on the Lord's day. This may have been Christmas or Easter. The reason I feel that such communication with the Lord is done this way and has been done this way since the resurrection is because our Spirit body can see more of the Lord than the limited human eyes and body can. However, this is contradictory to many Christian beliefs. Most Christian scholars I have discussed this with say that there is no such thing as out-of-body travel by Spirit. I believe that the evidence from many experiencers points to the contrary.

The second similarity between direct meetings with the Lord is found in the Book of Revelation, Chapter 1, Verse 17: "And when I saw him, I fell at his feet as dead. And he laid his right hand upon me, saying unto me, Fear not; I am the first and the last." As I have said in my two face-to-face meetings with the Lord, it is almost impossible to stand up in the presence of the Lord.

This point shows a true humility before the Lord. I have told this truth, about falling down to the Lord's feet, to unfortunately inexperienced persons who get angry when they feel that they may have to bow down before God. They perceive this as a power or ego phenomenon of God's. However, it is not so. Anyone who can withstand the Ecstasy and Glory of a sun, let alone galaxies of energy, is welcome to try and stand up. In the second meeting with the Lord, I did stand up, and was instantly crushed with more Glory (Innocence, Love, Ecstasy, Peace, Power, and Beauty) than I could stand to bear. Imagine being crushed with Glory so great it creates galaxies, and that it is far beyond human capabilities to withstand. That is true humility. It is the most beautiful experience of humility I have ever had. In fact, it is the only kind of humility that I will allow myself to fall unto.

In the Book of Revelation, Chapter 1, Verse 8: "I am Alpha and Omega, the beginning and ending, saith the Lord, which is, and which was, and which is to come, the Almighty." This is perhaps the deepest of all parables regarding the greatest mystery of the Lord. It is so vast in meaning I will only attempt to perceive and explain a fraction of it.

This is the Alpha point of the Lord, in Exodus, Chapter 19, Verse 21: "And the Lord said unto Moses, 'Go down, charge the people, lest they break through unto the Lord to gaze, and many of them perish.'" This is the Alpha point in what Jesus (then known as Jehovah) said thousands of years ago. Know that this is the Lord whom no one can gaze upon, because the power and the Glory are so great, it would destroy a being unless the Lord "allows a soul to gaze upon the Lord" by some mysterious power and transformation of the spirit. There is no other god, angel, saint or being ever mentioned who is so full of Glory that no one can withstand even a gaze unless they be pure in heart. This is not to say that the enlightened are not also full of the Lord's Glory and light and that their faces do shine very brightly. I have seen some of them and they do shine brightly. It is to say that there is a Supreme Being.

Many thousands of years later, the Omega point is revealed. We, as humans, could only see a point of observation at a time because the mind with which we operate is a fixed point and we are still in time. A being who lives in time cannot conceive of or experience that which always was and always will be, that which is beyond coming into existence and going out of existence. The human brain cannot grasp the mystery here. The Lord is not a being that came into existence and died on the cross the way we believe it. The Lord has always been. *The Lord was never "not in existence."* The Lord always was, is and will be.

Perhaps the greatest clue that supports what I witnessed directly in the Lord is that Jesus (the Omega) is one and the same as the Lord who appeared to Enoch and Moses (the Alpha), as found in the Book of Revelation, Chapter 1, Verses 13-14: "And in the midst of the seven candlesticks one like unto the Son of man, clothed with a garment down to the foot, and girt about the paps with golden girdle. His head and hairs were white like wool, as white as snow; and his eyes were as a flame of fire." Later, this same Lord who physically looks like God, and who appeared unto Enoch and Moses, speaks in Verse 18, saying: "I am he that liveth, and was dead; and behold, I am alive for evermore, Amen; and have the keys of hell and death."

Even though the Lord who here appears unto St. John the Divine has hair that is white as snow (The Ancient of Days), this is obviously Jesus transfigured into the Alpha point because only Jesus lived and died and now is alive for evermore (as the resurrected Christ). This concurs with what I saw in the Lord: Jesus is one and the same as the biblical Lord God, but even the biblical God is only a fraction of who Jesus really "is."

This is the further Omega point: Now in the Book of Revelation, Chapter 6, Verses 15-17: "And the Kings of the earth, and the great men, and the rich men, and the chief captains, and the mighty men, and every bondman, and every free man, hid themselves in the dens and in the rocks of the mountains; And said to the mountains and rocks, Fall on us, and hide us from the face of him that sitteth on the throne, and from the wrath of the Lamb; For the great day of his wrath is come; and who shall be able to stand?"

In this visitation of the Lord to St. John the Divine, the Lord appears with the same tremendous Glory as the Lord who appeared to Enoch and Moses. This is to show that by the same descriptions, the Lord Jesus seems to be one and the same, just as Swedenborg also had witnessed, as the Lord who appeared unto Enoch and Moses. In the time of Moses, the Lord had not taken unto a human birth yet. I know this statement may drive Jews and Christians insane, but it is what has been witnessed by this visitor unto the Lord Jesus Christ.

The Nag Hammadi Library offers two more spectacular pieces of evidence to support what I witnessed in the Lord. The first is found in The Apocryphon of John. In this book, John, the brother of James, is criticized by a Jewish Pharisee who mocks him: "With deception did this Nazarene deceive you, and he filled your ears with lies, and closed your hearts and turned you from the traditions of your fathers."

John then goes out of the temple and travels into the desert to grieve greatly. He must have been deeply depressed, perhaps even suicidal, to travel all the way out into the desert alone to grieve so greatly. He contemplates and starts talking to God.

It is written: "Straightway, while I was contemplating these things, behold, the heavens opened and the whole creation which is below heaven shone, and the world was shaken. I was afraid, and behold I saw in the light a youth who stood by me. While I looked at him he became like an old man. And he changed his likeness again becoming like a servant." Who is the servant John is seeing? This is really a great surprise. The text continues: "There was not a plurality before me, but there was a likeness with multiple forms in the light, and the likenesses appeared through each other, and the likeness had three forms. He said to me, 'John, John, why do you doubt, or why are you afraid? You are not unfamiliar with this image, are you?—that is, do not be timid! I am the one who is with you always. I am the Father, I am the Mother, I am the Son. I am the undefiled and incorruptible one.'"

The "servant" which John described was Jesus transfiguring himself from a youth, to an old man, and to what was obviously a woman, because Jesus reveals to John that Jesus is the Father, Mother and Son, all in one being. This gives astounding evidence to suggest what I witnessed in meeting Jesus, that Jesus is the Father/Mother as well as the Son of God. Now, this Apocryphon of John reveals the most astounding principle, that Jesus can also appear as the Mother.

When Jesus spoke the first words to me in October, 1994 ("I have appeared to a number of people throughout history, but at different levels of their spiritual ability. No one has seen me in my entirety. Even now, you are not seeing me in my entirety. It is not possible at this time"), Jesus delivered the message like the Lord did nearly 2,000 years ago. This is a powerful statement because, if I heard it correctly, if "no one" has seen Jesus in the Lord's entirety, this would mean that there cannot be anyone greater or spiritually more advanced in the universe than Jesus in Jesus' totality. That would mean that Jesus would have to be the great God, the Supreme Creator of all the universe. I realize this is a huge claim; however, it is not unfounded. The way the Bible has been interpreted, the statement I heard from Jesus would have to be considered false. The Bible scholars of yesterday and today only recognize Jesus as the Son of God, not God as the Lord's self.

Because I know I heard those words correctly when I met Jesus, I had to search for the evidence to support them. The evidence is found clearly in the Nag Hammadi Library, Trimorphic Protennoia, Page 521: "So, now, I was dwelling in them in the form of each one. The Archons thought that I was their Christ. Indeed I dwell in everyone. Indeed within those whom I revealed myself as Light I eluded the Archons. I am their beloved, for in that place I clothed myself as the Son of the Archigenetor, and I was like him until the end of his decree, which is the ignorance of Chaos. And among the Angels I revealed myself in their likeness, and among the Powers as if I were one of them, but among the Sons of Man as if I were a Son of Man, even though I am the Father of everyone."

This paragraph is so vast in knowledge, that to interpret it, one would be blind if they did not read the whole Nag Hammadi Library. Even then, they still may not know what it reveals. Jesus is showing here that, first, Jesus was dwelling in the form of each one of these great beings all at their own particular spiritual level of development, and there are many levels presented here. The highest beings are angels. To them, Jesus appeared as an angel, though obviously he is within and above the spiritual development of an angel. Below angels are the Archons (demi-gods) to which Jesus appeared, clothing himself as the "Son of the Archigenetor"—meaning the Son of the Chief of the demi-gods. This may even have been what Jesus meant, in part, when Jesus appeared to us on earth as the Son of God some 2,000 years ago. Still, this was only a fraction of who Jesus really is. The next spiritual level below the Archons is the Powers and Humankind. Jesus says that he appeared "among the Sons of Man as if I were a Son of Man" and that is what we saw on earth some 2,000 years ago. When Jesus appeared as the Son of Man, this was amongst one of the lowest levels of spiritual development that the Lord appeared in, as recorded in the Nag Hammadi Library.

I want to try and give even deeper insight to this most astonishing paragraph in the "Trimorphic Protennoia" because it gives climactic wisdom to the first words Jesus ever spoke to me, "I have appeared to a number of persons throughout history but at different levels of their spiritual ability. No one has seen me in my entirety. Even now, you are not seeing me in my entirety. It is not possible at this time." This paragraph in the "Trimorphic Protennoia" is a masterpiece!

Where Jesus says, "The Archons thought that I was their Christ," we have the example that the Archons (demi-god[desses]) reveal that Jesus also appeared to the demigods and goddesses and they thought that they had seen who Jesus really is. They even made philosophies about who Jesus is, that he was the Son of the God, Yaltabaoth (one of the gods of the Old Testament), who was, in their eyes, a higher being than Jesus. But, they did and do not know that Jesus was eluding them, as Jesus reveals, "Indeed within those in whom I revealed myself as Light, I eluded the Archons. I am their beloved, for in that place, I clothed myself as the Son of the Archigenetor, and I was like him until the end of his decree, which is, the ignorance of Chaos."

To understand that the Spiritual universe is made up of three larger realms of existence, found in all major religions, (Lower or Hell planets, Middle or demi-god[dess] planets (Archons), and Upper or Angelic Planets, (Aeons), Jesus is revealing here that "I eluded the Archons" because they, as we know, think they are the most advanced beings in the universe. They are blinded by the veil that prevents them from seeing the Aeon or Angelic Planetary realms where truly enlightened beings live much of the time above them. Jesus also tells here that the realm of the Archons is "the ignorance of Chaos" which is fitting because the Archons are the apex of the duality of good and evil. They are the highest beings in the realm of good and evil. But beyond and above "good and evil" the Angelic or Planetary realms of the Aeons dwarf them with the supernatural Light and Glory of God and Jesus in the Highest. This is where Jesus reveals in this paragraph, that "even though I am the Father of everyone."

This example in the Nag Hammadi Library agrees with the first words that Jesus spoke to me in October, 1994: "I have appeared to a number of people throughout history, but at different levels of their spiritual ability." For no one to have seen Jesus in his entirety, Jesus would have to be God, the Supreme Being, but having hid this truth as a great mystery. This is confirmed in the Nag Hammadi Library, Trimorphic Protennoia, when Jesus concludes: "Even though I am the father of everyone." Really, it is the Father-Mother of everyone, if you account for what John witnessed. All things considered, the Lord is so inconceivably great in Glory, the Lord will always remain a mystery to all.

Could we all have been fighting religious wars over the same Lord all of these years? By our fighting, what have we learned of love? How much love have each of us developed in our ability to feel, let alone Glory? The reason I am asking this is because the whole transformation will depend on this, and little, if anything, else. Wisdom is to grant us the intelligence to recognize all of our acts of violence, and to resolve them, to recognize our problems.

Religious wars are created out of ignorance and, by the wisdom of the Lord, must be avoided at all costs. We must evolve into a higher humanitarian togetherness if we are going to survive. Also, we must drop our barriers and recognize our talents and work together to solve international problems.

Large global populations cannot live by old tribal community formulas unless they develop clean science and technology. This is because, just on the basis of cooking food and staying warm, populations would have to burn nearly every tree, just as in India today. Just the need to bathe their bodies would pollute all rivers. By not evolving technologically as a large population, this becomes a form of severe violence to the ecology and each other.

Large populations relying on pollution-based energy technology would eventually reach critical mass and destroy the planet. Unless energy technology research at least starts developing natural gas for automobiles, heating and cooking, advanced solar power, aneutronic non-radioactive nuclear energy, zero point energy and hydrogen fuel for cars and homes, there cannot be a survival of the planet.

In an overpopulated world (a world without a clean energy base), critical mass will be reached sooner rather than later. Even though a family may appear calm and resided, but as a large family, especially a family that is not rooted in intelligence, this does not set an example of peace. Overpopulation appears to be a form of violence to each other and the earth.

Already, signs in the ecology of the destruction of our forests, air, ozone, each other, animals, mammals and smaller creatures is real and severe. Mutated frogs are being found all over the world. The Lord hears their suffering. Fish are mutating and dying by the thousands of a strange disease. The Lord hears their call. The little creatures at the base of the seafood chain are dying. The Lord even hears their calls.

What is it going to take before we are willing to change? Do we really want to live in a self-created hell? Or, do we want to shine with Love and evolve in Glory? If we choose love and Glory, we will be able to withstand the transformation of the Holy Ghost, and evolve in the Lord's Heavens. And, when the Lord does come (at what time no one knows, not even the Lord) those who live in Love and wisdom will see the Lord and be filled with as much Glory as they can partake in. It will be the greatest celebration ever.

What will happen when the Lord does come? When I saw the Lord both times, I had no doubt that the Lord had the power to create planets and galaxies at will. It is entirely evident in the Lord's Glory. Even Angels, who are "as one" with the will of the Lord, can create new paradise worlds all on their own with ease, and Supremely Enlightened ones whole galaxies. The reason no one tells anyone what to do in the Heavens is clear, in that this is the only real freedom possible. Many persons believe that if they surrender to God, they loose their freedom. They loose their freedom to be bonded to an ego only. There is so much more freedom in the Lord than there is in any world where egos (good and evil) clash and oppress each other. In fact, there is hardly any freedom on earth at all compared to the Heavens. The Lord said to me and you, "Because the Heavens are suspended in love, everything is created out of love. So nothing unholy can manifest here." This is total freedom.

When the Lord comes to earth, I feel it is entirely possible that all of the elements in our bodies and earth will seem to dissolve into spirit energy. The Lord is so powerful, that this could actually happen. This is because the Lord is so much greater in the Lord's resurrected body of light than the Lord appeared while in a human body as Jesus Christ.

In the Book of Matthew, Chapter 24, Verse 23-26: "Then if any man shall say unto you, Lo, here is Christ, or there; believe it not. For there shall arise false Christs, and false prophets, and shall show great signs and wonders; in so much that, if it were possible, they shall deceive the very elect. Behold, I have told you before. Wherefore if they shall say unto you, Behold, he is in the dessert; go not forth: behold, he is in the secret chambers; believe it not."

Verses 29-30: "Immediately after the tribulation of those days shall the sun be darkened, and the moon shall not give her light, and the stars shall fall from heaven, and the powers of the heavens shall be shaken: And then shall appear the sign of the Son of man in heaven; and then shall all the tribes of the earth mourn, and they shall see the Son of man coming in the clouds of heaven with power and great glory."

Where will the Lord go to sit when the Lord arrives on earth? In the ancient Book of Enoch (Chapter XXIV), there is a clue. While Enoch is flying with the holy Angels, getting a tour of the Heavens and mysterious places on earth: "He answered me, saying, That mountain which thou beholdest, the extent of whose head resembles the seat of the Lord, will be the seat on which shall sit the holy and great Lord of glory, the everlasting King, when he shall come and descend to visit the earth with goodness."

The mysterious question is, where is this mountain on earth that the Lord will come and sit upon? I will tell you that the ancient Russian Shamans and the Tibetan Buddhist know more about where this place is than most Christians on earth. It is a secret hidden place in the mountains. If you read the Book of Enoch, you will get a clue. There is a city of the Lord's Angels based on earth since the earth began, but no one may enter before the Lord returns, unless it is the will of the Lord. Few have been there. Even fewer have returned. What the Tibetans and other Buddhists know about it is elaborate because the Buddha himself had visited there.

The Buddhist prophecy of the end of times is almost identical to the Christian Revelations. Very briefly, it goes like this: Once the evil king Rudara Chakrin (anti-Christ, or anti-love and Glory) had conquered the whole earth and destroyed all the armies, the mysterious mists cleared and revealed the entrance to the hidden secret city, which had been sealed until the end of times. In the hidden city live great numbers of gods and goddesses (angels) who have tremendous spiritual powers, ready to remove the evil king from the earth. The Buddhist gods and goddesses here have what is called the "power of the mirror." It is written that they just mirror the violence of the evil king Rudara and his armies, all of his attacks, back into him, and he is destroyed by his own violence.

The Buddhist example of the power of the gods and goddesses is not unlike the powers that angels have, as described by Swedenborg in his book *Heaven and Hell.* On page 167 it reads: "The power angels have in the spiritual world is so great that if I were to cite at this point everything I have seen, it would be beyond belief. If there is something left there that needs to be removed because it is an opposition to the Divine design, they raze and destroy it by sheer force of will, with a look. I have seen mountains, under the control of evil people, razed and destroyed, sometimes shaken from boundary to boundary as if by an earthquake, the central peaks parting into a chasm, the evil ones on them engulfed. . . . A multitude is powerless against them."

We can see from the Word that angels have similar power in the natural world (earth) when they are allowed to use it. In the Second Book of Samuel, Chapter 24, Verse 17: "The angel stretched out his hand upon Jerusalem to destroy it; [the Lord] repented him of the evil, and said to the angel that destroyed the people 'It is enough; stay now thine hand.'"

Some might ask the question, Is it true that nothing unholy can manifest in the Heavens because everything there is suspended in love and Glory and all is created out of it and by it? The answer is: There are rare interactions between spirits who live in hell planets or war planets trying to establish contact or set up bases in the higher Heavens or planets. This could not be possible for humans, but only for the angels that fell into inner conflict when they try to regain what they lost. The only place this could happen is on the border of the First Heaven planets and the Astral world which is just below.

As described in the *Tibetan Book of the Dead* by Robert Thurman, the ancient Tibetans point out that the anti-gods/goddesses (fallen angels) are always trying to take over the planets of the gods/goddesses but they never win. The anti-gods or Titans are warriors (proving they live in conflict), and appear much greater than human beings.

Rudara Chakrin, who must be an anti-god, is known as the evil king because he misinterpreted the meaning of Nirvana (enlightenment) as being beyond good and evil, and therefore one can do whatever one wants to and there is no judgment. Rudara's reckless interpretation leads to a society of chaos and war and corruption.

Once Rudara found the hidden city, he sent his armies in to take it over. However, the gods and goddesses who live there are so powerful, possessing the power of the mirror, that they destroyed the evil king with ease—the same kind of ease that Swedenborg witnessed the angels had in removing opposition. Because they do this with such ease, it can also hardly be called a war because it would only last for a short time.

Getting back to the Lord's return arrival on earth, what finally happens after the Lord's angels easily remove the anti-christ armies, is easy to deduct.

Because beings who are not learned and evolved in love are so terrified of love and Glory, it appears to them as a "wrath" because the Lord's love and Glory are so great they will writhe in pain and flee in terror just on the arrival of the Lord alone.

None of these anti-gods or fallen angels will be able to be near the Lord, even within scope.

Is it going to be important to actually physically be near to where the Lord is going to sit when the Lord arrives? The answer is "no." Firstly because very few will be able to stand that close because of their own lack of spiritual development. Secondly because when each of us is called, or long before, our bodies will transform into Celestial bodies, and we will be taken from any point on the earth to the Lord. Don't worry. This may sound like a great miracle, but when you see how much power and Glory the Lord has, you will also say that it is so easy for the Lord.

Each will be taken as spirits, and it will be as was revealed to me in this message. Most will hide their faces and be in the Lord's presence for a very short duration, unless they can withstand the Glory, and the Lord will not turn those away. Just because you may only last one or two seconds, does not mean you will not live in one of the Heavens or the New Earth. Direct contact with the Lord is so great, even the highest angels cannot penetrate the full view of the Lord in the Lord's entirety. No one can. But to live in the Lord's emanations (Heavens) is much easier. Those who cannot withstand the cleansing by the Holy Ghost, they will flee in terror and create hells on their own, by their own lack of love and wisdom, just as they did on earth. Then the Lord will decide what to do with them.

In the Book of Matthew, Chapter 24, Verses 40-42: "Then shall two be in the field; the one shall be taken, and the other left. Two women shall be grinding at the mill; the one shall be taken, and the other left. Watch therefore: for ye know not what hour your Lord doth come."

What will you do, and how will you live your life from this day on to prepare yourself to withstand the Lord's Love, Ecstasy, Peace, Power, Light, Beauty, Innocence, Graces, and more?

I pray that you all choose love, wisdom and healing for each other and the beautiful creation we have been given to live and evolve on, our very own earth.

Peace, all peace!

CHAPTER FOUR

Meeting with Mary and Third Meeting with Jesus Christ

Astral (Middle) Universe
February 16, 1999, 1:40 AM

XXIII

Vision of Mary, Mother of Jesus,
January 10, 1999, 3:00-3:30 A.M.

This was my first Vision of the Virgin Mary. I was taken by the Holy Spirit out of body. It was so beautiful. Mary was shining in the most radiant and graceful, easy, peaceful light inside the middle (purgatory) realm above a tall skyscraper. There were Angels shaped like doves flying in and out of her body of light as though she were a portal between heaven and earth. It was so beautiful to see this.

Then, she transfigured herself into a ball of light that was so beautiful and soft, it reminded me of the Biblical descriptions of "The Burning Bush" which spoke to Moses. Suddenly I could not remember what she looked like before she became the ball of light, but why? Impossible to remember. Perhaps it is a mystery. I approached the ball of light (which was Mary) and it moved right inside of my chest (heart) and soothed and filled my heart with immense peace, beauty and grace. It was a very different light than the Light of Jesus Christ, yet is contained in the Light of Jesus Christ. After meeting Jesus I could clearly see that Jesus is the source of the light and all is contained in Jesus, while, my inexperienced and humble opinion is that Mary is a recipient and reflection of the Light of Christ, yet reflects the Light of Christ perfectly. It was also the most feminine and softly loving light I had ever known. The light was easy to look at, easy to bear the Glory of, and not so bright as the sun, which made it easy to look at.

After experiencing the ball of light (which was Mary in a transfigured form) I went down to purgatory (Astral realm) below and told everyone there that I had seen the Virgin Mary. They asked, "Where is she?" and I said, "Up above." I then started to fly upwards to go and greet her once more and suddenly another transfigured form of the Mary appeared below me, in a white gown, crying tears of blood which flowed onto her white gown. Her eyes were flowing with blood. This part of the vision was so terrifying to experience that anyone who does not understand her compassion would die of fright. She was carrying the suffering (sins) of those in the lower worlds (purgatory and hell) and trying to release some of their suffering so that they might come to know love. How deep her compassion is, I thought.

Only if the suffering souls felt love, could they know what love is, and by love, begin redemption from their sins. She carried so much suffering it was incredible. As she was carrying the sins of the souls in Purgatory and Hell, she was full of love and smiling. The pain and suffering of those souls, although she bore it, did not affect her experience of God's love, all pervading her being.

As I flew upwards to greet the Mary Above (the higher form of Mary) this compassionate form of Mary (who appeared to be about 14 years old) grabbed hold of my feet. The words "You are a Stigmatist" came into my mind which I thought I was telling her because I thought the Virgin Mary was above in the light and why was this form of Mary below holding my feet bearing the wounds of stigmata? A mystery? This was Mary showing me that she simultaneously exists in Heaven (the splendid form of Mary always radiating and reflecting God's Glory of Innocence, Love, Ecstasy, Peace, Graces, Wisdom and Beauty), and she simultaneously exists in the formless holy spirit (the Ball or Globe of light) and also in her most compassionate form (as the bearer of sins crying tears of blood because she tries to wipe away the suffering of souls in purgatory and hell). The implications of this are staggering and so sophisticated, it will take much research and compilation of ancient texts to explain some of the most miraculous wisdom of our Lord: how our Lord can simultaneously exist in Heaven while also manifesting in the lower worlds to help other lost souls.

Suddenly, as we flew together upwards, my feet began to experience the most intense physical pain I have ever felt, as though nails were piercing my bones. I was screaming in pain and agony, flying upwards when the message "These are the sins of the world. Experience them as they offend God's purity." She was having me experience the sins of the world inside the pain in my feet which was so excruciating I thought I would bleed from the pain. It was as though I was experiencing the nails in Christ's feet during the crucifixion, but on no other place on my body (not my hands, side nor head) did I feel pain.

Then I felt the most terrible evil inside the pain (sins) of the world against God. I heard the words, "Feel the evil the sins of the world have caused." Again Mary was unaffected by this evil because she is a perfect reflection of the Light of our Lord. The evil was a void icy and cold where no love or Glory of God existed. It was terrible. I could not bear the pain nor the evil of the world and I came back into my body because I could not bear the pain in the vision any longer. Yet when I returned into my body, I could still feel the pain in my feet so intense I was sure I was bleeding, but I was not. Then the pain subsided and I saw brilliant peaceful light filling my head. I was awake for hours and said many "Hail Mary"s.

This experience shows that the sins of the world against God are a Crisis in the eyes of God. They are far worse than any person can imagine. Mary has to emanate herself down to these lower worlds and bear the sins (take the suffering of them into herself) of sinners to help them experience love. It is only by experiencing and living a life of love that one can enter heaven and be saved. She is so merciful in doing this. The ultimate mercy. The expression on her face, as she was crying tears of blood, was unfathomable joy and compassion. Can you imagine a mother crying, knowing her children are suffering so much, and not one ounce of their suffering affects the continuous flow of compassion and love she has, yet she bears it? This is because Mary "is" the embodiment of feminine compassion and Heavenly Grace.

As she had me experience the pain of the sins of the world, she was asking me to help take away the sins of others by bearing their pain. This is the example of compassion. When a mother holds a child that has injured itself, she does not take away the pain, but her love and compassion makes the pain bearable. The child becomes absorbed in its mother's compassionate love and transcends pain. It is the experience of compassion itself, and when the one who suffers absorbs their consciousness in the compassion, it as if carries them out of the pain. This is how the experience of compassionate love transcends sin. Sin causes a soul to experience spiritual pain and suffering in the here-now and in the after-life. If a soul suffers too much, they will cause suffering and grief to others. This is what an evil person is: a soul who has sinned too much and feels too much spiritual pain, and thus causes others to suffer the same by cruel deeds. Evil souls cause others to suffer by their anger, greed, corrupted lusts, violence, and lack of love: hence, evil and spiritual pain are closely related.

Mary's example of compassion shows that, first, because of sin a human being will suffer and not experience the omnipresent Glory of God. Depending on how severe the sins of a person are, if they have a lot of sin, the more their soul will suffer spiritually. To suffer spiritually means that a person is stuck in pleasure and pain both (the human condition). This is to say that when a rich person escapes physical and some mental suffering, that they are not free from sin. However, if a rich person has compassion for a poor person, and they both experience the blessing of compassion, both of them may begin to heal and rise above sin. But if compassion does not arise in the rich person's heart for the poor, and the poor suffering person does not experience compassion, both will remain in sin. If the rich person is too stubborn to have compassion, the rich person will remain aloof from God's love. If the poor person is too proud to accept the compassion of another human being (and give compassion), this poor person will remain in their spiritual suffering and have a difficult time rising above the human condition of pleasure and pain (sin).

After this meeting, I cannot express the importance of compassion, to give it and to receive it. It is almost a miracle that when we suffer, if compassion is born in us, for our own suffering and of others, that this blossoming of compassion is the wave that we can ride and take us out of sin and into the experience of love, and ultimately through Heaven's proverbial Gates.

Jesus has said in "The Acts of John" from the "Hymn of Christ" to the disciples before being crucified: "What I am you shall see when you come. If you knew how to suffer you would be able not to suffer. Learn how to suffer and you shall be able not to suffer."

Is the reason we suffer just so that we learn "compassion," the very miracle that carries us out of suffering? Is this what Jesus meant? If so, we have so much to learn about compassion, the giving and receiving of it, and our own purpose in evolving out of our own suffering. It could even mean, that while we are sick and dying, if we heal others and give to the poor, while we are the ones who suffer, that by even this we shall be set free of our sins.

XXIV

"The Passing of Mary"
as written by James, the brother of Jesus.

In that time before the Lord came to His passion, and among many words which the mother asked of the Son, she began to ask Him about her own departure, addressing Him as follows: O most dear Son, I pray Thy holiness, that when my soul goes out of my body, Thou let me know on the third day before; and do Thou, beloved Son, with Thy angels, receive it."[2]

Then He received the prayer of His beloved mother, and said to her: "O palace and temple of the living God, O blessed mother,[3] O queen of all saints, and blessed above all women, before thou carriedst me in thy womb, I always guarded thee, and caused thee to be fed daily with my angelic food,[4] as thou knowest: how can I desert thee, after thou hast carried me, and nourished me, and brought me down in flight into Egypt, and endured many hardships for me? Know, then, that my angels have always guarded thee, and will guard thee even until thy departure. But after I undergo suffering for men, as it is written, and rise again on the third day, and after forty days ascend into heaven, when thou shall see me coming to thee[5] with angels and archangels, with saints and with virgins, and with my disciples, know for certain that thy soul will be separated from the body, and I shall carry it into heaven, where it shall never at all have tribulation or anguish." Then she joyed and gloried, and kissed the knees of her Son, and blessed the Creator of heaven and earth, who gave her such a gift through Jesus Christ her Son.

In the second year, therefore, after the ascension of our Lord Jesus Christ, the most blessed Virgin Mary continued always in prayer day and night. And on the third day before she passed away, an angel of the Lord came to her, and saluted her, saying: "Hail, Mary, full of grace! the Lord be with thee."

And she answered, saying: "Thanks to God."

Again he said to her: "Receive this palm which the Lord promised to thee." And she, giving thanks to God, with great joy received from the hand of the angel the palm sent to her. The angel of the Lord said to her: "Thy assumption will be after three days."

And she answered: "Thanks to God."[6]

Then she called Joseph of the city of Arimathaea, and the other[7] disciples of the Lord; and when they, both relations and acquaintances, were assembled, she announced her departure to all standing there. Then the blessed Mary washed[8] herself, and dressed herself like a queen, and waited the advent of her Son, as He had promised to her. And she asked all her relations to keep beside[9] her, and give her comfort. And she had along with her three virgins, Sepphora, Abigea, and Zaël; but the disciples of our Lord Jesus Christ had been already dispersed throughout the whole world to preach to the people of God.

Then at the third hour[10] there were great thunders, and rains, and lightnings, and tribulation, and an earthquake,[11] while queen Mary was standing in her chamber. John the evangelist and apostle was suddenly brought from Ephesus, and entered the chamber of the blessed Mary, and saluted her, and said to her: "Hail, Mary, full of grace! the Lord be with thee."

And she answered: "Thanks to God." And raising herself up, she kissed Saint John. And the blessed Mary said to him: "O my dearest son, why hast thou left me at such a time, and hast not paid heed to the commands of thy Master, to take care of me, as He commanded thee while He was hanging on the cross?"

And he asked pardon with bended knee. Then the blessed Mary gave him her benediction, and again kissed him. And when she meant to ask him whence he came, and for what reason he had come to Jerusalem, behold, all the disciples of the Lord, except Thomas who is called Didymus, were brought by a cloud to the door of the chamber of the blessed Mary. They stood and went in, and saluted the queen with the following words, and adored her: "Hail, Mary, full of grace! the Lord be with thee." And she eagerly rose quickly, and bowed herself, and kissed them, and gave thanks to God. These are the names of the disciples of the Lord who were brought thither in the cloud: John the evangelist and James his brother, Peter and Paul, Andrew, Philip, Luke, Barnabas, Bartholomew and Matthew, Matthias who is called Justus,[12] Simon the Chananaean, Judas and his brother, Nicodemus and Maximianus, and many others who cannot be numbered. Then the blessed Mary said to her brethren: "What is this, that you have all come to Jerusalem?"

Peter, answering, said to her: "We had need to ask this of thee, and dost thou question us? Certainly, as I think, none of us knows why we have come here today with such rapidity. I was at Antioch, and now I am here." All declared plainly the place where they had been that day. And they all wondered that they were there when they heard these things.

The blessed Mary said to them: "I asked my Son, before He endured the passion, that He and you should be at my death; and He granted me this gift. Whence you may know that my departure will be to-morrow.[13] Watch and pray with me, that when the Lord comes to receive my soul, He may find you watching." Then all promised that they would watch. And they watched and prayed the whole night, with psalms and chants, with great illuminations.

And when the Lord's day came, at the third hour, just as the Holy Spirit descended upon the apostles in a cloud,[14] so Christ descended with a multitude of angels, and received the soul of His beloved mother. For there was such splendour and perfume of sweetness, and angels singing the songs of songs, where the Lord says, "As a lily among thorns, so is my love among the daughters,"[15] that all who were there present fell on their faces, as the apostles fell when Christ transfigured Himself before them on Mount Thabor, and for a whole hour and a half no one was able to rise. But when the light went away, and at the same time with the light itself, the soul of the blessed virgin Mary was taken up into heaven with psalms, and hymns, and songs of songs. And as the cloud went up the whole earth shook, and in one moment all the inhabitants of Jerusalem openly saw the departure of St. Mary.

And that same hour Satan entered into them, and they began to consider what they were to do with her body. And they took up weapons, that they might burn her body and kill the apostles, because from her had gone forth the dispersions of Israel, on account of their sins and the gathering together of the Gentiles. But they were struck with blindness, striking their heads against the walls, and striking each other.[16] Then the apostles, alarmed by so much brightness, arose, and with psalms carried the holy body down from Mount Zion to the valley of Jehoshaphat. But as they were going in the middle of the road, behold, a certain Jew,[17] Reuben by name, wishing to throw to the ground the holy bier with the body of the blessed Mary. But his hands dried up, even to the elbow; whether he would or not, he went down even to the Valley of Jehoshaphat, weeping and lamenting because his hands were raised to the bier, and he was not able to draw back his hands to himself. And he began to ask the apostles[18] that by their prayer he might be saved and made a Christian. Then the apostles, bending their knees, asked the Lord to let him loose. And he, being healed that same hour, giving thanks to God and kissing the feet of the queen of all the saints and apostles, was baptized in that same place, and began to preach the name of our God Jesus Christ.

Then the apostles with great honour laid the body in the tomb, weeping and singing through exceeding love and sweetness. And suddenly there shone round them a light from heaven, and they fell to the ground, and the holy body was taken up by angels into heaven.

Then the most blessed Thomas was suddenly brought to the Mount of Olivet, and saw the most blessed body going up to heaven, and began to cry out and say: "O holy mother, blessed mother, spotless mother, if I have now found grace because I see thee, make thy servant joyful through thy compassion, because thou art going to heaven." Then the girdle with which the apostles had encircled the most holy body was thrown down from heaven to the blessed Thomas. And taking it, and kissing it, and giving thanks to God, he came again into the Valley of Jehoshaphat. He found all the apostles and another great crowd there beating their breasts on account of the brightness which they had seen.

And seeing and kissing each other, the blessed Peter said to him: "Truly thou hast always been obdurate and unbelieving, because for thine unbelief it was not pleasing to God that thou shouldst be along with us at the burial of the mother of the Saviour."

And he, beating his breast, said: "I know and firmly believe that I have always been a bad and an unbelieving man; therefore I ask pardon of all of you for my obduracy and unbelief." And they all prayed for him.

Then the blessed Thomas said: "Where have you laid her body?" And they pointed out the sepulchre with their finger. And he said: "The body which is called most holy is not there."

Then the blessed Peter said to him: "Already on another occasion thou wouldst not believe the resurrection of our Master and Lord at our word, unless thou went to touch Him with thy fingers, and see Him; how wilt thou believe us that the holy body is here?"

Still he persists saying: "It is not here." Then, as it were in a rage, they went to the sepulchre, which was a new one hollowed out in the rock, and took up the stone; but they did not find the body, not knowing what to say, because they had been convicted by the words of Thomas. Then the blessed Thomas told them how he was singing mass in India—he still had on his sacerdotal robes. He, not knowing the word of God, had been brought to the Mount of Olivet, and saw the most holy body of the blessed Mary going up into heaven, and prayed her to give him a blessing. She heard his prayer, and threw him her girdle which she had about her. And the apostles seeing the belt which they had put about her, glorifying God, all asked pardon of the blessed Thomas, on account of the benediction which the blessed Mary had given him, and because he had seen the most holy body going up into heaven. And the blessed Thomas gave them his benediction, and said: "Behold how good and how pleasant it is for brethren to dwell together in unity!"[19]

And the same cloud by which they had been brought carried them back each to his own place, just like Philip when he baptized the eunuch, as is read in the Acts of the Apostles;[20] and as Habakkuk the prophet carried food to Daniel, who was in the lions' den, and quickly returned to Judaea.[21] And so also the apostles quickly returned to where they had at first been, to preach to the people of God. Nor is it to be wondered at that He should do such things, who went into the virgin and came out of her though her womb was closed; who, though the gates were shut, went in to His disciples;[22] who made the deaf to hear, raised the dead, cleansed the lepers, gave sight to the blind,[23] and did many other wonderful things. To believe this is no doubtful matter.

I am Joseph who laid the Lord's body in my sepulchre, and saw Him rising again; and who, before the ascension and after the ascension of the Lord, always kept his most sacred temple the blessed ever-virgin Mary, and who have kept in writing and in my breast the things which came forth from the mouth of God, and how the things mentioned above were done by the judgment of God. And I have made known to all, Jews and Gentiles, those things which I saw with my eyes, and heard with my ears; and as long as I live I shall not cease to declare them. And her, whose assumption is at this day venerated and worshipped throughout the whole world, let us assiduously entreat that she be mindful of us in the presence of her most pious Son in heaven, to whom is praise and glory through endless ages of ages. Amen.[24]

XXV

I am taken out of body by the Holy Spirit aboard a space/temple ship to meet Jesus Christ, February 16, 1999, 1:40 A.M.

The mystery of Jesus' first words to me in October, 1994 are evolving deeper, that "I have appeared to a number of people throughout history, but at different levels of their spiritual ability. No one has ever seen me in my entirety. Even now, you are not seeing me in my entirety. It is not possible at this time."

These words of Jesus to me in October, 1994, are confirmed in scripture once again, found in the book *New Testament Apocrypha* (edited by Wilhelm Schneemelcher), "The Acts of John," when Jesus has appeared to John inside of a cave in a blaze of light during his own crucifixion. Jesus tells John, "For what you are you see, I have shown it to you; but what I am is known to me alone and no one else. So let me have what is mine; what is yours you must see through me; but to see me truly is, as I said, not possible, except for what you are able to know, being a kinsman."

Written in "The Gospel of Thomas," Jesus said, "Let him who seeks continue seeking until he finds. When he finds, he will be astonished, and he will rule over the all." This third meeting with Jesus I am about to share with you is baffling and disturbing to human minds about how great the Lord Jesus Christ really is. It is so baffling, I do not fully understand what Jesus showed me in this vision, but I will try my best to reveal what I do understand about it.

As I have mentioned before, there are three basic levels of the spiritual and physical universe common to all major religions. First, as noted in Christianity, Islam, Judaism, Hinduism and Buddhism, there is hell or otherwise known as planets of war and ignorance. Secondly, noted by all these religions is a middle region known by Catholicism as Purgatory, by Emanuel Swedenborg as "The World of Spirits," by Hinduism as the planets of the demi-god(desses) (and by many Hindu Yogis as the Astral Universe filled with paradise planets), and by Buddhism as the realms of the anti-gods and god(desses). And third, as noted by all these religions is Heaven or "The Heavens," in Catholicism as Heaven, by Emanuel Swedenborg as "The Heavens" (plural because they ascend into higher and higher heavens), by Hinduism as the planets of the enlightened which evolve into higher and higher planets (and by some East Indian yogis as the Causal realms), and by Buddhism as the realms of the Buddhas, or clear light realms, which ascend into higher and higher (up to nine) clear light realms. These are the highest of spiritual realms known to great saints.

Noted by almost all these religions, there are lower and higher hell realms, lower and higher astral realms, and lower and higher clear light Heavens. From my own experience of being taken by the Lord through Seven of these ascending clear light heavens, I can attest that these are very real truths.

In the Nag Hammadi Library (page 521), "Trimorphic Protennoia," we find a clue of Jesus appearing throughout these different levels of the spiritual universe, eluding the Archons (the demi-god[desses] from the Astral or middle of the spiritual galaxy or universe), who indeed thought that Jesus was their Christ: "So now, I was dwelling in them, in the form of each one. The Archons thought that I was their Christ. Indeed I dwell in everyone. Indeed within those in whom I revealed myself as Light I eluded the Archons." How did Jesus elude the Archons, who thought that they had known and seen the real Christ?

While Jesus eluded us and all of the spiritual beings in the spiritual and physical universe, the entirety of Jesus Christ remains an unraveling mystery to us all. This will set the stage for this third, such astounding and baffling meeting with the Lord Jesus Christ.

I moved out of my body by the Holy Spirit and was taken aboard an enormous space craft/spiritual temple, into an oval room or chamber which must have been 25-30 yards in diameter. I say that this spiritual temple was a spacecraft because it appeared in outer space. This leaves me with no other explanation other than the temple or craft was in space; thus I call it a space craft. There were lower and upper levels of this chamber inside the enormous spacecraft. I was taken through the walls and into the lower part of the chamber.

Because the notion of being taken in spirit into a spacecraft is notably disturbing to many of us, even if the spacecraft is a spiritual temple manifested by the power of God rather than a piece of machinery, I will present evidence from the vision of Enoch, the first Biblical saint, before we move into this meeting further.

In the Book of Enoch, Chap. XIV, we find evidence. "I perceived in my dream. . . . Behold, in that vision, clouds and a mist invited me; the running of stars and flashes of lightning impelled and pressed me forwards, while winds in the vision assisted my flight." The "running of stars" suggests that Enoch was flying through space so fast that stars were running by. Then Enoch is taken into a structure he describes: "Its floor was on fire, and above were lightnings and the running of stars, while its roof exhibited a blazing fire." Now that he is inside this object, he sees again "the running of stars" going by, which suggests the temple or space craft is moving through space also. Then Enoch goes to meet the Lord God in an exalted throne blazing with light, which is described as an orb or circular temple: "Attentively I surveyed it, and saw that it contained an exalted throne; The appearance of which was like that of frost, while its circumference resembled the orb of the brilliant sun."

Now this sounds like a circular temple or craft which shines and is shaped like a bright sun. But, Enoch describes, "From underneath this mighty throne rivers of flaming fire issued." Does this suggest a propulsion system for this temple of God? Enoch continues, "To look upon it was impossible. One great in glory sat upon it; Whose robe was brighter than the sun, and whiter than snow. No angel was capable of penetrating to view the face of Him, the Glorious and the Effulgent." This suggests that even the Lord God can appear to someone in this fashion, and sets the example of what I was about to experience and see.

So, I was inside of this spiritual spacecraft, as I define it. There were about twenty to thirty people there, many of whom were deluded by demons of egotism, argumentation, and spiritual blindness, some of whom were humans from the planet earth, and there were spirits who were clearly from other worlds.

These people seemed to be experiencing a spiritual deficiency; something was wrong with many of them. I did not have my answer right at this point, but it was about to be revealed to me.

There was an enlightened being aboard the ship, and it was my turn to go up and meet this being. I levitated or floated up through a portal in the center of the craft and was taken to a high room above, which had a high white dome for a ceiling. There was a master there who would not make himself seen. As this master was hidden in the shadows, the room was dark. I was offered some great East Indian food but I was not hungry. I could not see the master but heard his voice and knew he was there.

XXVI

Jesus gives a message about the spiritual dangers of using narcotics, hallucinogenic drugs and alcohol.

It should be duly noted that I do not use drugs, smoke, or drink alcohol at all. The message from Jesus is important to all persons, using drugs or alcohol or not. I was shown by some of the people on the craft that many, but not all, of the people who had come to be in this ship were under the influence of special hallucinogenic and other drugs. It was by the use of such drugs that they came into their pseudo-spiritual visions. This explained to me what I was sensing about these souls: that they were persons seeking God and traveling on their spiritual path with the aid of drugs. They appeared to be very proud of their visions and spiritual abilities to "see" the higher worlds, so they thought. I could see a darkness in their spiritual bodies. Soon I would have an even deeper answer to what I was sensing about all of these souls.

Suddenly, Jesus Christ floated through the walls of the spaceship. Jesus had a sudden sense of urgency and purpose.

The Lord moved swiftly. I was so happy to see Jesus again. While Jesus moved about swiftly, I tried to gaze upon the Lord's most beautiful face. Only when I looked directly upon Jesus' face, only then did his face shine about as bright as our sun with a white-golden-yellow light. Jesus let me see the Glory shining from his face for a short while. Because Jesus was moving about very quickly, I did not get to look into his eyes for a long time. This time, Jesus' hair was blonde, shining with a bright golden-yellow light of its own. Jesus wore an emerald colored robe with a fuchsia colored extra robe covering the first. His clothes glowed with a light of their own. The light that shone from Jesus' face was the most holy and silent light, so much that it stilled my mind and made it perfectly clear, bright and expansive just to see it. In this, Jesus was showing me the lesson of perfect mental clarity. My mind became so clear that I experienced clear expansion into cosmic space and spiritual oneness with all the souls aboard this ship.

Suddenly Jesus came before the master of this spaceship, who revealed himself out of the shadows as another Jesus: A direct copy of Jesus it appeared. This baffled me to no end. The copy of Jesus looked identical to Jesus but it had a deficiency with its light. Its light had a shadow of grayness in it, as though it were a mirror to the grayness I saw in the souls aboard the ship. I could see and experience that the light of this Second Jesus appeared to be imperfect. This appearance could have just been seen by me as an "appearance" (a reflection of what the other souls saw when they looked at Jesus through their minds). It had gone as if out of balance. It was an astral copy of Jesus which was appearing to people aboard this spaceship, and to many who were using hallucinogenic and other narcotics.

While I stood next to Jesus, as though I had x-ray vision, I could see that the souls of the persons who were using narcotics had two faces and bodies. One face was the dark-luminous (a deficient spiritual light) astral body and face which they all saw of each other, which appeared normal (many of these souls were not from earth, but were humanoids). Simultaneous to me seeing their normal faces, I could also see another face and body glowing with a very dark light inside of each one of them. This second face, which was present in every one of these souls, was a demon. They were very ugly, looking like little monsters. These demons attached themselves to these souls after their natural spiritual light became deficient from using drugs. These demons are attracted to deficient light.

There is an epidemic of persons using drugs thinking that it is a great way to expedite their spiritual growth. By this message, Jesus is showing us that these persons are all being seriously deluded. They do not know that the light they see in their narcotic pseudo-spiritual visions is a deficient light. I could actually feel just how deficient the light in the drug experience is. It was so clear while standing next to Jesus Christ in a state of cosmic consciousness, gazing at these souls from all over the galaxy.

Just in the United States, the Office of National Drug Control Policy, according to national surveys in 1996, estimated 13 million Americans admitted to using an illicit drug during the last month. The study reported that in 1996, there were an estimated 1.1 million new hallucinogenic drug users, 805,000 new inhalant users, 171,000 new heroin users, 2.5 million new marijuana users, 675,000 new cocaine and crack cocaine users, and 4.3 million new users of alcohol.

If all of these drug and alcohol users could see what happens to their spirituality when they use such drugs, as the Lord was showing me very clearly, they would never use drugs or abuse alcohol again. As I could see very clearly, the drug abuse, and perhaps even alcohol abuse was causing a gray deficient light to corrupt the natural light of the souls who were now in the presence of the Lord. Could this explain why so many persons using drugs and abusing alcohol commit violent crimes such as rape, murder, theft, acting as liars, deceit, greed, and corrupted lusts; because of the demons such persons attract and have living inside of them? I hope all of such persons reading this message choose to clean themselves of such habits and learn to eat healthy food, pray, meditate and fast to become clear and pure again.

Because of the people using drugs and manifesting demons, which were clearly seen by me, their demons, acting on their minds as impurities, had tarnished and made this copy of Jesus' light darker; thus the light of this copy of Jesus became deficient (or was seen as deficient by drug users). In other words, perhaps this copy of Jesus was just "appearing" in a deficient light to simulate what happens, and how deficient the light drug users experience while hallucinating under the influence of narcotics or alcohol abuse. Could this be the mystery Jesus was revealing?

It is said that when spiritual masters take upon the sins of their disciples, the master's aura darkens temporarily, and then the master washes him or herself of the sins which have been taken away from the disciples. I believe this is what I was seeing.

This message goes out to drug users who think they are seeing Jesus Christ in their visions. Your minds are not clear, and you are not seeing the real Jesus, but a hallucination of Jesus or other spiritual beings in a spiritually deficient light. Although the Lord has compassion for you all because you really do seem to wish to know Jesus. Because you are using drugs, you are polluting your minds with manifest demons and polluting the form of Christ you are seeing through your own minds. The Lord asks me by this vision to warn you not to use drugs of any kind. To use drugs is to pollute your astral body with the dark light (the deficient light); thus demons are attracted to pollute and influence your mind, body and soul. This will become more clear to you when this third meeting is finished.

There is a story from Medjugore similar to this. It was told to me by a man who has traveled there many times. He said that once Mary appeared to many of the villagers in Medjugore in a body of light, but a light body that could be touched by human hands and felt as real. She told some of the villagers to reach out and touch her hand. When they reached and touched her, the glow of her body of light became darker. When they let go of her hand, her body of light returned to its brightness. She told them that the sins of the world are so dark that they offend the light of God, and this is why people must be made clean before they can enter heaven. This is similar to what I was seeing about this manifestation of Jesus which had become darkened.

What appeared to be the real Jesus, which was Jesus in an Astral, or middle spiritual universal form body, approached this manifestation of himself. Suddenly there was a bright flash of light extending itself from the perfect Jesus into the copy of Jesus. The flash affected everyone on the spaceship. I cannot tell you how deeply it affected us all, but I felt, in the oneness of it all, minds becoming instantly clear. Immediately (in just a few seconds) the copy of Jesus' light was made perfect. Suddenly this copy began to glow with a perfected and much brighter light, which made everyone's minds even more clear. The clarity of mind was astounding, as though I had become one with the cosmic mind of God.

When the Jesus with the perfect light caused the manifested copy of Jesus to become light, the sins and demons of all present vanished and I actually felt them all relieved of their demons and saw the demons leave from behind their faces. Everyone's mind on the craft was made much more clear and bright. It was a great miracle. Now that all of these persons seeking God through the use of drugs were washed free of them, the Lord hopes that they do not return to such drug and alcohol abuse, but repent.

This was Jesus demonstrating the power of the Holy Ghost washing away people's sins. I looked closely at many of them, and suddenly they began to speak the truth, relieving themselves of lies they had told previously in their lives. I saw a little girl freed of her inner demons and she was so happy to see me in her new light. Perhaps she was a victim in childbirth of her parents' use of such contaminants.

Jesus took me through the central walls of the spaceship and contained the lower vibrational Astral copy of himself in a miraculously formed circular glass-like force field that would not allow others to see that there were two Jesus Christs. I guess Jesus did not want to confuse or baffle these beings. I was now standing with Jesus outside the clear glass-like force field looking through it at his copy, and they were both dressed in the same colored robes, and had brightly glowing golden-yellow hair. They both glowed with a perfect white-golden-yellow light as bright as our earthly sun, and both appeared as enlightened beings. I was so taken and shocked with the wisdom and insight of this vision I became deeply astounded. How could there be more than one Christ at the same time? How could one of the copies become deficient in its light and the other correct it? Now for the next great mystery.

XXVII

Jesus reveals more of the mystery of appearing in many places in the unvierse at the same time.

I was so astounded because, first, neither of these two manifestations of Jesus Christ was anything like the clear and bright forms of Jesus I met in 1994 and 1997. In those meetings, Jesus' face shined brighter than 1,000 suns. The power in the Glory was so great in those meetings, I collapsed at Jesus' feet, and could hardly bear the inescapable Glory of Innocence, Love, Ecstasy, Peace, Power, Beauty, Graces and Wisdom the Lord beheld in those first two meetings.

The Jesus in this third meeting was very colorful looking (with emerald and fuchsia colored robes and golden yellow hair), had a face that shined as bright as our own sun (but only when I looked directly at it), and I did not collapse at this Jesus' feet. It was clearly a different vibration, yet an incredibly holy, manifestation of Jesus Christ.

I chased after the Jesus who corrected the deficiency of the Jesus who was aboard the spacecraft. Yet, when I turned to face the Jesus still on the craft, concealed behind the force field, I could not tell them apart because they were both enlightened beings. I knew that neither of them were the higher heavenly body of Jesus I had met in 1994 and 1997. This revealed that Jesus can and does manifest in bodies of light that are of higher and lower spiritual vibration. When I turned to run after what I thought was the real Jesus, he was gone. I was left staring at the second Jesus who was glowing with a light as bright as our sun and clear mind consciousness. I stared at this Jesus totally astounded and unable to move for what I had seen. I was so astounded I could not bear the mystery and experienced the greatest sense of wonder, but I could not bear the wonderment.

This is to show that Jesus simultaneously exists in many spiritual bodies at the same time; the highest clear light heavenly forms and the middle or Astral forms, and even physical forms who manifest on earth and other planets. Perhaps Jesus can appear to many beings in the universe at the same time by way of these numerous copies of the Lord's self, each vibrating at a rate of spiritual light relative to the spiritual potential of enlightenment for beings who live in this particular region of the universe.

As it is written about the Lord in the Nag Hammadi Library, "Trimorphic Protennoia," "So now, I was dwelling in them, in the form of each one." For Jesus to suggest that Jesus dwells in the form of each one, suggests that Jesus can manifest, not only at different levels of spiritual ability and levels of the universe, but in myriad forms at the same time. I am astonished at how this is possible, but I saw and experienced it in the Lord.

This phenomenon is commonly known in Hinduism and Buddhism as a great quality of enlightened spiritual beings. In Hinduism and Buddhism, there are numerous accounts of saints who can appear in two places at the same time. In Buddhism, it is said that a full Buddha (Tathagata) can manifest in many places in the universe at the same time, and can also manifest as a Bodhisattva, which can also manifest in many places in the universe at the same time.

A Bodhisattva a being who eventually attains higher enlightenment than Nirvana, Nirvana being the Seventh Clear light, and a Bodhisattva ultimately attaining the Eight and Ninth clear light (see Buddhist *Lankavattara VIII Sutra)*. It is said that such beings can also manifest in 1,000 places in the universe at the same time to help sentient beings on their spiritual path. These manifestations radiate a light proper to the beings it serves, yet hides the full radiance of the total Bodhisattva. This is because the full radiance of a Bodhisattva is even brighter than a being who has attained Nirvana. The full meaning of this is a great mystery in Buddhism.

The Tibetan Buddhist leader, the Dalai Lama, is said to be an emanation/incarnation of the Supreme Bodhisattva Avalokiteshvara (one of the eight great Bodhisattvas named in the Dhamapadha). An emanation means one of perhaps a thousand emanations (emanations are light bodies that can appear) or incarnations (incarnations are emanations that have actually been born in a physical body somewhere in the universe) of such a glorious being.

While I have not found evidence for this in Christian gospels, Christian manuscripts or the Bible, there is some evidence of this in the visions of the Christian mystic, Emanuel

Swedenborg. Swedenborg describes in his book, *Heaven and Hell,* that the highest angels, such as the Archangel Michael, is not one angel, but that a whole community of angels who make up the whole Angel Michael. Thus, one could deduct that such an angel can make appearances to hundreds or thousands of beings in the universe at the same time. Each of these sub-component angels radiates less than the total enlightenment of the highest vibration in which it lives (the community).

It is written in Swedenborg's book, *Heaven and Hell,* page 56: "From time to time, therefore, a whole angelic community may appear as a unit in the form of an angel, a sight which the Lord in fact has let me see. Michael, Gabriel, and Raphael are nothing but angelic communities, given their names by reason of their functions." By this wisdom, it is easy to deduct that each of the Angels can appear in many places in the universe at the same time also.

If the highest angels can manifest in thousands of places in the universe at the same time, of course Jesus Christ can do this and more also. But how great such a one must be to exist simultaneously in thousands of places in the universe at the same time? Is this one of the powers of omnipresence? Can omnipresence actually be a physical phenomenon as well as a consciousness?

If we took the notion of a God who could only be in one place at any given time, this would make God very inefficient at serving and helping and communing with all beings on their spiritual path in the universe. Now, with the aid of giant space telescopes, we know that the universe is filled with countless galaxies. Galaxies are filled with billions of stars and planets. Now if God could only appear in one place, on one planet at any given time, in the whole creation, the Lord could not serve the Lord's creation with any kind of efficiency. The creation would starve for spiritual aid. To suggest by direct experience that the

Lord can manifest all over the universe at different levels of spiritual ability at the same time, is to suggest a very efficient God. This is why the Lord is very efficient indeed.

To give evidence, another example of a spiritual person experiencing Jesus manifesting in a body of lower and higher spiritual vibration at the same time comes from the story of a great East Indian Mystic named Krishnamurti. He was said to be an enlightened master from India, who lived his last years of life in Ojai, California. I attended a lecture by Krishnamurti on his last birthday in Ojai, California. He passed away the next year. Krishnamurti was, in my opinion, one of the greatest thinkers of our time.

In the book *Krishnamurti, The Years of Awakening,* the story of this master's awakening years reveals an out-of-body meeting he had with many great masters, including Jesus Christ. But was this one of the Astral copies of the real Jesus Krishnamurti met? I believe it was so because the mystery lay before Krishnamurti with such astonishment and sophistication, his bewilderment revealed why he did not wish to speak about it.

Krishnamurti is led out-of-body by his spiritual mentor, Mrs. Besant, who travels out-of-body with him. He writes of his initiation into "The Great White Brotherhood," on January 12th, 1910: "When I left my body the first night, I went at once to the master's house and found him there with the master Morya and the master Djwal Kul. Then we all went together to the house of the Lord Maitreya, where I had been once before, and there we found many of the Masters—the Venetian Master, the Master Jesus, the Master Hilarion and the two masters, Morya and K.H. Kuthumi. The Lord Maitreya sat in the middle, and the others stood around him in a semicircle." Krishnamurti then goes through a long process of being initiated into the "Great White Brotherhood" of all these great saints.

With the Lord Maitreya in the middle of this circle, we see Jesus as a member of the group but not the Supreme Lord I am proposing Jesus Christ to be. Maitreya is another one of the eight great Bodhisattvas listed in the Buddhist Dhamapada. He is prophesied in Buddhism to be waiting to incarnate as the next great Buddha destined to lead the Buddhist people and the world to enlightenment. I know this appears disturbing to the presentation I have made in this book. But, if you are patient, you will see how the mystery of Christ reveals itself to Krishnamurti with absolute astonishment.

At the end of this initiation, a great Silver Star flashed out over the head of his master Maitreya. Gautama the Buddha and another great saint named Mahachohan appeared on either side of this star. This shows Guatama the Buddha and Manachohan shining above all of these great saints. The Silver Star is later to be known as the greatest being of all, said to be the King, which shines above even Guatama the Buddha and Manachohan. Krishnamurti's master Maitreya says, "In the name of the One Initiator, whose star shines above us, I receive you into the Brotherhood of Eternal Life."

Later in the vision, Krishnamurti meets the King (the manifestation of the great silver star) in person. He describes it in his diary: "The next night I was taken to see the King, and that was the most wonderful experience of all, for He is a boy not much older than I am, but the handsomest I have ever seen, all shining and glorious, and when He smiles, it is like sunlight. And the Silver Star we have just seen is just part of Him—not sent there, for He is there and everywhere all the time, but just somehow made so that we can see it." The mystery is, who is this great King who shines above all of the great saints? Why doesn't Krishnamurti tell us who the boy King is? Why does he say that "He is there and everywhere all the time, but just somehow made so that we can see it"? Obviously he was deeply mystified.

The truth is revealed by Mrs. Besant, Krishnamurti's spiritual mentor, who must have been out-of-body in that vision with him, because it is she who described just who the mysterious and supremely radiant boy King was, writing to Krishnamurti January 12: "And then Shambhalla in the presence of the King. How much I should like to talk it over with you. The dear boy looked so beautiful, like a picture of the child Christ, with his large solemn eyes, full of love and trust. Does he remember it all?"

Now we have our answer. The most supremely radiant boy King, who shines above all these great saints was the child Jesus Christ. Krishnamurti must have been so baffled as to why, while he thought he had seen Jesus amongst many masters below, this most supreme being appeared to be Jesus shining above the Jesus he met with the other masters. What a great mystery. Mrs. Besant questioned if Krishnamurti had remembered because he never spoke about it. Was he so mystified to find Jesus Christ shining above all of many of the great saints of India? Is this why he never spoke about it again? I have read so many of Krishnamurti's books and seen so many videos, he never spoke of this again. Why?

There is more evidence to what I saw and experienced in Jesus Christ, Jesus can appear in the Astral universe as a great enlightened saint, so much so that those who meet this Jesus there will swear that this is who Jesus is: a saint among saints. But, there is a much higher and more Supreme form of Jesus as the Lord, the King of Kings. This story of Krishnamurti reveals the evidence that another person, who is more spiritually advanced than I am, did see the same phenomenal wisdom of the Lord. Jesus eluded us all. Jesus hid the truth from everyone and the mystery unravels.

Jesus Christ, as the Nag Hammadi Library "Trimorphic Protennoia" reveals, "The Archons thought that I was their Christ. Indeed I dwell in everyone. Indeed within those in whom I revealed myself as Light I eluded the Archons." Jesus eluded the Archons and even the enlightened beings (Aeons) just as the Lord eluded Krishnamurti until the Lord revealed the Lord's self to him shining above all.

Does the Supreme Form of Christ know what all of the myriad manifestations of the Lord's self are doing all over the universe at the same time? Or, are the myriad manifestations of Jesus Christ enlightened beings who have become enlightened unto Jesus Christ, and have become likened unto Jesus? This is a great mystery that cannot be solved but will surely leave even the angels of all religions baffled when they see and experience this great mystery.

In the New Age community, there are a few accounts of persons who have been taken out-of-body aboard a space-ship and have met Jesus Christ, who is also known there as "Lord Sananda (Jesus Christ)." Jesus appears to these great beings aboard their spaceships as their Supremely Enlightened Spiritual master. There are accounts of beings who call themselves "Arcturians" from the star Arcturus (Bootes Constellation) who operate these enormous space ships.

On November 15, 1998, I had the chance to meet these Arcturians. While out-of-body, I flew up to a cloud where I felt the presence of large space ships. Two bright balls of light came out of the clouds, one was glowing with red light, the other a blue-violet light, and they announced to me that "We are Arcturians." I had a brief encounter with them which I will not go into now.

I had to research into who these beings were because I had never heard the name "Arcturian" before. I found a book called *We the Arcturians* by Dr. Norma Milanovich. I read her book and found it to be fascinating. In her book, the Arcturians say that Jesus, "Lord Sananda," beams aboard their spaceships, and they love this form of Jesus as the most radiant being in the universe. Is this the form of Jesus which I just met in this Third meeting? Is Lord Sananda a copy of the Supreme Lord Jesus Christ helping to govern one small part of the Universe, our local galaxy, while those who see him remain unaware that Sananda is perhaps one of thousands or millions of manifestation bodies of Jesus Christ which is relative to their spiritual vibration? By descriptions people have made about Lord Sananda, it just might be so.

By the examples of this Third Meeting with Jesus Christ, and the recent before mentioned meeting with Mary, Mother of Christ (appearing in three different forms simultaneously), it is clear that Mary and Jesus exist simultaneously in the Highest heavens while manifesting throughout the other levels of the physical and spiritual universe.

How could Jesus exist simultaneously in Heaven while manifesting all throughout the spiritual and physical universe? There are great parables in the Bible where I believe Jesus was trying to reveal to the Lord's disciples this very same phenomenal mystery. But did we miss what Jesus told long ago?

There are a number of times in the Bible where Jesus reveals that the Father is in Heaven, such as in Matthew, Chapter 10, Verse 33: "But whosoever shall deny me before me, him I will also deny before my Father which is in heaven." This is to show that Jesus reveals that the Father is in heaven while Jesus is on earth. But watch what happens as Jesus reveals the mystery in the book of John, Chapter 3, Verses 12-13: "If I have told you earthly things, and ye believe not, how shall ye believe, if I tell you of heavenly things? And no man hath ascended up to heaven, but he that came down from heaven, even the Son of man which is in heaven." This is the greatest mystery revealed that Jesus, the Son of man, "is" in heaven. But why would Jesus say that Jesus "is" in heaven when we see Jesus walking on the earth?

The mystery gets deeper. We now know from Jesus that the Father is in Heaven, "And no man hath ascended up to heaven, but he that came down from heaven." We know that Jesus came down from Heaven, where the Father is, right? We also know that Jesus, the Son of man "is" in heaven while Jesus also came down simultaneously. Now, in John, Chapter 6, Verse 46, an even greater mystery: "Not that any man hath seen the Father, save he which is God, he hath seen the Father." Here Jesus reveals that no one has seen the Father but God? If God sees the Father, then God must be the Father, right? In John, Chapter 10, Verse 30, Jesus tells us that: "I and my Father are one." This means that, because no one has seen the Father but God, and for Jesus and the Father to be "one," Jesus must be God, the Father who art in heaven while simultaneously walking on earth. This shows that Jesus can exist in Heaven as the Father while simultaneously appearing on earth. Could the Jesus who walked on earth nearly 2000 years ago have been one of hundreds, thousands, millions or billions of manifestations of Jesus Christ walking on planets and living amongst beings all over the universe at the same time?

Jesus finishes the mystery in John, Chapter 14, Verses 7-10: "If ye had known me, ye should have known my Father also: and from henceforth ye know him, and have seen him. Philip saith unto him, Lord, show us the Father, and it sufficeth us. Jesus said unto him, Have I been so long time with you, and yet hast thou not known me, Philip? He that hath seen me hath seen the Father; and how sayest thou then, Show us the Father? Believest thou not that I am in the Father, and the Father in me? The words that I speak unto you I speak not of myself: but the Father which dwelleth in me, he doth the works."

I am so humbled by these meetings with Jesus. I have seen that, although many have seen Jesus, including the many disciples Jesus had on earth nearly 2000 years ago, no one has ever seen Jesus in the Lord's entirety. Even when Jesus became transfigured into a great light and the disciples fell as dead on the ground, even so, they did not see the Lord in the Lord's entirety. I have not seen Jesus in the Lord's entirety, even though I have seen what I am capable of, which leaves me with the reminder

Jesus gave to his disciple John (The Acts of John) nearly 2000 years ago: "... but to see me truly is, as I said, not possible, except for what you are able to know, being a kinsman." This wisdom and this light leaves me humble before the greatest mystery and the greatest Glory in the universe.

XXVIII

Prophecy.

These revelations were delivered to St. John the Divine by the Lord Jesus, the Lord's self. *This section alone is not a direct message from Jesus.* I, David, read these Revelations of St. John the Divine, and this is my personal insight into them:

From Revelations, Chapter 12, Verse 1: "And there appeared a great wonder in heaven; a woman clothed with the sun and the moon under her feet, and upon her head a crown of twelve stars." Interpretation: The woman is Mary (with the moon under her feet and a crown of twelve stars), the mother of Christ.

Chapter 12, Verse 5: "And she brought forth a man child, who was to rule all nations with a rod of iron; and her child was caught up unto God, and to his throne." Interpretation: She brought forth a man child who "was" to rule all nations with a rod of iron; her child was caught up unto God, and to his throne. This is Jesus Christ after the resurrection. He was sent here to save us but we killed him, rejected God incarnate on earth, and he went back up to God and sat on the Lord's throne.

Chapter 12, Verses 7-9: "And there was war in heaven: Michael and his angels fought against the dragon; and the dragon fought and his angels, 8. And prevailed not; neither was their place found any more in heaven. 9. And the great dragon was cast out, that old serpent, called the Devil, and Satan, which deceiveth the whole world; he was cast out into the earth, and his angels were cast out with him." Interpretation: Obviously the fallen angels and their leader fell to earth.

Verse 13: "And when the dragon saw that he was cast unto the earth, he persecuted the woman which brought forth the man child. And the dragon was wroth with the woman, and went to make war with the remnant of her seed, which keep the commandments of God, and have testimony to Jesus Christ." Interpretation: This was after the crucifixion, the resurrection, and after the fallen angels came to earth. To make war with "the woman" would be to make war against the greatest earthly power that represented Jesus Christ, and that would have to be the Catholic Church, because only that church is where the woman "Mary" could be found *as an Icon* in Christianity. If Satan could gain control over the Church, Satan could deceive and corrupt even the religious elect. It is well known that the visionaries of Fatima delivered a terrifying message that Mary told them to keep secret until a certain date. The Catholic Church stored that message for them. However, the Church did not release the message to the public. It was only leaked out by a few faithful ones in the church. In that message, it was revealed that "The time of great trials will also come for the Church. Cardinals will oppose Cardinals, bishops will oppose bishops, Satan will march among them, and there will be changes in Rome. The Church will be darkened, and the world will be overturned by terror."

From Revelations, Chapter 17, Verses 1-2: "AND THERE came one of the seven angels which had the seven vials, and talked with me, saying unto me, Come hither; I will show unto thee the judgment of the great whore that sitteth upon many waters: 2. With whom the kings of the earth have committed fornication, and the inhabitants of the earth have been made drunk with the wine of her fornication." Interpretation: I say the "great whore that sitteth upon many waters" is the MYSTERY OF ALL MYSTERIES hidden in the Vatican. Interpretation: The kings of the Earth are the owners of the central banks who are bankrupting economies all around the world today, so that they may bring forth their new world order (one world government).

Chapter 17, Verses 4-6: "And the woman was arrayed in purple and scarlet colour, and decked with gold and precious stones and pearls, having a golden cup in her hand full of abominations and filthiness of her fornication. 5. And upon her head was a name written, MYSTERY, BABYLON THE GREAT, THE MOTHER OF HARLOTS AND ABOMINATIONS OF THE EARTH. 6. And I saw the woman drunken with the blood of the saints, and with the blood of the martyrs of Jesus: and when I saw her, I wondered with great admiration." Interpretation: We know the fallen angels went to make war to gain power in the most powerful organization on earth, the Vatican (Revelations, Chapter 12, Verse 17), where the mere "image" of Mary could be used by Satan to hide behind, to deceive the world. The woman is now a MYSTERY because things are not the way they seem in reality to the masses. The image of Mary of Jesus is being used by the hidden, mysterious part of the Catholic Church, for image purposes only, and is being used (Verse 4) arrayed in purple and scarlet color, and decked with gold and precious stones and pearls, having a golden cup in her hand. "Decked with gold and precious stones and pearls" means that the mere image of Mary is being used as a puppet to make "money"—the root of all evil. In Verse 5, we see how deep this mystery is; things are not as they appear now. The woman (the image of Mary being used for profit and power by the same legal body that had Jesus crucified, Rome) is now drunken with the blood of saints, and the blood of the martyrs of Jesus.

For Rome and the Catholic Church to be drunken with the blood of saints would have to be proven, if it were the Catholic Church, or some force in it, that was terribly corrupt. Here is that proof: Jesus Christ himself was persecuted and assassinated by the Jews' use of the Roman legal system.

More proof: In September of 1978, Albinoni Luciani (Pope John Paul I) asked his secretary of state, Cardinal Jean Villot, to begin an investigation into the corrupt Vatican Bank operations, because Pope John Paul I knew that this bank was the most powerful bank in the world, and that the leaders of most of the world's banks, the Mafia and others did business with the Vatican Bank because of its tax-free status.

This Pope wanted the corruption to be removed from God's church and bank. On September 28, 1978, Pope John Paul I gave Cardinal Villot a list of people who were to be transferred, asked for their resignations and began the cleansing of the Vatican Bank. All the people on the list were suspected to be members of a secret religious Freemason or Illuminati group called the "P2." Just one day later, September 29, 1978, Pope John Paul I was found dead in his room. Then, Cardinal Villot issued false statements to the press, deceiving the nations about the circumstances surrounding the death, and ordered the body to be embalmed without an autopsy (see *In God's Name* by David Yallop).

Chapter 17, Verses 7 and 9: "And the angel said unto me, Wherefore didst thou marvel? I will tell thee the mystery of the woman, and the beast that carrieth her, which hath the seven heads and ten horns. 9. And here is the mind which hath wisdom. The seven heads are seven mountains, on which the woman sitteth." Interpretation: Note that the beast carries the woman (Mary and the Catholic Church) and the city, which is Vatican City, deceiving the nations. This is a mystery because the hidden powers in the Vatican are using the mere "image" of Mary and Jesus but are a den of thieves (taking the money powers of the world for corruption).Verse 9 tells us that she sits on seven mountains. Vatican City sits around seven large hills or mountains.

Chapter 17, Verse 18: "And the woman which thou sawest is that great city, which reigneth over the kings of the earth." Interpretation: The woman now is that city, which reigneth over the kings of the earth. Now all the key central bankers, such as the Rockefellers, Morgans, Rothschilds, and so on, and all their banks, do business with the Vatican Bank, which is the most powerful bank in the world.

Many theorists say that this woman city is London, England and the Royal Family, but look at the Book of Revelations, Chapter 2, Verse 13: "I know thy works and where thou dwellest, even where Satan's seat is: and thou holdest fast my name, and hast not denied my faith, even in those days wherein *An'-ti-pas* was my faithful martyr, who was slain amongst you, where Satan dwelleth." An'-ti-pas? This is Vatican-Rome, not England. But it also says that Satan dwells there. That means Satan's seat is somewhere inside the Vatican walls.

From Revelations, Chapter 18, Verse 4: "And I heard another voice from heaven, saying, Come out of her, my people, that ye be not partakers of her sins, and that ye receive not of her plagues." This is not to say that the whole Catholic Church is under the control of Satan, rather, as the scripture reveals, that Satan went down to earth to make war and send a flood after the woman (Mary and the Catholic Church). This means that Satan would try to take control over the Lord's temple on earth. Because gaining control of the "money" in one of the world's largest, and perhaps the largest and most powerful bank in the world, would be how Satan could use this power to deceive and control the world, where in the Vatican would Satan attack? The bank! Who is the head of the Vatican bank today? Paul Marcinkus, and there are others with him.

From Revelations, Chapter 2, Verse 9 tells us: "I know thy works, and tribulation, and poverty, (but thou art rich) and I know the blasphemy of them which say they are Jews, and are not, but are the synagogue of Satan." Adolph Hitler was a Christian fanatic, and any fanatic would read Revelation. Jesus is only talking about those Jews who say they are Jews, and are not, but are the synagogue of Satan. Many of the owners of the United States Federal Reserve Banks (a private corporation) are the same owners of most of the world central banks and appear to be Jews, but are not—they are masters of the secretive Freemason (P2, the Vatican Bank Heads) and Illuminati religions. They have their symbology in the seal of the United States, U.S. currency, and all of the money systems it creates around the world.

Revelation, Chapter 3, Verse 9, says: "Behold, I will make them of the synagogue of Satan, which say they are Jews, and are not, but do lie; behold, I will make them to come and worship before thy feet, and to know that I have loved thee." Hitler must have gone mad with this idea. I think it was terrible of him to assassinate so many innocent people, yet he was so close to this terrible irony and truth about Jews "who were not really Jews," but the P2 banks who make the world its slaves by power and mastery over the money system on earth.

From Revelation, Chapter 17, Verses 15-18: "And he saith unto me, The waters which thou sawest, where the whore sitteth, are peoples, and multitudes, and nations, and tongues. 16. And the ten horns which thou sawest upon the beast, these shall hate the whore, and shall make her desolate and naked, and shall eat her flesh, and burn her with fire. 17. For God hath put in their hearts to fulfill his will, and to agree, and give their kingdom unto the beast, until the words of God shall be fulfilled. 18. And the woman which thou sawest is that great city, which reigneth over the kings of the earth." Interpretation: All the world has been giving donations to the Church thinking it would do good and serve causes and serve the poor with their money, as Jesus would have it, but they were deceived. In fact, if there was any environmental technology or any healing project that was in need of funding, and was unable to get funding elsewhere, that project should be able to get assistance from the Church, but the Church is not doing this compassion work with our money. It is building a system of economic slavery instead. Compassion is the proper role of the Church and its money supply.

In 1997, the United Nations Voluntary Trust Fund for Assistance in Landmine Clearance revealed that the Holy See (The Vatican Bank) only donated $4,000 U.S. dollars to the cause, while even poor countries like Iceland donated $10,000. Where did all those donations go? Why does this powerful bank refuse to donate sufficient amounts of money to great causes to alleviate suffering, as it should?

The ten horns, I believe, are people in the Catholic Church, such as Pope John Paul I, who exposed this crime and now many follow and are working to remove the corruption in the Vatican Bank, and all of its subsidiary holdings. It is said that the ten horns shall "burn her with fire." This means that Jesus has placed honest and true servants of the Lord inside the Catholic Church, as always, who will stop Satan and the fallen angel servants from controlling the Vatican Bank, even if they have to do it by fire.

It is important to understand that the Freemason religion has contact with beings of supposed manifest light, who are said to be ascended masters. The New Testament warns us that Satan could appear in a light that would deceive men and make them think he, Satan, is a god. This Satan would teach men to create power, oppressions, and elite societies that are not of love and goodwill to all, just as these Freemasons have done.

What are the Freemasons doing with all that money they have been stealing from our banks for the past few hundred years? Could they be building a superior "control" technology to enslave us further?

UFO experts document how the secret government, infiltrated into our own government, has been working with aliens and advanced technologies within the military since the late 1930s. What are they preparing us for? If they want to get the whole world's attention to dawn the New World Order, could it be a seemingly fantastic miracle that they are preparing?

Revelation, Chapter 13, Verse 7 says that the beast would have power over all the kindreds, tongues and nations. Could this be the United Nations we have today? The United Nations was started on Rockefeller land in New York City. David Rockefeller is the head of the Council on Foreign Relations (planners of the New World Order), the head of the Trilateral Commission (planners of the New World Order), and is a major shareholder in the Federal Reserve bank (bankrupting America), which runs the American currency, and David Rockefeller's subsidiary holdings span across the globe. He meets very secretly with heads of the Vatican Bank and the P2.

Revelation, Chapter 13, Verses 13-14 tells of the beast bringing *fire down* from heaven *on earth* in the sight of men, and of the many miracles that the beast will bring. "Fire in the sky" is classic UFO terminology. Could the years 2000 to 2010 hold a surprise that will catch the world's attention? Could it be an even later date?

There are many books available in print where top U.S. Army personnel tell of how our government has been working with aliens and their advanced technology since the late 1930s. Timothy Good's *Alien Contact* is a fantastic book to read.

I say that to get the whole world's attention, the central banking kings are bankrupting the economies of the world, bringing all nations into despair. They used their moneys to copy UFO alien technology and will land UFOs in every major city in the world all at the same time. Maybe in the years between 2001 and 2011. They will offer friendship with all our governments and finalize the New World Order through the United Nations. They will offer the cure for AIDS, cancer and many other diseases, and to become part of the new system, everyone will receive a computer chip implant in their wrist or forehead. (In Sweden today, over a hundred-thousand people are receiving computer chip implants in their wrists as an experiment.) All people should be warned not to take the mark of the beast! God save us all! Do not be deceived when these miracles appear, because the same ones who made the world a living hell are now offering us a salvation that is false.

There is a deep reason why the Lord God warned us not to bow down to the many lesser gods. It was out of compassion and wisdom, but we did not listen.

In the Book of Exodus, Chapter 20, Verses 1-5: "AND GOD spake all these words, saying I am the Lord thy God, which have brought thee out of the land of Egypt, out of the house of bondage. Thou shalt have no other gods before me. Thou shalt not make unto thee any graven image, or any likeness of any thing that is in heaven above, or that is in the earth beneath, or that is in the water under the earth. Thou shalt not bow down thyself to them nor serve them. . . ."

The answer to this becomes more and more clear when you understand the problems that come with bowing down, worshipping and praying to any of the fallen angels (Buddhist anti-gods), angels, or even early stage enlightened beings. None of them are perfected yet. It is quite possible that these Freemasons have done just that: served the order of those anti-gods who appeared to them. If you are one of them and read this message, I pray that you turn against the fallen ones and reveal their plan to the world. I pray that you abandon the fallen angels' plan of world domination by "control" technologies. Do not sell your soul.

It is more intelligent to pray to the enlightened, but even that can be limiting. The dangers increase when the blind bow down and serve, not knowing just how evolved the gods may be that the blind are making themselves subservient to. These lower gods may limit your path to God and the Heavens because they are filled with the Glory, but not fully wise as to the many ways that lead to God and Heaven, including your own way. By making yourself subservient to them, you may even find yourself following the wrong path instead of the one that was made unique by God, just for you. It certainly could not be harmful, and could be beneficial to be friends and love any of them, but to bow down to them as the Supreme Being would be foolish and limiting.

Why not bow, ask for guidance and serve the Supreme Being, the Lord. After all, the Lord is the most intelligent, omnipresent, loving and Glorious being of all that are creating this universe. I pray that you make that choice, based on your own intelligence.

By this message, I predict that the first aliens that have been visiting and working with our military installations are *mostly* of the order of the fallen angels, because they are militant and educating our governments about "control" technology. This order of aliens and fallen angels will try to bring about the New World Order. They will identify an alien threat from above and try to get us to help them fight the outside threat with them. That outside threat, I predict, are the ascended angels who are in service to the Lord.

As the Padma Sambhava Buddha has revealed in the *Tibetan Book of the Dead,* "the anti-gods are always trying to make war with the gods and take over their more evolved planets, but they always lose."

I predict that those fallen angels/anti-gods have sent their robots here, to first of all show our governments how to gain control over the masses, us, by "control" technology. Also, Satan has gained control of our money supply and the banks, is using that money to finance our underground military bases and secret corporations to build a fleet of spacecraft and advanced weapons (many of the UFOs we see today), to use as a force to fight the gods, the ascended angels, that will arrive here to free us from Satan's bondage.

With all the power I have seen that the Lord has, it will be a laughing matter to the Lord to remove Satan's army and the armies Satan tried to get us to join. It is not even a war for the Lord. It is like shining a mirror into the eyes of violence. The violence mirrors back into the fallen ones as a force, not created by the Lord, but the same force the fallen ones created, and mirrored back unto them. They will fall with such ease. There is no worry. The thing to watch out for, if you are a soldier in the military, is to not join Satan in this attack against the Lord, the angels and the gods *because you will lose more than your life. There is not even a 1% chance that Satan will win the battle, because for the Lord and the Lord's Angels it is not even a war. It is a cleansing.*

The same thing happened, say the Hindu scholars of the *Bhagavad Gita* and the Vedas, some 7,000 years ago (3,000–5,000 BC) when the Hindu Supreme Being Lord Krishna appeared during a great battle on earth at the end of a great cycle. Krishna just had to merely arrive in his Glorious, universal form and all the fallen angels and demonic beings fled in terror.

It is written in the *Bhagavad Gita* on page 581 in Text 36, "Arjuna, after hearing from Krishna about the outcome of the Battle of Kuruksetra, became enlightened, and as a great devotee and friend of the Supreme Personality of the Godhead he said that everything done by Krishna is quite fit. Arjuna confirmed that Krishna is the maintainer and the object of worship for the devotees and the destroyer of the undesirables. His actions are equally good for all. Arjuna understood herein that when the battle of Kuruksetra was being concluded, in outer space there were many demigods, siddhas, and other intelligentsia of the higher planets, and they were observing the fight because Krishna was present there. When Ajuna saw the universal form of the Lord, the demigods took pleasure in it, but others, who were demons and atheists, could not stand it when the Lord was praised. Out of their natural fear of the devastating form of the Supreme Personality of the Godhead, they fled."

There is a modern-day Christian stigmatist from Italy named Giorgio Bongiovanni who has bled with the wounds of Christ (hands, feet, side and forehead) every day for eight years. No other stigmatist in history has had the wounds of Christ manifest every day. Giorgio was visited by the Blessed Virgin Mary and Jesus many times. He was told that the reason so many UFOs are being seen on earth today is because there are many beings who Jesus preached to in other worlds and many others who wish to be here on earth for the Second Coming, just to see Jesus in his Supreme and Glorious body of light. They are said to be traveling in spacecraft from other galaxies just to be here for this rare event. Just to see Jesus in his Supreme Form is so rare, that it is a great journey for them just to be here. Imagine how greatly they must be aware of the Lord to travel so far?

This sounds so familiar to the 5–7,000-year-old tale of the Hindu Lord Krishna arriving here on earth at the end of the great battle of Kuruksetra, with the many demigods watching from outer space. Could this process of prophecy be repeating itself? Is Jesus the same as Krishna? Are the UFO beings coming here today for the Second Coming of Christ, just like the ancient demigods came to earth to watch the ancient battle of Kuruksetra, and, even more so, to see Krishna in his universal form body?

Krishna is said by the Hindu scholars to have been on earth some 5–7,000 years ago. 3,500 years after Krishna would take us to 1,500 BC, around the time that the Lord God appeared to Moses on Mount Sinai. Another 3,500 years later brings us to the year 2,000 AD (today's times).

Giorgio Bongiovanni says that Jesus told him that Krishna and Buddha (as well as many other saints) will be with Jesus during the Second Coming, which he predicts will happen soon. The whole spiritual hierarchy will be made manifest. There should be gods and goddesses flying in their spacecraft all under the direction and guidance of the Lord Christ, all here to help us into an age of peace. The bad news is—Giorgio was told the same thing I was—that there are too few loving souls on earth right now; so few, in fact, that Mary has appeared to him weeping tears of blood for humankind's ignorance. If we do not change, she said, a natural or human-made disaster will annihilate the majority of humankind.

This great force of gods, goddesses and Angels is what the warrior-like (Satanic) armies are going to try and get us to fight against. There is no way that any army, including one with nuclear weapons, can fight the power of the Lord, let alone an Angel.

Last prophecy: Because of the damage that we have done to our earth, its myriad creatures and each other, a negative shockwave from the suffering of the earth and its deformed and tormented creatures was sent out into the universe. Because God hears the suffering of all the myriad creatures and the very earth itself, the Lord will mirror a response to that suffering in the form of a growing number of natural disasters (because we caused suffering to nature), the final of which may culminate in a most destructive event unless we change our ways. Again, in the Lord there is no wrath, but that which the Lord mirrors or reflects back to us by natural law appears as wrath.

If you see comets coming towards the earth to destroy it, ask not where you will be safe, but ask what you can do to heal the earth, even at the last minute. If we change, even at the last minute, I predict the greatest miracle all humankind has ever or will ever see: comets changing in their course towards earth and being driven away.

May you all be intelligent and choose true love when it faces you. May you choose true love over and above all that is false below the glorious feeling of love. May you be wise and find the right meditation or prayer practice that best suits you. May you find true peace by dissolving the inner conflict. May you all enter the Heavens and evolve eternally.

Peace, all peace. I thank you my Lord and Master Jesus Christ for allowing me to deliver this message unto humankind as it moves into the new millennium. I pray that humans use it well to live in harmony with the earth and as a helpful guide to evolve into the Heavens.

Guide to Healing Technologies

1. Dr. Bogdan Maglich's non-radioactive aneutronic nuclear power. See *Omni Magazine* article "Bogdan Maglich Knows How To Make Non-Radioactive Nuclear Power, So Why Isn't He?" in the February 1987 issue. To make investments, write to: APA Group, Inc. 6000 University Station, Irvine, CA 92616-9998.

2. To make donations or investments to transmuting nuclear waste into more stable and less harmful matter, write to Hal Fox, Fusion Information Center, P.O. Box 58639, Salt Lake City, UT 84158.

3. To make donations to the American Hydrogen Association, or to invest in Harry Braun's Phoenix Project (Solar Power Hydrogen Power Plant Project), contact the AHA at 1739 West 7th Avenue, Mesa, AZ 85202-1906. www.Clean-Air.org

About the Author

DAVID SEREDA (born in Edmonton, Alberta, Canada) was first introduced to meditation by his father, Dr. Lynn Sereda (Psychology, U.C. Berkeley), when he was 13 years old. This began a deep and lasting quest to find God and the answers to many of life's most perplexing questions. He has met and studied with many Hindu, Buddhist, Native American and Christian teachers, while maintaining a daily meditation practice for over 17 years.

David has worked mainly as an environmentalist. He has planted over 900,000 trees in British Columbia, Canada, helped clean up oil spills, and directed the L.A.-based" Tesla Foundation" which promoted scientific discoveries for a better environment. He was president of The Green & Blue Corporation, trying to bring eco-technology projects to private investors and corporations, and was president of HiEnergy Microdevices, a small company developing leading-edge technology for the detection of buried landmines.

In 1994, during the darkest hour of his life, David had his first face-to-face meeting with Jesus Christ. David collapsed at Jesus' feet and began to receive messages. On Easter morning, 1997 and again in 1999, Jesus appeared to David again to continue with the messages, which are all contained in this book.

While grateful to all his past teachers, David became a disciple of Jesus Christ at the moment of the first meeting, as he felt he was in the presence of the most divine being in the known universe.

Printed in the United Kingdom
by Lightning Source UK Ltd.
121518UK00001B/271/A

9 781577 330325